LOVE, SONGS, WAR
L'Amour, les chansons et la guerre

Colette Gauthier Myles

LOVE, SONGS, WAR
L'Amour, les chansons et la guerre

Memoirs. Volume One

©2011 by Colette Gauthier Myles

All rights reserved. No part of this book may be reproduced or transmitted in any form or by any means, electronically or mechanical, including photocopying, scanning or by any information storage and retrieval system, without written permission.

Publisher's Cataloging-in Publication Data:

Gauthier Myles, Colette
Love, Songs, War: L'Amour, les chansons et la guerre, a memoir / by Colette Gauthier Myles.

The Mousetail Press
Sonoma, California
ISBN 978-0-9827435-1-5

1. World War, 1939-1945 – Personal narratives, French. 2. France- History – German occupation, 1940-1945. 3. Paris (France) – Social life and customs – 20th century. 4. Fontenay-sous-Bois (France) – History. I. Title

In memory of my parents
Louis Gauthier and
Germaine Gauthier (née Cessot)

ACKNOWLEDGMENTS

First and foremost I wish to thank Fred Kellogg, who designed the book and advised me with infinite patience on choosing the best way to display the numerous photographs. I am especially grateful to him for his encouraging words on what turned out to be a lengthy project. I also wish to thank my daughter, Kisaya Myles Jones, who provided her professional expertise in helping me design the cover. I am grateful to my friends, Richard Kempton, Colette (Brun) Sabatier, Adoum Dazi and to my supportive cousins, Dr. Bernard Labbé and Marie Christine Gisselbrecht, who read the manuscript and offered valuable comments. My sincere thanks go to my cousin Denise Balordi who was gracious enough to sit for an interview and to my cousin Jacques Larmaz who reminded me of family anecdotes I had forgotten. Finally, I wish to address posthumous thanks to several members of my family for sharing with me their memories when this book was just a distant project: my dear aunts Valentine Éoche and Yvonne Labbé, and the cousins I miss so much, Roger Éoche, Paulette Lammaing and Michèle Michaud.

INTRODUCTION

I was born in France in 1935. At the age of twenty-two I came to live in the United States. This is the story of my family and a memoir of my youth. In this story, entangled with the history of France, I share the lives of my relatives as they go to war, cry for their loved ones, fall in love, and, in the warmth of family reunions, sing their songs, their *chansons*.

Although this memoir was written for my children and grandchildren, others might wish to read it. Foreign visitors often say that it is not often one gets invited into a French home. I hope that by introducing my family members, visiting the rooms of their houses, sharing their conversations and their meals, I have helped satisfy an outsider's curiosity.

By using many French words and expressions, I have sought to give the impression that the text is "almost written in French." For those who read French, it will be easy to recognize the words. For the others, I have provided translations. I hope that this stylistic peculiarity will amuse (and perhaps sometimes instruct) English speakers who love France and the French language. Finally, I want to mention that there is no hatred, no revenge, and no horrible revelation in these stories, and that my childhood, although spent during World War II and its aftermath, turned out to be as normal as possible despite the circumstances.

CONTENTS

	Maps	x
	Family Tree	xii
1	**First Threads**	13
	An Old Letter – The Jumelins – A Fancy Great-Aunt – The Gauthiers – More on Great-Aunt Valentine	
2	**1910-1935**	37
	Arthur and Louise – The Cessots – Louis and Germaine – My Brother	
3	**An Interview with my Cousin Denise**	71
4	**1935-1941**	83
	First Memories – The War Begins – My Parents' Bedroom – Tante Marthe – Maman – Cinema – Tante Valentine – Villa de l'Ouest– My Bedroom	
5	**1941-1945**	137
	Life during the War – Mother's Day – School and More Villa de l'Ouest – Flashes of Awareness and Papa's Ideas – The Kitchen – The War Ends	

CONTENTS

6 1945-1946   179
Lost Love and Still More Villa de l'Ouest – Nasty Events – Cemetery – Tante Yvonne – Brittany – The Dining Room – Peaceful Days

7 1946-1948   229
Songs and a Trip to Le Havre – My Mother's Death – Tante Valentine, Oncle Baptiste and Roger – Things Are Starting to Change – Tante Yvonne, Cousin Bernard and a Black Elephant – Grand-mère Cessot – Childhood Readings

8 1948-1950   281
New School and Colette – Sainte-Aubierge – A Lot about Printing and a Little about Kissing – Corsica – Papa Finds a Wife

9 1950-51   321
Friends and Teachers – Quatorze Juillet – Life at Home – The Hairdresser and the Stocking Mender – Sixteen

10 1951-53   359
Sophie Germain – Barcelona – Party at Bernard's – Inside the Schuschmann's Household – Papa and Fréda – Colette in Ireland – Bound for Other Things

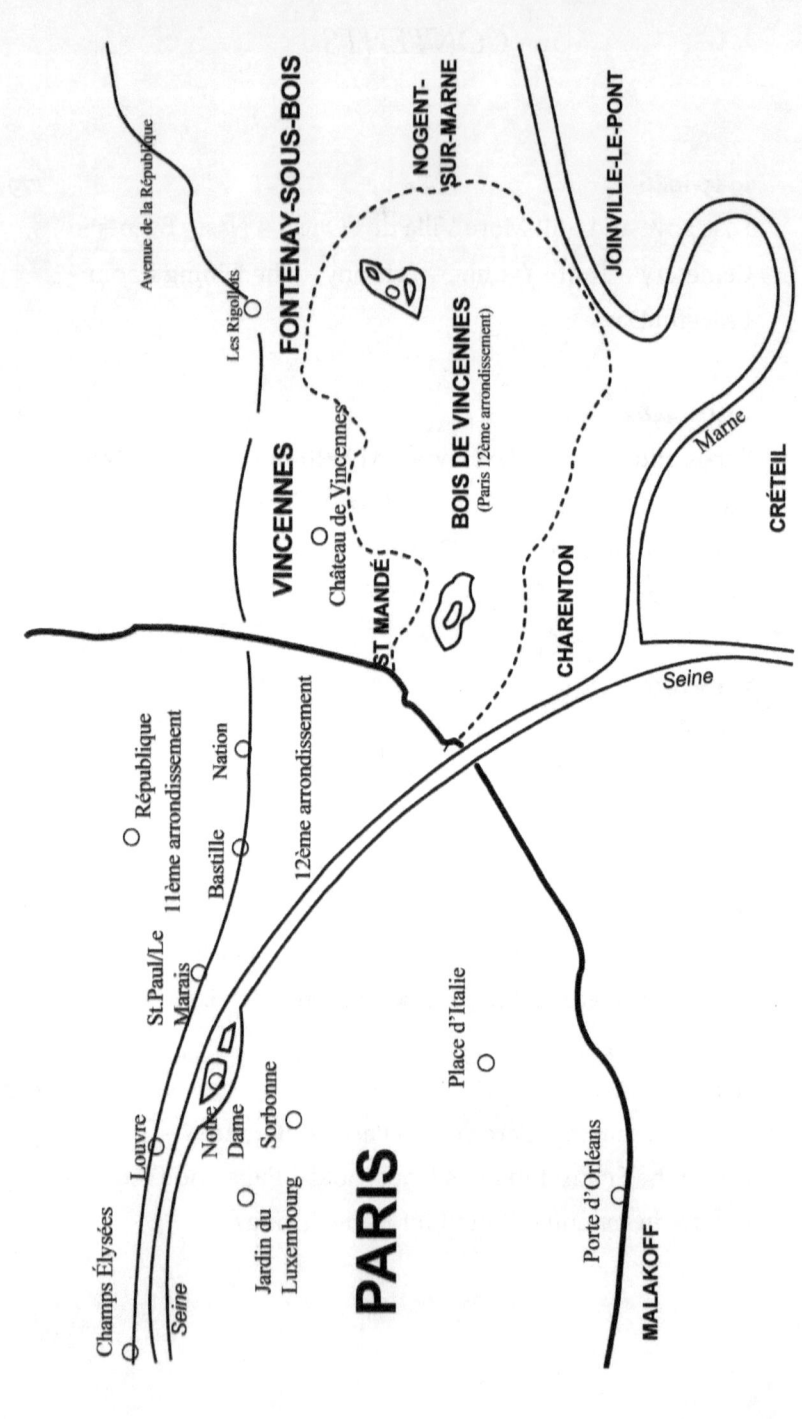

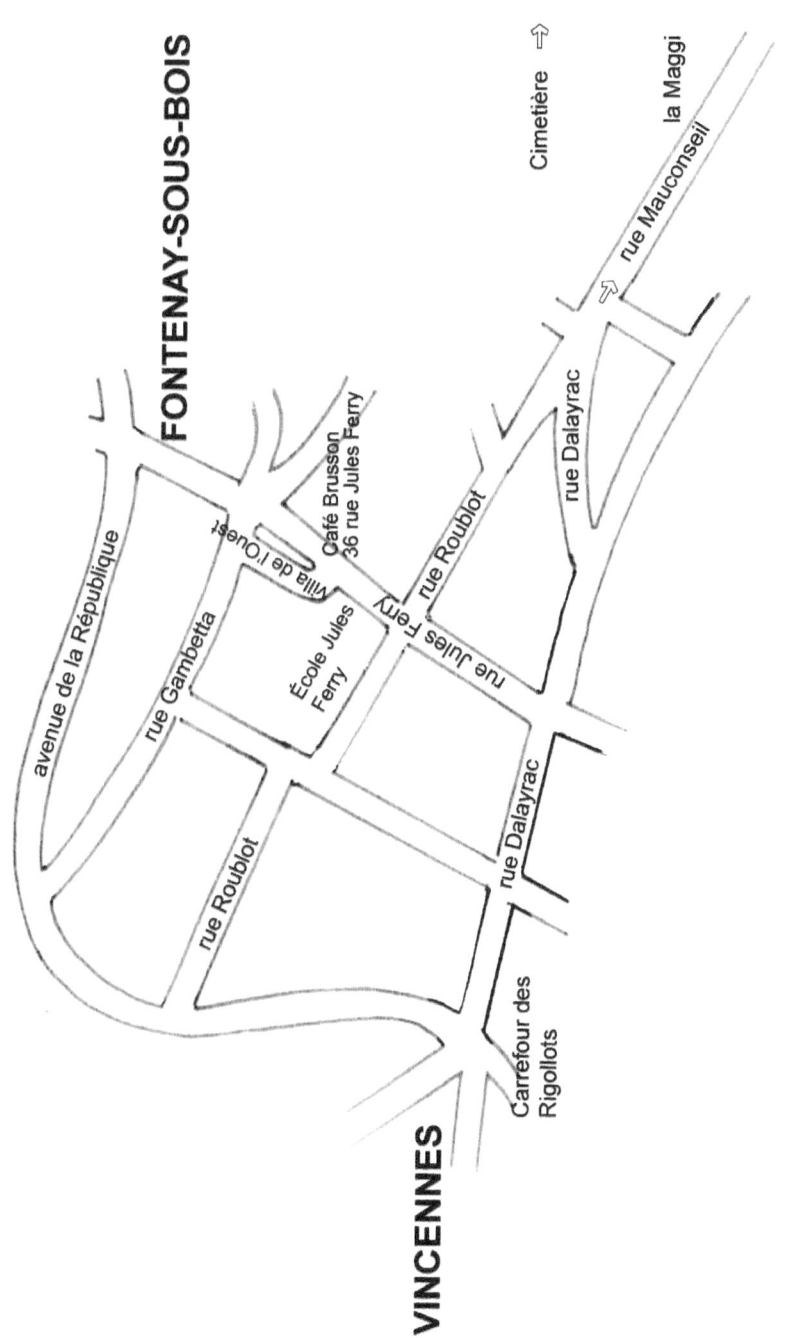

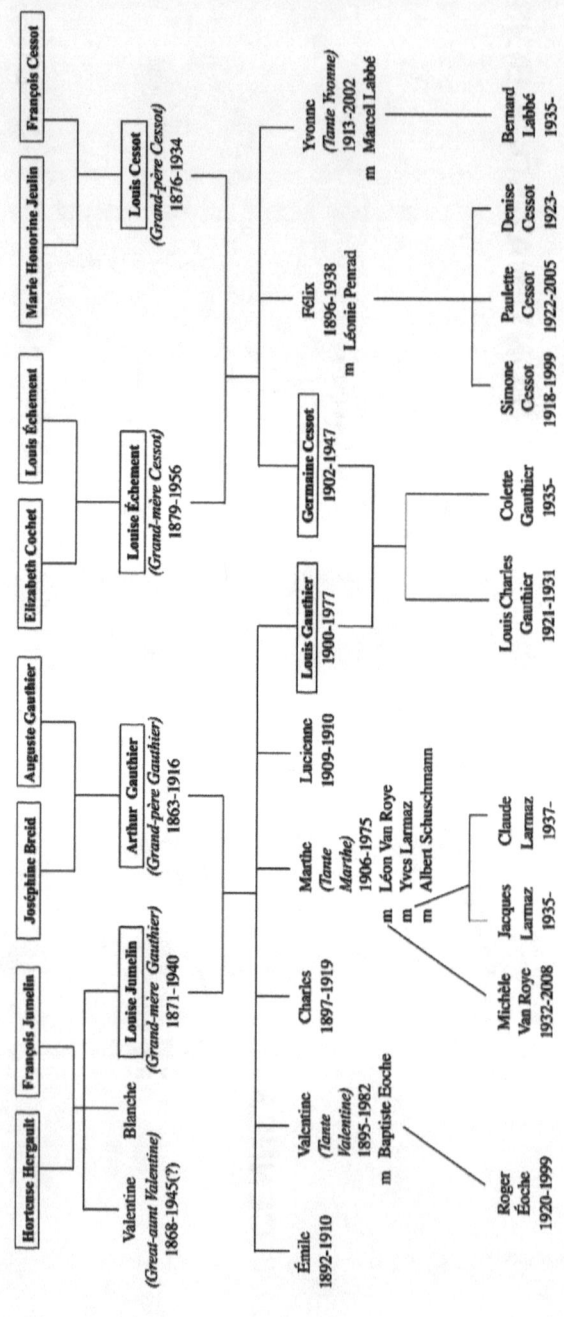

November 2010

xii

ONE

First Threads

1
An Old Letter

... Your brother Augustin stopped at Englefontaine last May 28th as he returned from the wedding of our Emperor. He came to our house and asked for your address. Apparently he had something personal to write to you. He came on horseback and spent only one night. He had entrusted his other horses to his companions and left the next morning to join them in Mons, and from there to Namur and to his post. He has become so mighty (*puissant*) that one could barely recognize him.

I often wondered about the word *puissant* in this French letter sent on January 28, 1811 to my great-great-great-grandfather by a cousin of his. What did the cousin mean by *puissant*? Had this soldier of Napoleon become so powerful, so imposing that his family could hardly tell who he was? The 19th century Dictionnaire de l'Académie Française gives several definitions of the word. Indeed, *puissant* meant (and still means) "mighty," "powerful," but it could also mean "physically strong." It could even signify "heavy," as in the example: "This man has become very *puissant* by lack of exercise." In other words, "fat." In our case, however, it is evident that it was the soldier's powerful physique that had so much struck the cousin.

This New Year's letter, written on soft gray paper and secured by a seal of red wax, was addressed to *Monsieur Louis Pierre Jumelin, Maréchal à la*

Commune de Pitre, proche le Pont-de-l'Arche, département d'Evreux, dit de l'Eure. (Mr. Louis Pierre Jumelin, Marshal in the town of Pîtres(s), near Pont-de-l'Arche, in the Evreux *Département,* also known as "Eure").

The letter was sent from Englefontaine, a village in French Flanders, near the Belgian border. There was something else about this letter that puzzled me. What did *"Maréchal* (Marshal) *à la Commune"* mean? Although it sounded like a military rank, I soon found out it was not. No, Louis Pierre Jumelin was not a *maréchal* in the army: he was the *maréchal-ferrant* (the blacksmith) of the Pîtres municipality, a position important nevertheless at a time when the horse was central to farming, transportation, and the economy in general.

The towns of Pîtres, Pont-de-l'Arche, and Évreux are in Normandy, about fifty miles northwest of Paris. Pîtres, near Rouen, built at the confluent of the Eure and Andelle rivers, is renowned for its Neolithic and Gallo-Roman archeological sites. First known as Pistus, it is found mentioned as early as the year 660. In the 9th century, when it became a center of resistance against the Viking invasions, Pistus was the site of a royal residence for King Charles the Bald. At that time Pistus included both the communities of Manoir and of Romilly-sur-Andelle, the town where my family would settle.

The letter contains news of various relatives, as well as information on the cost of goods:

> Your nephew continues to take lessons from the same master in Valenciennes. The students are twenty-eight in number, and by his diligence, he now ranks among the first.
> ... Wheat here presently costs eight francs per sack ...
> Tobacco in powder and other kind just rose to seventy *sous* per pound since the last three weeks.
> ... Your brothers and sisters and their children send their best wishes to you and your little family. The wife of your esteemed brother just gave birth to a boy two months ago. Your aunt Victoire Benoit died last March twenty-fifth at the age of eighty...
> ... My sister, your cousin, was ill for seven months last year. Without great care and attention, it would have taken little for

her her to perish. Thank God, she is doing well enough at the present. She is able to do her work.

All your relatives and friends salute you and are in good health.

Your cousins,
François and Marie-Claire Crappez

The elegant handwriting and easiness of style attest to the literacy of the writers at a time when not everyone was privileged to go to school. Furthermore, the first newsworthy item: the fact that a nephew studies in the nearest big town, seems to show that the family valued education.

The most interesting part of the letter is the paragraph I first cited. On May 28th Augustin Jumelin, a soldier (perhaps an officer), was returning from the wedding of Napoleon and Marie-Louise which had taken place in Paris on April 1st and 2nd, 1810 (the civil ceremony in the Galerie du Palais de St. Cloud, the religious ceremony in the Salon Carré du Louvre). It is probable that Augustin was part of Napoleon's *Garde impériale*, serving either in the *Chasseurs à cheval*, a light cavalry unit who usually provided personal escort to Napoleon, or even in the *Grenadiers à cheval*, an elite unit composed of men selected for their strength and stature and mounted on strong black horses—which might explain why he was found so *"puissant"* by his relatives. After his stop at Englefontaine he went to Belgium, first to Mons, then to his post in Namur where Napoleon had positioned part of his Northern Army. Whether this great-great-great-uncle of mine ever returned to his home, or perhaps died in 1812 during the disastrous invasion of Russia, or in 1815 at Waterloo, I do not know.

About the writers of the letter, we only find that they were the dispensers of family news and that they bore the uncommon name of Crappez. This name was also born by one Emmanuel Crappez, Master in Surgery, who is documented to have resided in 1795 in Wargnies-le-Petit, a village very near Englefontaine. Although it is not certain that Doctor Emmanuel Crappez was a relative of my distant cousins, the fact that he bore the same name, was a contemporary of theirs, and lived only eight miles away makes it more than likely. Doctor Crappez found his place in history thanks to a medical report he wrote on the alleged victims of the notorious bandit Moneuse.

Toward the end of the French Revolution, under the *Directoire*, France crossed a grave financial crisis. This crisis gave rise to a period of disorder during which bandits roamed the countryside and frequently attacked people. In the Northern provinces of France and in Belgium, a brigand named Moneuse, together with his large band, conducted highway robberies, looted farms, stole horses, and organized attacks on wealthy citizens. He circulated openly, his boldness and his allure making him somewhat of a legend. Several books have been written about him, particularly one by Albert Jotrand, in 1932 (from which I gleaned most of my information), and another by Alfred Gallez, in 1959. Moneuse has also been the subject of many articles and of a French television program. For several years the brigand managed to escape the law, thanks to the protection of some, who gave him alibis, or the silence of others, who were too frightened to testify against him. In the court archives of Judge Harmegnies we read:

> "His bearing is proud and bold. He usually wears a long open coat with a red collar, a silk jacket striped in purple, red and white, iron-gray pants made of cloth and black leather, very clean boots, and either a round cap or a russet straw hat adorned with a fox tail. He rides a gray-white horse, and is armed with pistols (at least one pair) and good ammunition." (Translation mine).

We also learn that he was handsome, tall and thin, with a pronounced aquiline nose and a scar on his left cheek. Also, that his hair was black and curly, his eyes piercing, and that women were mad about him.

In October 1795, a horrible murder was committed at the isolated inn of La Houlette. The innkeeper, his wife, his children, and one of his lodgers were found assassinated. In all, nine people, including a baby, were found dead—all savagely stabbed. The police called on two local physicians to prepare a medical report on the crime; one of these physicians was Doctor Emmanuel Crappez.

Public opinion immediately accused Moneuse of the crime, and he was arrested. However, because it was suspected that some enemies of the Revolution (perhaps French émigrés on their way to Belgium) might have been involved, and because Moneuse managed to obtain an alibi, he was released and continued his banditry. Sometime later, however, he was arrested again and imprisoned for robberies. In 1798, after a long and complicated trial, he was put to death by guillotine. Later, his name was given to a Belgian beer (strong and mean, I suppose), "la Moneuse."

I know I went astray talking about Moneuse and the good Doctor Crappez, but the story was worth telling, I think. Anyway, I do apologize for the detour.

My father jokingly boasted about the Jumelins, his maternal ancestors. He even suspected that "way back" they may have been aristocrats. Showing us his narrow wrists, he would say, *"Regardez mes attaches fines!"* (Look at my narrow joints!) "Isn't that proof of noble breeding? If I had lived in the old time, I might have been d'Artagnan!"

He may not have been completely wrong. If we go back far enough, we are bound to discover a noble ancestor—or at least one who was an ace at wielding the sword.

2
The Jumelins

For at least two more generations the Jumelins remained close to their Normandy roots. My great-grandfather, François Honoré Jumelin, lived in Romilly-sur-Andelle, a village only two and a half miles from Pîtres. There, he married Hortense (born Hergault), also from Normandy. Not long after their marriage, the young couple decided to leave their village and move to Paris. Soon, they had two daughters: Valentine, born in 1869, and Blanche, in 1870.

Not long after Blanche's birth, Hortense found she was pregnant again. At that time, France was in great turmoil. The Franco-Prussian war had begun in July 1870. The German army, which had invaded Lorraine and captured Napoleon III, arrived in Paris in September 1870. The Parisians put up a sharp resistance but were besieged by the Germans. The Siege of Paris, which lasted from September 19 to January 28, 1871, brought terrible hunger to the population, who resorted to eating cats and rats. On May 10th, 1871, the Treaty of Frankfurt, which marked the defeat of France, ceded Alsace and a part of Lorraine to Germany (a clause that would eventually lead to World War I). But although the war had ended and Napoleon III had been deposed, although the Third Republic had been proclaimed, the situation in Paris was not yet calm. In March 1871, idealistic political activists together with workers formed *La Commune de Paris*, an independent government that lasted from March 18 to May 21, 1871. Soon, *La Commune* was mercilessly attacked by the regular French army. The *Communards* burned several monuments, among them the Hôtel de Ville de Paris, the Palais des Tuileries and the Palais de la Légion d'Honneur. During *"la Semaine Sanglante"* ("Bloody Week") which lasted from May 21 to 28, 1871, more than 20,000 people were killed by the government's repressive forces.

It is easy to understand why Hortense Jumelin was frightened by these violent events. While staying with relatives in Vassy (Bourgogne), she had her baby. Louise (my future grandmother) was born on May 13th, 1871. Soon after her third daughter's birth, Hortense took her two young daughters and her baby to Normandy, and then returned to Paris to join her husband. Only, she did not bring back her new baby daughter. She left her behind in the care of her parents, the Hergaults.

Great-grandmother Hortense Jumelin (born Hergault) Paris. (c. 1895)

Great-grandfather François Jumelin. Paris. (c. 1895)

Louise's grandparents, who probably resented having this baby dropped in their lap, treated her with little kindness. As soon as she was able, Louise was made to do chores that were beyond her age. She would later remember how she was whipped with nettles whenever she was disobedient. Besides treating her roughly, her grandparents never sent her to school. She would remain in Normandy until she was ten.

Meanwhile, in a Paris that had recovered and was now preoccupied with construction and progress, such as building the Sacré-Coeur and installing electric lights on Avenue de l'Opéra, the Jumelin family was concentrating on bringing up their two daughters. The oldest, Valentine, was the favorite. From the time she was five or six she was a real charmer, always ready to entertain her parents' friends by singing her little songs. Soon, Hortense had Valentine take lessons from a nearby piano teacher, and, determined to bring her up as a *demoiselle*, sent her to a finishing school where she was taught *les bonnes manières*. If Valentine had a pretty round face, shiny brown eyes, full lips and curly hair, her sister Blanche was quite plain. Worse still, she was cross-eyed. Hortense, who could not bear having a cross-eyed daughter, could never bring herself to be nice to her. Well-aware of her mother's feelings, Blanche took the habit of talking back to her. This made for an unhappy relationship that would never be completely mended.

At last, Hortense decided that it was time for Louise to join the family. She went to pick her up at the railroad station. As Louise got off the train, wearing her gray smock, black stockings, and heavy galoshes, she saw an elegant lady looking at her.

"*Excusez-moi Madame*, are you Valentine's mother?" she asked.

"Your mother too, stupid goose!" Hortense answered.

When Louise arrived home, Valentine and Blanche couldn't help laughing at her peasant accent. And, how awkward she was! She broke some fine glasses as she was drying them. Soon, however, Louise lost her country ways and the three sisters learned to get along.

Their father earned a decent salary as a clerk in a government office, but their mother, who loved fancy things, often ran out of money. When Louise was thirteen, Hortense decided to send her into service in a bourgeois family. The girl was, after all, used to hard work! In her new position, Louise was treated unfairly. At first she was too shy to say anything, but after a while, she did not let people abuse her. Whenever her employers were mean to her, she left them and found another family to work for. Her indomitable spirit had begun to show. Moreover, proud as she was, she could not tolerate remaining ignorant. She taught herself to read and write, learning her letters by spelling out the names of stores and street signs. Finally, swearing to never work as a maid again, she looked for another line of work. However, having no qualifications, the only job she could find was as a reeler in a silk factory.

The reelers, who sat at long work tables in front of complicated machines, unraveled the fine silk threads from silkworm cocoons. Gathering several filaments, they guided them through holes in a system of gears and pulleys. Not only did the workers have to be very fast, but since the cocoons were kept in hot water (the hot water killed the silk worms and softened the threads), they were confined in factories steamy and unbearably hot. Silk reeling, an exhausting and low-paid job, was done almost exclusively by women.

Louise bore with the work without complaining. Now eighteen, she had become a good-looking young woman. A photo taken at the time shows her as calm-looking and poised. Tightly corseted in a fashion that accentuates her chest and small waist, she bears an expression that is serious, perhaps beyond her age. In her almost perfect oval face, her features are regular and pleasant. Her brown hair is tied in a bun. If her hairstyle makes her look a little severe, her soft hazel eyes give her away. Honest, spirited, resolute, she was well-liked by her girlfriends at the factory. The girlfriends must have had brothers. The brothers must have had friends. All these young people must have gone out together. It is perhaps at such outings that Louise met Arthur Gauthier, a watch repairman from the Jura region, who had recently moved to Paris. She probably was not able to resist the charms of this handsome man with his high forehead, wavy hair and well-combed mustache. But it must have been the kind look in his intelligent eyes that Louise found so appealing.

Grandmother Louise Gauthier (born Jumelin). (c. 1890)

Grandfather Arthur Gauthier. (c. 1890)

3
Great-Aunt Valentine

Before continuing with Louise and Arthur, I will begin the story of Valentine, Louise's oldest sister, the accomplished "demoiselle" of the family. The cute little charmer had turned into a true beauty. Encouraged by her mother, she now worked as a fashion model for the Haute Couture House of Jeanne Lanvin. With her large bosom and tiny waist, she had the perfect figure to incarnate the ideal feminine body of *La Belle Époque*.

She soon met Alphonse Meyer, the son of wealthy cloth merchants. Alphonse, handsome and *amoureux* would be the love of her life. They got engaged in spite of the fact that they faced opposition, not only from Valentine's parents who objected to the marriage (Alphonse was a Jew), but from Alphonse's parents who had hoped for a Jewish bride. To keep Alphonse away from Valentine, his parents sent him to America. But Valentine, who was determined to join her beloved, saved on her salary and took the boat. As soon as she arrived in New York, she and Alphonse got married. They soon returned to France where they had to get married again when they found that their American wedding was not considered legal. Faced with the fait accompli, both sets of parents accepted the situation.

Valentine was well received at her in-laws' house. Except for the fact that her dishes and silverware were handled separately, her in-laws treated her as any other member of the family and were very nice to her.

Alphonse worked at La Samaritaine, a department store prestigious at the time. (The Samaritaine building, a mixture of Art Nouveau and Art Deco, is still one of Paris architectural attractions.) There, Alphonse was manager of the semi-autonomous fabric department. He earned a good living, but Valentine who loved to go out or give dinners for their friends, kept an extravagant lifestyle. Money slipped through her fingers.

The couple lived on rue Francoeur in Montmartre in a luxurious apartment tastefully furnished in the style of the time. My father told me that when they were young boys, he and his brother Charles loved to visit their elegant and perfumed aunt Valentine. They rolled on the fluffy white carpets, saying, *"Ça sent ma tante! Ça sent ma tante!"* ("It smells like auntie!")

Valentine had a maid named Louise, like her sister. In order to avoid confusion, the maid was nicknamed "Louise-la-Rouge" (Louise-the-Red) because of the color of her hair. Seduced by Alphonse's brother, the maid became pregnant. Marriage was out of the question, because of class difference, of course. However, it might have been a good thing as Alphonse's brother (although he was very intelligent and spoke several languages) did not work, preferring to live at the expense of his family. Louise-la-Rouge was soon married off to a cousin from the Hergault branch of the family. She did not love her husband, but to everyone's relief, the future baby had a father.

In spite of her society life, Valentine was bored. She took a few lovers, but the one she really adored was her husband. She called him "Mireil." Why? No one knows. As he adored her also, he forgave her peccadillos. Then she had the idea of opening a business in the hope that it would help her at month's end. She opened a jewelry store on the Passage des Princes, near the Grands Boulevards. Did she confuse gross income and benefits? I cannot tell. In any case, business declined. Moreover, it was against the rules for the wife of a floor manager to run a business. Poor Alphonse got fired from the Samaritaine. He found another position, but his salary was lower. The jewelry store had to be sold. The young couple had already moved to Boulevard Voltaire, in an apartment less luxurious than the first one. Now they had to move again. They found a cute little apartment in Auteuil, but this time there was no maid. Then Alphonse fell ill and soon died. It was a great shock for Valentine, who not only lost her beloved husband but was now deprived of his financial support. After his death the household savings quickly melted, leaving Valentine almost penniless. What was she to do? We will see later what happened to Great-aunt Valentine. For the moment, let's return to her sister Louise's paramour, the clockmaker Arthur Gauthier.

4
The Gauthiers

If the Jumelins (except for Louise) had succeeded in attaining a certain social status, the family of my future grandfather, Arthur Gauthier, was more modest. Arthur's mother, Joséphine Breid, was an unmarried factory worker at the time of his birth. Unmarried she was, it is true, though she could have had a husband: the baby's father had asked her several times to marry him, but she had refused.

Joséphine Breid lived in Morez, a town of eastern France in the high part of the Jura Mountains. Close to the Alps, Morez was less than eight miles from the Swiss border. The town, deeply ensconced between two high mountains, consisted mostly of a main street lined with houses, shops, and numerous factories where clocks, watches, and eyeglasses were manufactured. If one wonders why all these factories were perched so high in the mountains, the explanation is that watchmaking, an occupation practiced by local people, had become a full-fledged industry when a number of business-minded *Jurassiens* had the idea to develop it and centralize it in Morez. They rendered the industry profitable by building factories, simplifying and dividing the tasks, and employing local people at low wages.

Joséphine Breid got up at five o'clock in the morning to be at six at the clock factory. It was very cold; the only source of heat in her small apartment was a wood-burning stove in the kitchen. Outside, almost everything was buried under the snow. At least, she was lucky to be living in a town where she could easily get around; in nearby villages, snow would block all roads for two to four months of the year. She worked ten, sometimes twelve hours a day assembling clock parts. She did not earn much, but she had no choice: here, those who were not well-to-do were either small farmers or factory workers. Since hardly anything grew at such high altitude, the only way for farmers to survive was to keep a cow or a few sheep and goats, and make and sell cheese. Life in the villages was very hard, especially in the winter. It is no wonder that the majority of small farmers left the land to work in factories.

Morez was the clock and eyeglasses manufacturing capital of France. It was there that were made most of the watches and wall clocks, as well as the stylish horn-rimmed glasses that were sold in France and exported to the rest of Europe and the United States. In this town of only 5,000 inhabitants there were more than twenty-five eyeglass factories and fifty clock or watch factories—and the industry was still growing.

Joséphine was born in 1835, in Champagnole, a town twenty miles north of Morez and a little smaller. Champagnole, built along the river Ain and crossed by two old stone bridges, was quite picturesque, but work was hard to find there. When Joséphine was still a baby, her parents, Jeanne (born Blondeau) and Mathias Breid, unable to find steady employment, had decided to move to Morez. When Mathias died, Jeanne, left with several children to raise, had to go work in a clock factory. Her eldest child, Joséphine, helped as much as she could with caring for her brothers and sisters, but as soon as she turned ten, she too went to work at the factory.

Years later, Joséphine, now pregnant with a child almost due, was still working at the factory. As she sat at her work bench doing repetitive work, one can imagine that she asked herself whether or not to marry the father of her baby. She probably had tender feelings for him. He certainly was a handsome man, while she herself couldn't pretend to be a beauty with her moon face and upturned nose. But he drank too much, much too much. One didn't have to be a wizard to know he wouldn't make a good husband. No! She wasn't going to marry him. For sure, her mother was going to fret and cry, and even claim she was going to die of shame, but she'd eventually get used to the idea. After all, Joséphine thought, I'm twenty-seven, not a young girl any more. Besides, in this town, these sorts of things happen all the time!

Her son, Arthur, was born on January 15, 1863 in Morez. When Arthur was one year old, Joséphine met a very nice man, Auguste Gauthier (Pierre Auguste Gauthier). Soon, Joséphine and Auguste decided to live together. Even if Joséphine still thought about her lover, she was glad to have found Auguste, who acted like a true father to her son.

Auguste worked at an eyeglass factory. A little younger than Joséphine, he also was from the Jura region. He was born in Saint-Laurent, just a few miles away. His parents, César Gauthier and Marie (born Chevassu) lived in La Rixouse, a small town about ten miles south of Morez.

One cannot say that Auguste was very good-looking, but he was thoughtful and hardworking. On April 19th, 1869, Joséphine and Auguste got married, first at the Morez City Hall, then at the church. He was twenty-nine, she was thirty-four. Auguste gave his name to Arthur who officially became: Louis Arthur Gauthier. My future grandfather Arthur was called by his middle name, as seems to have been the custom.

One may think that with two salaries the young couple was able to live comfortably. In fact, their life remained very hard. Even after working long hours they barely earned enough to feed themselves and their child.

The French leaders of the time did not show much concern for workers' needs. Napoleon's Empire, the Restoration, the Second Republic had all come and gone; the new regime, Napoleon III's Second Empire, was mostly preoccupied with taxes and wars. It was not surprising that many people wondered why France had found itself involved in a war in Crimea, and why the French had continued to fight in Mexico in spite of their defeat on the *Cinco de Mayo*. Although some social reforms would eventually take place toward the end of the Second Empire, at the moment the workers had no hope to better their condition. It was not surprising: the factories' owners or their cronies held all the official positions from mayors and chiefs of police, to lawyers and judges. It was a state of affairs with no recourse. In England, the situation was similar. At a time when Queen Victoria reigned over the vast British Empire, a wealthy middle class profited from the rapid growth of industry while workers labored for minimal wages.

In the United States of America, the situation appeared to be different. "In America, it's easy to become a millionaire," Joséphine and Auguste heard people say at work. It was written right there, in the newspaper *La Sentinelle du Jura* (owned by Frédéric Gauthier, who probably was not a relative, the name Gauthier being quite common).

Whether or not that was true, at least it was nice to hear. It made one dream when, at lunch time, the news was shared by a few literate workers. Had it not been for these people, Joséphine and Auguste would not have known what was happening in France and in the rest of the world; they had never been to school and did not know how to read or write.

In 1888, when Arthur reached the age of twenty-five, he decided to leave the Jura to try his luck in Paris as many had before him. One can easily imagine that he cast a last look at the town of his birth, a town he would never see again. Morez was still asleep. The sun was beginning to rise; soon his parents and all the other workers would get up to go to the factories.

Arthur, who had been working since the age of eleven, had had enough; especially, he could no longer bear to see his parents wearing themselves out. If he succeeded in making a living in Paris, he pledged he would send for them. His mother cried when he left that morning, but his father put on a brave front. Leaving was difficult because he knew his parents still needed his help, but he had to do what he knew was right.

Like his parents, Arthur was illiterate. Education, which had been mostly controlled by the Church, was now secular, free and obligatory since the Jules Ferry laws of 1881-82. These laws came too late for him.

Medical care was still minimal. When the workers got sick, they were attended by a few nuns at the municipal hospice. Arthur felt lucky to be in good health but was worried about his mother. Joséphine had a goiter, an enlarged thyroid gland, a condition common among mountain people. By way of treatment, she bought potions at the Morez or the Champagnole annual fairs where hawkers peddled remedies, but these potions did not work. As a consequence of her ailment, Joséphine was often irritated. When something went wrong she got easily upset, and was known (and often mocked) for screaming in a high voice and stomping her feet like a child. Good thing her husband had the patience of an angel! Arthur told himself: if I can ever bring my parents to Paris, the first thing I'll do will be to take my mother to a doctor.

About himself he was not really worried; he was ready to start a new life. Although he had mostly worked on the assembly line, he had studied on his own the complete mechanism of clocks and watches and was confident he would be able to find work in Paris.

Carrying a knapsack with a few clothes, Arthur sat by the side of the road. His bag also contained a bottle of wine, a couple of round loaves of bread, and some cheese and cold chicken that his mother had packed for him. He was waiting for a friend who was to take him to the nearby town of Saint-Laurent in a horse-drawn cart. There, he had some relatives who would take him by cart a little further. But after that, he would be on his own to walk all the way to Paris.

Many people have heard of the Jura. This is because, due to the great number of fossils found in the sandstone and limestone of the area, the name of the region is associated with the Jurassic period. However, paleontology is irrelevant in this story. Rather, it was Arthur's knowledge of local geography that was going to serve him well. He knew that the Jura region looked like a huge staircase with high mountains at the top, vineyard-covered hills at the next level, and a fertile plain at the bottom. With only a few francs in his pocket, he had chosen to leave at the time of the grape harvest. On his way to Paris he was planning to work in vineyards, earning food and shelter as he went. It was a good three hundred miles to Paris. Before starting to walk, Arthur took off his shoes, tied them up by the laces, and threw them over his shoulder (he would need good shoes in Paris). The trip would last several weeks but the road did not frighten him.

When my grandfather Arthur arrived in Paris, he had difficulties at first but eventually found work in a shop as a clock repairman; by the end of the year he was pretty much established with a job and a small room. Going out with his friends, he soon met a nice girl, Louise Jumelin, who worked in a silk factory. Whether or not Louise and Arthur met while visiting the 1889 Paris *Exposition Universelle*, the main feature of which was an enormous celebration for the inauguration of the Eiffel Tower, I do not know, but after going out a few times on their Sundays off, they decided to spend their life together.

Entrance to the Exposition Universelle, 1889. Painting by Jean Béraud

My grandparents Arthur Gauthier and Louise Jumelin were married on May 31st, 1890. Louise was nineteen, Arthur twenty-seven. They were happy, but even though they both worked very hard, they didn't make much money. Still hearing people say that life in the United States was easier than in France, they decided to emigrate to America to seek their fortune. Before booking their passage they went to say their good-byes to Louise's relatives in Normandy.

"Don't go!" the relatives told them. "You will die on the ship! And even if you get to America alive, you may not be able to find work! You will end up hungry and miserable, and without family to help you!"

They must not have been too determined in the first place for they heeded their relatives' advice, abandoned their plans and returned to Paris. There, my grandfather found another watchmaking job, and my grandmother, who by then was expecting their first child, took in laundry to make ends meet. It was around that time that, as he had promised himself, Arthur sent for his parents Joséphine and Auguste Gauthier, to come to Paris. They settled not far from their son and his new wife, and never returned to the Jura.

Louise and Arthur were to share good times and hard times. Alas, hard times would be more frequent than good times, as we soon shall see. For the moment, let's just record that during their marriage, they had seven children. Their first son, Émile, died in infancy. Their second son, also named Émile, died at eighteen. After Émile came a daughter, baptized Jeanne but called Valentine in honor of Louise's sister. Then came two more sons: Charles, who died at twenty-two, and Louis, my father. Six years after Louis' birth, a daughter, Marthe, followed. The youngest child, Lucienne, died at nine months. Of their seven children, only three would live beyond their twenties: Valentine, Louis, and Marthe.

But for now, they were still newlyweds. After their marriage, the young couple had settled in an older apartment building in one of Paris' poorest *quartier*, near Boulevard Voltaire in the 11th arrondissement. They moved a few times, but always stayed in the same district. My father told me that whenever his parents moved, they rented a handcart, piled all their possessions on it, and pulled it on the cobblestones, the small children following behind. In 1906, tired of the hard life of the city, they relocated in Créteil, an eastern suburb of Paris. At that time, the small town of Créteil had almost the feel of a village.

5
More about Great-Aunt Valentine

What was happening to Great-aunt Valentine? After the death of her dear Alphonse, her "Mireil," she was devastated. Also, with most of the household savings now spent what choice did she have left but go to Normandy and settle in the village of Romilly-sur-Andelle, in the now vacant family house? By then, both her sisters were married and had children. Louise's oldest son, Émile, was already a teenager. Blanche, unable to have children, had adopted a girl, Pauline, who was almost ready to get married herself.

As far back as she could remember, my great-aunt Valentine would have loved to have children. But, like her sister Blanche, she could not have children of her own. When she lived in Montmartre with Alphonse, she had the idea that it would be nice to take care of Jeanne, Louise's oldest daughter, a child who not only was her niece, but also her goddaughter, and who (at her suggestion) had been "renamed" Valentine like herself. She was ready to give her a good education and had already made arrangements for her to receive piano lessons. But her hopes were quickly dashed. Little Valentine had just spent a week with her when Louise came to pick her up. Without malice, the child, who was about six or seven at the time, told her mother, "From now on, Aunt Valentine will be my mommy and you will be my aunt Louise!" Louise became so upset that she took back her daughter for good.

"Tu resteras pauvre, mais avec moi!" "You will stay poor, but with me!"

This is why my great-aunt Valentine neglected her niece Valentine, and instead pampered her other niece, Pauline, Blanche's adopted daughter—although Pauline, of a rather cold nature, gave her little satisfaction.

Blanche died in her fifties. Not long after her mother's death, Pauline got married and had a little girl. Valentine, eager to leave Normandy and the boredom of village life, went to live with Pauline and her family in Lyon. It was decided that they would all move to Algiers and open a jewelry store. I don't know the details of their life in Algiers, but after a time they sold their business and returned to Lyon. There, Pauline and her husband became owners of another jewelry store.

Before World War II began, Great-aunt Valentine married Monsieur Cuenot, a nice gentleman who lived on a government retirement pension. She and her new husband settled in Marseilles.

But I will yield the pen to Great-Aunt Valentine herself. Up to now, while I was drawing a rough sketch of her life, I knew full well that some secret remained. I had heard rumors, both from my own Tante Valentine and from my father. Was there any truth behind these rumors? I am convinced there was. Some time ago, I imagined that my great-aunt opened her heart in a letter to a woman friend of hers. I do admit that these are not Valentine's real words, but it is her voice, I suppose, and I am willing to bet that such a letter may very well have been written.

> Marseilles, September 1st, 1933
>
> My dear A.,
>
> I have never revealed to anyone what I am about to tell you today, but our long friendship urges me to free my mind, and, should I die unexpectedly, at least I would feel relieved to know that you were aware of my past errors. So here it is, my dear friend, and may I be so bold as to beg for your indulgence.
>
> I am sixty-four now, on my way to becoming an old woman. I do not try to hide this fact from myself, though perhaps I still try to hide it from those around me; but let us not talk about that now! What I want to tell you is something that happened more than twenty years ago. I feel ashamed of my mistake. The thought of it makes me blush still, and I know that it will to the end. But was it really a mistake? Am I really guilty? Whatever one may say about me, "La Belle Valentine," as they used to call me, I didn't kill Émile. He would have died that summer. That, I know. Everyone knows.

But first, my dear A., let me tell you a little about my life when I was a much younger woman. I have shared with you only partial confidences: the stories of my husbands, of my lovers, but you do not know much about my family life.

My sister Louise and her husband Arthur had several children. When I was married to Alphonse and lived in Montmartre, some of the children sometimes came to visit. I wanted to take care of my little niece Valentine, but it didn't work out. I think that my sister Louise was jealous of me. Once in a while I went to visit Louise and her family. They lived in such a poor district of Paris! I hated to go there; their apartment was so dark, so crowded. At that time their oldest son, Émile, was about fifteen. He was a nice-looking boy, tall, but thin and pale. I found him a little shy.

"He plays the violin," Louise had said with admiration, "he wants to enter the Music Conservatory."

I could not help thinking how ridiculous it was to try to make music in this noisy slum, but I made an effort to be kind, and said nothing. I could see that at Louise's Émile didn't have the quietness he needed; in order to block out the animal noises of his brothers and sisters, he had to lock himself in a room and cover the opening under the door with old rags. He owned a cheap violin, with a meager metallic sound.

In 1910, Émile fell ill. By that time, after the death of my dear Alphonse, I had gone to live in Normandy, in Romilly-sur-Andelle. Louise asked me if she could send Émile to stay with me for a while, hoping the country air would do him good.

The last time I had seen Émile was when he was fifteen. In the last three years he had changed so much that when he arrived at my house I almost did not recognize him. He was as pale as before, but taller and stronger. He had become a man. Unmistakably, the very minute I greeted him, I was stirred by the sensual look in his eyes. (Remember! I had been living alone for a while!) In spite of the age difference, which—I hate to say—was of twenty-three years, I began to fall in love with my nephew, my feelings taking the same form as in years past, my love showing itself as a servile display of affection.

I think that Émile was slightly embarrassed by my attentions, and although I tried my best to adopt a maternal air (I, who never had children!), a kind of uneasiness existed between us. I knew he was not ready to admit it, but I felt he was captivated by my well-chosen dresses and my elaborate hairstyles. You remember that I was a fashion model in my youth; at that time many a woman had envied my generous chest and diminutive waistline (I could barely breathe in my corset!). I know that all this was a long time ago, but my shape had barely changed, and my body was still firm. I also had kept my little secrets of makeup and perfumes. Following a "secret" formula given to me by my mother, I still prepared special drops to make my eyes shine. Today, I smile at these *coquetteries*, but at that time, they were important to me.

In the mornings, as I did not want Émile to get up too early, I always brought him his *petit-déjeuner* in bed, staying with him while he had his bowl of café au lait and his slices of buttered bread. We looked at one another, happy. He was handsome and disheveled. I could see in his eyes that he was feverish. I knew he desired me. He told me his bizarre dreams, and, in the afternoon, when we sat together in the garden, I told them back to him—and he laughed, for he had already forgotten them.

Émile had brought his poor cheap violin and practiced every day. One day, the doctor of Romilly, who came for regular visits, had mentioned that he wanted to sell his very good violin. I immediately noticed Émile's eyes light up. I knew he wanted the violin very badly. When his birthday arrived, I thought of the violin, and, without saying anything to him, I decided to buy it (a folly!).

On the morning of his eighteenth birthday, I entered Émile's room as he was still asleep. When I caressed his forehead, he opened his eyes. He seemed to be waiting for someone, and I knew that this someone was me. I offered him the violin. He was so happy that tears came to my eyes! I sat on his bed, and the thank-you kiss he gave me became a kiss that did not leave us any doubt. He opened my blouse, took out my too-ready breasts, and let himself drift into a desire sometimes childish, sometimes more manly than I dare to describe.

Days passed. Little by little I lost all willpower, or (should I say?) all common sense. I called love the weakness that has always prevented me from resisting a young and handsome man touching my body. I spent my days desiring and caressing Émile. I spent my nights loving and devouring him.

His health was becoming worse; a fever and an awful cough did not let go of him. I knew he needed rest, but when he asked me to stay with him, I could not leave his room. Then his illness took over. There was nothing the doctor could do.

My pain became unbearable. I felt helpless! I adored this child! He had barely been at my home three months when he died.

My sister Louise came to Romilly for the funeral. She was wearing black as I did. By the way, I must say that mourning clothes did nothing for us, except perhaps accentuate the discoloration of our aging skin. For a long time I was afraid to look into Louise's eyes, but finally I sensed that she suspected nothing. He and I were the only ones who knew. But now he is dead. As for me, I have nothing to do but hark back to my memories, memories that are dear to me, but fill me with unease. It is as though I stretch my hands over a fire that refuses to warm them.

Oh, my dear friend, how comforting it is for me to have told you all this! Please do not blame me too much. Think of me as a woman whose weak heart was overcome by love.

Your devoted friend,

Valentine

Well! It could have been like that! I was never told exactly what happened, although it was strongly hinted that La Belle Valentine had become indecently fond of her nephew. I am sorry I never had a chance to meet this fancy great-aunt of mine, but she lived in Marseilles, far from my parents', and I was just a child when she died.

This chapter almost marks the end of the first Valentine's adventures. Except for a mention of two brief visits paid to her, one by my parents in 1932, the other by an uncle of mine in 1940, the second Valentine, my father's sister, my dear "Tata Gâteau" will be the only Valentine in the rest of this story.

From right: Great-aunt Valentine in her sixties, my mother, my parents' friends. Marseilles. (1932)

Two

1910 - 1935

1
Arthur and Louise

Arthur and Louise Gauthier had now settled in Créteil. My grandfather Arthur, who was illiterate when he left the Jura, was now able to read the newspapers, having been taught how to read and write by my grandmother, who used with him the same method she had used to teach herself.

In spite of hardship, the Gauthiers raised their children the best way they could. They also shared whatever they had with my grandfather's parents, Joséphine and Auguste, who never regretted having left their native Jura. Old Joséphine had become senile, but Grand-mère Gauthier never complained about having to take care of her mother-in-law. As for my great-grandfather Auguste, I was told that he was a darling and liked to help with the cooking. If my grandparents never had much, they at least had dreams. My grandfather joined the "League of Landlords," but, unfortunately, never became a landlord himself.

Unlike many of their neighbors, the Gauthiers never used corporal punishment; instead, Grand-mère enforced discipline by giving her children *"les gros yeux"* ("the eye"), and Grand-père pretended to untie his belt whenever the situation called for it. This method seems to have worked very well. Theirs was a loving household in which everyone got along.

All the children were musical: Émile played the violin, Charles and Louis joined the municipal band, Valentine never missed a town concert, and Marthe had a beautiful singing voice. They were quite well-behaved, except for my father, Louis (P'tit Louis), who was the naughty one of the bunch. Apparently, he had a terrible temper and could not stand being teased. His brother Charles would chant a little ditty, *"Rage, rage! T'auras du cirage!"* ("Rage, rage, you'll get shoe polish!") at which my father would fly into a tizzy. My aunt Valentine told me that when Papa was a little kid, he would get angry at the slightest criticism and would threaten to drown himself by sticking his head in the toilet (but my father always protested, "No, no, it's not true! I never did that! She is making it up!").

The Gauthiers were Catholic but their church-going was mostly limited to attending mass at Easter and Christmas, plus of course for baptisms, first communions, weddings, and funerals. While all the children were baptized and went through the ceremony of their first holy communion, the one who was the most closely associated with the church happened to be my father: it was thought advisable that P'tit Louis, the testy, hard-headed child would learn to behave in the care of the cloth. But my father did not become an angel! When he and the other altar boys were told to take heavy jugs of holy water to devout old ladies who lived far away, they poured out the blessed water as soon as they were out of sight, carried the empty bottles, and, just before arriving, filled them up at a fountain. Whether they added a few drop of pee might have just been my father's way of embellishing the story. He also told me of a priest who closed his eyes and pretended to pray when the altar boy poured the mass wine in the chalice, but as soon as the boy added water to the wine, the priest quickly "woke up" and energetically gestured: Stop! Stop!

It was now 1910. In January, my grandparents' last-born daughter, Lucienne, died of the measles when she was just nine months. Everyone mourned the death of the beloved baby, not yet knowing that it was only the beginning of the tragic events that would soon befall the family.

The eldest son Émile, who was particularly gifted, practiced his violin and dreamt of entering the Paris Conservatory. In the spring of 1910, at eighteen, he fell ill with tuberculosis. Hoping that the air of the country would be good for him, Louise sent him to stay with her sister Valentine who had moved to Normandy after the death of her husband. Sadly, Émile did not recuperate and died in Romilly-sur-Andelle, a few months later. His grieving parents took a train from Paris to attend his funeral.

At the time of Émile's death, my father, Louis Auguste Gauthier (born in Paris, 10th arrondissement, on October 27, 1900), was ten years old, his sister Valentine, fifteen, his brother Charles, thirteen, and his little sister, Marthe, four.

In 1914, World War I broke out. From the very beginning it was a terribly bloody war. Thousands of soldiers were killed. The suffering in the muddy trenches of Flanders was more than anyone could have imagined. Grand-père Gauthier, who was a patriot, enlisted in the army at the age of fifty-one. The departure of the head of the family made conditions worse at home. My aunt Valentine, my uncle Charles, and my father became the main providers. For added income, my grandmother became a *nourrice*, taking in small children to raise, often fostering them for several years. This was to be both a curse and a blessing, for the family got terribly attached to the little boarders and broke up in tears every time they went back to their own families. (Sadly, one of these children, Adolphe Schtoel, a little Jewish boy beloved by my father and his siblings, would later die during World War II, victim of the Nazis.)

My uncle Charles, who had started working as a telegram delivery boy for the Créteil Post Office, was soon able to obtain a good position at City Hall, thanks to his keen intelligence. Besides being very smart, he was also handsome, with curly black hair, beautiful dark eyes, a little mustache, and a devilish smile. Papa told me that his brother was highly appreciated by the Post Office ladies, who did not shy away from granting him special favors. My father had a particular bond with his brother; they were, he told me, "like twins," sharing confidences and dreams of the future.

At the age of fourteen my father left school to start working. Like his brother, he started at the Post Office, delivering telegrams on his bicycle throughout the city of Créteil. A year later, in 1915, Charles, as all eighteen-year-olds, got drafted to go to war. Soon, my father had to find a better job, since he and his sister Valentine were the only ones left to help

The Créteil Post Office. Papa sitting on the ground at right. (1914)

Papa on second bicycle from the left. (1914)

their mother provide for the family. Valentine worked as a salesgirl. She had, by then, fallen in love with a young man who had been sent to the front. My father found work delivering goods to grocery stores. At that time deliveries were still made by horse cart. It is not without pride that my father, at fifteen, became the driver of a two-horse delivery wagon. Of all the stories he told me about his youth, the ones I enjoyed most were those about his horses. I especially remember Bijou, the horse with a mind of his own, who wanted to return to the stable whenever he took the fancy, obliging my father to use all kinds of tricks to convince his friend to work a little longer. I know my father made up some details "to embroider the stories," as he said, but I can still feel the love he had for "his" horses. But the war was still raging, causing immense suffering to the people of Europe. In 1916, my grandfather came home from the front suffering from pneumonia caught in the damp trenches of eastern France. He had seen soldiers die around him, blown up, fallen by illnesses, or gassed by the enemy. He didn't recover, and died at home.

Tante Valentine. (c. 1916)

My uncle Charles was still at the front. Before going to war he had fallen in love with a young woman, Lucienne, who by her sweet disposition had earned the affection of the whole family. She and Charles had planned to marry as soon as the war was over.

Uncle Charles, second from right. (1917)

After four years of war, the Armistice was finally signed on November 11th, 1918. My aunt Valentine was overjoyed at the idea of seeing her brother and her fiancé again. She went to Paris to join the celebrations on Armistice Day. There were huge festivities with thousands of people in the streets, all embracing, shouting and rejoicing. For a time the crowd was so dense that it became dangerous, to the point that Tante Valentine found herself almost squeezed to death (she would forever remain afraid of crowds). But it was with a broken heart, shortly after the Armistice, that she found out her fiancé had been killed in the war.

My uncle Charles came back. After the death of two of her children in 1910 and of her husband in 1916, I can only imagine my grandmother's joy at seeing her son again. The whole family was basking in happiness at Charles' return, especially my father. His dear brother was back! It was an uplifting time, a moment of great rejoicing.

Charles. (1919)

Charles and Lucienne's wedding. (1919)

As planned, my uncle Charles and Lucienne got married as soon as Charles was returned to civilian life, in 1919, and their wedding brought still more joy to the family. But happiness was not to last. Six weeks after the wedding, Uncle Charles died of a cerebral hemorrhage at the age of twenty-one. Everyone was devastated. Why did it have to happen? The legend is that Uncle Charles missed Lucienne so much, and was so deprived of love during the war that when he finally was able to take his young wife in his arms, he made love to her too much, and died of love. My father cursed God. There would be no more God in his life.

At Charles' funeral, the Créteil Municipal Band marched in the procession. My father told me (and I still remember the expression on his face), "You cannot imagine how sad it is to hear music at a funeral!" I could. I could almost see the mourners' tears.

But life had to go on. Papa, who was then nineteen, decided to study tool-making. He found a job at ACAM, a metal shop, rue Amelot, Paris, 11th arrondissement, owned by a young entrepreneur named Pierre Boyer, and soon became proficient in his trade. The shop manufactured parts for maritime companies. Also working at ACAM was Maurice Joly, a tall, handsome fellow who would remain my father's best friend for life. It was at that time that Papa became involved in sports, especially bicycle racing, and entered (and often won) many competitions.

My father, the only surviving son of the family, still lived with his mother and his younger sister Marthe (his older sister Valentine, who had recently married a young man from Brittany, Baptiste Éoche, had moved out). Papa had many friends. He liked to joke, go out at night, drink, smoke, and have fun with women. But, if he believed such a lifestyle was suitable for himself, he was of another opinion when it came to Marthe, his teenage sister, and was very strict with her. When he found out that she had kissed Maurice Joly (I assume it was just a kiss), he gave her a slap she would long remember. (I hope he got equally angry at Maurice!)

My father's sister Valentine and her husband Baptiste Éoche. (1919)

My father loved women and women loved him. They liked his energy, his wit, his zest for life. They also liked his strong body and handsome face. How could they resist his dark-brown curly hair, sexy green-hazel eyes, square chin, and exquisitely drawn lips? He was busy enjoying his conquests, when, as he turned twenty, two things happened at the same time: he was called to the military service and he met my mother, Germaine Cessot (pronounced "say-so"), a beautiful young woman who lived in Paris with her parents and her little sister Yvonne.

My father on first bicycle at left. (c. 1920)

My father (at left, second row, sitting) during his military service. (1920)

2
The Cessots

This beautiful young woman, my mother, is now entering the story, but before catching up with the young lovers, I will briefly introduce the eccentric Cessot family.

My mother's mother, who used Louise as her first name, was born Eugénie Louise Échement in 1879, in Paris, 15th arrondissement, near Montparnasse. I do not know much about her ancestry, except that her mother, Elisabeth Esther Cochet, and her father, Louis Stanislas Échement, who were from the Ardennes region, had moved to Paris in their youth. My grandmother told me that her parents would have liked to see their province again before they died; however, they never did. I pressed her for more details, but could only learn that her father was a coachman and her mother a seamstress. When I was a little girl myself, I remember asking her, "*Mémé*, when you were a little girl did you wear long bloomers under your dresses?" Her answer was simply "No." She never talked much about her parents or siblings. I understand her father died when she was quite young.

In return, my mother's father, Louis Cessot, and his relatives were much more colorful and even could boast of Gypsies and rebels in their midst. According to family tradition, François Cessot, my grandfather's father, was a schoolteacher. The only photo of him that I have shows a very good-looking man, with large dark eyes, arched eyebrows and a small mustache. On the photo, he wears a satin vest, a frock-coat and bow-tie. My mother's sister, Tante Yvonne (always trying to impress) claimed

Great-grandfather François Cessot. (c. 1880)

that her grandfather François was *Professeur à la Sorbonne,* which is most unlikely, one of the reasons being that his wife, Marie Honorine, was a pushcart vendor, *une marchande des quatre saisons,* a hawker of fruit and vegetables. This discrepancy did not prevent Tante Yvonne from creating a rather picturesque tableau: on his way to teach at the Sorbonne Grand-père François pushed his wife's vegetable cart wearing his top hat and frock-coat!

There is another family tale about the Cessots, this one accepted by all. It is that my great-grandfather, François Cessot, the schoolteacher (a.k.a. The Professor), was the son of a Gypsy. It is said that he was educated with money sent to his Parisian mother by his father, a Gypsy from Germany's Black Forest, probably of the Manouche clan. His mother being a *gadjo,* a non-gypsy, a marriage could not take place. The Gypsies, or I should say, the Rom, whose ethnic origins can be traced to India, have kept many of their physical traits to this day. The exotic look and dark complexion of many members of my family seem to indicate that there is some truth to the family lore. Both my grandfather and his son, my uncle Félix were nicknamed *"Peau-d'boudin"* by their friends at work, which translates (not very well) to "Blood-sausage skin," meaning that their skin was (almost) as brown as what the British call "black pudding."

Great-grandmother Marie Honorine Cessot (born Jeulin). (1899)

A little more is known about my great-grandmother Marie Honorine Cessot (born Jeulin), the pushcart vendor. She was a strong-willed woman. In 1871, during the Commune, when the citizens of Paris were attacked and starved by the army of the French government, she defied the authorities. She had several children, but, unlike my great-grandmother Jumelin, she did not have the opportunity to leave Paris for the countryside. Instead, she joined the *Communards* and protested with them on the streets (or was it the barricades?), shouting, "We want bread for our children!"

My aunt Yvonne, still a little girl when Marie Honorine died, remembered that her grandmother used to call her by the fetching names of *ma petite liberté* or *ma petite France*.

One of the youngest of my great-grandparents' children was François René Cessot, born on April 4th, 1876, in Paris, 6th arrondissement, near the Luxembourg, who would be known under the name of Louis Cessot, and would become my grandfather. Lively and smart, he received a good primary education and began an apprenticeship as a printer. He worked, first as a typographer, then as a plate maker in newspaper printing houses.

When he was nineteen my grandfather met my grandmother, Louise Échement, who was sixteen. It was a typical story: they fell in love, made love, she got pregnant. Innocent and frightened, Louise asked her sweetheart, "How do babies come out? Will the doctor have to cut my stomach open?" When she told her mother that she was expecting a baby, her mother chased her out of the house. My grandmother had to go to a home for pregnant women, rue d'Alésia in Paris, where she gave birth to her son, Félix. It must be said that shortly after Félix' birth, she returned to live with her mother—who had forgiven her by then. Unlike Grand-mère Gauthier who never had any schooling, Grand-mère Cessot attended school till the age of thirteen, at a time when the educational level was quite high in primary schools. She was knowledgeable in literature, history and geography, and wrote in very good style.

In 1899 my grandparents got married. The wedding took place at the City Hall of Paris 14th arrondissement. My grandmother was twenty, my grandfather twenty-three. Their son was three years old. My grandmother did not wear a white dress but a long dark frock with a frilled lace collar. In keeping with the groom's wish, it was little Félix who carried the orange blossom.

On their wedding picture one can identify my grandfather's dignified older brother, his rather boorish street hawker mother, and a couple of his stern-looking (not to say mean-looking) sisters. My grandfather himself looks very young and a little foolish with his hair pasted flat on his forehead; however his lively spirit shines through his dark eyes.

My grandparents' wedding. November 11th, 1899. Front row, from left: the bride's mother; Félix (3); the groom, Louis Cessot; the bride, Louise Cessot; the groom's brother; the groom's mother. Back row: the groom and brides' siblings and their spouses.

Louis and Louise Cessot. (c. 1900)

From right: my grandparents Louise and Louis Cessot, my mother Germaine Cessot. Standing in back: Félix. Others are unidentified. (c. 1906)

After Félix (and another son who died in infancy), my grandparents had two more children: my mother Germaine, born in Paris, 6th arrondissement, on March 6, 1902, and my aunt Yvonne, born in 1913.

My grandmother also apprenticed to become a printer for newspapers. She only worked during the first years of her marriage, first as a lithographer, then a typographer. After that, she stayed home. Yet, from what I heard, she was never interested in being a homemaker. When her children were small she did not take care of them herself, but sent them *"en nourrice,"* shipping them out to the country to be brought up by a foster family for a modest monthly fee. My mother, who as a child had been very unhappy at her foster parents' home, did not want her little sister to endure the same fate. She strongly objected when

Maman and Tante Yvonne. (1917)

little Yvonne was sent away to be brought up by the rough "Maman Yéyette" and her clan. After a time, when it was judged that my mother was old enough to take care of her little sister, Yvonne was taken away from her foster home and sent back to Paris.

During World War I, both my grandfather and Félix were called to the army. Both wrote from the front on postcards showing photos of themselves with their soldier friends. Félix later suffered from the consequences of having been gassed in the trenches. In 1918, with the men absent, my grandmother decided to work in a "war factory," and had my sixteen-year-old mother work there also. But not for long: it was almost the end of the war and the men soon came home.

In 1919, Alsace was returned to France. The country now crossed a period of economic growth and modernization. Grand-père Cessot, who had resumed his work at the newspaper printing plant, was active in supporting the trade unions and their claims to obtain new benefits for the workers.

I never knew Grand-père Cessot, who died the year before I was born, but I heard quite a bit about him. The first thing everyone said was that he was an acrobat: *"Il faisait les pieds-au-mur sur le ciment"* ("He could do handstands on the concrete") is a sentence I heard repeated dozens of times, and which was usually followed by: "Even at fifty-one, he could do handstands on one hand, with his other hand in his pocket. He could turn cartwheels. He could do all sorts of things. He was a contortionist."

My grandfather was apparently quite a character. Physically, he was attractive with a slight but well-shaped body. His face, round in his youth, became angular as he grew older. With his piercing dark eyes shining with intelligence (when they were not hazed by alcohol), he looked in his middle age quite a lot like Picasso.

Besides being noted for his physical prowess, my grandfather was respected for his original mind. He was also an absolute whiz at spelling, and his love for the written and spoken word was well-known to everyone. Fond of saying to his children: "A spelling mistake hurts my eyes, a grammatical mistake hurts my ears," he insisted on their acquiring a good knowledge of language, and frequently tested them. His son Félix followed in his path. So did my mother and Tante Yvonne, who both had perfect spelling and grammar (Tante Yvonne often annoyed people, especially children by correcting them). My Cessot relatives, most of them in the printing business, relished their constant contact with letters, words, and with writing in general.

My grandfather was remembered by everyone as a great wit. When I went to the newspaper printing plant with my father, many people still talked about *"le père Cessot"* long after he had died, recalling especially the colorful nicknames he had bestowed on his colleagues (*le vicomte, le cabossé, Gueule-de-travers*). He was well-liked and had lots of friends. But two major faults dominated his life: drinking and gambling.

While Grand-père Cessot played every game possible—cards, dice, roulette—he claimed that it was *"les dadas, les toutous"* ("the horsies, the doggies") that would bring his ruin in the end. More than once, he lost his wages at the track. That was sad. However, when he won, he and my grandmother were happy again, as they celebrated with friends. Then, wine flowed liberally—a bit too liberally for sure, since everyone ended up good and drunk. With their young children boarded out, my grandparents had plenty of freedom to enjoy the good life. Later on, when my mother was a teenager, she tried her best to keep order in the household and provide her little sister Yvonne with surroundings as stable as she could possibly make them.

Maman loved her sister "Vovonne." She played with her, and improvised for her *un petit théatre* in front of the dining room curtains, training her to sing and recite poetry *avec les gestes* (with gestures). Tante Yvonne told me that, besides being coddled by her big sister, she also was her parents' pet: they let her do whatever she wanted.

"They treated me very nicely," she told me, "but my mother was not always nice to my big sister Germaine. When Germaine came home one day, her hair cut *"à la garçonne"* and wearing mascara (as was the fashion in the twenties), Maman slapped her face." Tante Yvonne also told me that my mother held it against Grand-mère Cessot to have forced her at the age of sixteen to work in a factory *"pour faire des bombes"* ("to make bombs"). I don't know if my mother actually "made bombs," but a remarkable photograph of a large group of workers in front of a factory shows my beautiful mother, with her well-cut coat, long scarf and laced boots, looking as if she were starring in a war movie, as she stands next to working women in plain black smocks and wooden shoes.

Center: my mother and grandmother. (1918)

It would be wrong to assume, although he gambled and drank, that my grandfather led a totally dissolute life; he was in fact responsible enough to keep his job as a newspaper printer, and even for a time to run his own printing business in the Quartier Latin. He was, besides, very much involved in leftist politics. A photograph shows him with my grandmother participating in a SFIO rally. The SFIO (*Section Française de l'Internationale Ouvrière*, the original French Socialist Party), led by Jean Jaurès and Jules Guesde, was founded in 1905 to support workers' interests. The rally must have taken place close to 1905, as both my grandparents look very young on the photo. In 1920, the communist members of the Socialist Party split to form the Communist Party. I don't know if at that point my grandfather remained a socialist or affiliated himself with the Communist Party, but I remember that when I was young my grandmother claimed to be a communist; and while she did not actually belong to the party (or, for that matter, had much interest in politics), she did vote communist, and was proud to know the words to the *Internationale*.

When it came to religion both my grandfather and grandmother were passionately anti-Catholic or, I should say, anti-church. They or their children never participated in religious activities. These feelings, as they filtered themselves through my mother and Tante Yvonne, became less an aversion for the Catholic Church than a sort of indifference toward religion in general.

My grandparents Cessot and my mother lived at that time rue Châtelain, Paris 14th arrondissement, not far from Montparnasse.

By 1917, my mother's brother Félix had married Léonie Penrad. They had a daughter, Simone, whose birth would be followed by the birth of two other daughters. A few years later, it would be my mother's turn to get married.

My grandparents on vacation. At left: Grand-père and Grand-mère Cessot with Yvonne (child) in the water. (c. 1919)

3
Louis and Germaine

Curious to know how my parents met, I asked Tante Yvonne, who told me the story of their first encounter (taking the opportunity to remark that the Cessots were much better than the Gauthiers). The meeting, she said, had taken place in a sports field. My father was playing soccer and my mother was watching from the side. At that time, it would have been difficult to find a girl prettier than my mother (who was eighteen then), with her jet black hair, fair skin and light green eyes. During a break, a fellow walked to her and gave her a flower. I like to imagine that it was a rose, but maybe it was just a simple flower, picked among the ones growing nearby. My mother took the flower, and seeing my father approaching, turned toward him and offered it to him.

After that they fell in love and soon, of course, made love. It happened at night, perhaps even by the soccer field. Tante Yvonne told me how my mother hated to have lost her virginity on the muddy ground. But isn't that a common thing with us women? Don't we hate the fact that we lose our virginity in ordinary places, and not on the satin sheets of Prince Charming's wonderful bed?

My father had to answer the call of the Army. In 1920, he was drafted to begin his two-year military service in the heavy infantry. He was first posted at the École Polytechnique, an elite military school for engineers, where, as a private, he had little contact with the cadets, most of them officers or future officers who belonged to the upper class. But soon, perhaps because of the tender feelings he had kept for his delivery horses, he somehow ended up in a cavalry unit. A photo of the time shows him sitting straight and proud on a tall black horse. Before long, however, his regiment was reunited with the main part of the infantry, at which time he was assigned to drive military trucks. While in the service he spent all his leaves with my mother. After one of these leaves, in the summer of 1920, Maman found that she was pregnant. I have some of their correspondence

My father, Louis Gauthier. (1920)

during this period, written on romantically illustrated post cards, telling of love, of worry when the mail was late, of joy shared during the leaves. On a postcard, where mauve flowers encircle a blue-helmeted soldier kissing a woman on the cheek, my father wrote this tender rhymed poem:

Les beaux jours se sont enfuis
Pour faire place à l'ennui
D'être séparés l'un de l'autre
Par ce métier qui n'est pas le nôtre
A nous jeunes gens pleins de jeunesse
Qui n'appartenons qu'à la tendresse.
Mais après la libération
Finies toutes les punitions!
Chacun reviendra à l'aimée
Qui l'aura attendu deux années.
La joie sera encore plus grande
Notre bonheur ne se laissera prendre
Et nous reviendrons dans notre Créteil
L'amour d'antan sera pareil
Nous redeviendrons les jeunes amoureux
Car ma foi nous ne serons pas beaucoup plus vieux.

The beautiful days have fled
leaving only the sadness
of being kept apart
by this trade forced upon us.
We are young people full of life
whose only master is Love.
But after our liberation
Farewell to all punishments!
Each one of us will return to the loved one
who had been waiting two long years.
Our joy will be greater then,
our happiness will not let itself be ensnared.
And we'll return to our Créteil,
our love of yore unchanged.
We will be the young lovers we once were,
for, truly, we won't be much older.

A little before my father's departure for the army, my mother had started to work *"dans la presse"* (in the press). She had been recommended for the job by her printer father and was now a linotype operator for a Parisian newspaper, a profession that required training and skill.

On another one of the postcards in my collection, this one depicting two fancily-dressed lovers holding hands on the bank of a river, my mother wrote:

Mon petit homme chéri,

You will be angry at me because it has been two days since I last wrote to you. But, please do not blame me too much. I am so tired now that I work the night shift that in the morning, when I come home, the only thing I want to do is fall on my bed. I would like to have the day shift again as I am now feeling sick with nausea.
Besides this card I am also sending you a letter.
A long kiss, and I will love you forever,
Your Maine

Papa was granted a special leave to get married. My parents' wedding took place on September 4th, 1920 in the City Hall of Paris, 14th arrondissement. (Tante Valentine couldn't attend: her son, my dear cousin Roger, was born on September 2nd). The wedding picture shows Papa wearing his uniform and Maman wearing a white dress not too tight around the waist. They both look very serious (Maman even looks sad), but I know they must have been happy. Their love, indeed, would last forever.

At the end of the twenties and in the early thirties, my parents often took trips to the Normandy beach resorts of the English Channel, mostly Deauville, Trouville and Criel-sur-Mer. These resorts were popular with Parisians who could easily travel there for weekends or short vacations.

My parents' wedding, September 4th. (1920)

My mother. (1924)

My mother. (1924)

My father. (c. 1925)

My father (in leather coat) with people in front of a bicycle and motorcycle shop. (c. 1925)

My parents had many friends. One photo shows them at the end of a dinner (the coffee and liqueurs are on the table). My mother smiles, but if my father doesn't look happy, it is not (I am sure) because a young man is contentedly leaning on my mother, but because Papa had adopted the habit of looking serious on photographs.

Sitting at right: my mother and my father (with cigar). Others are unidentified friends. (c. 1930)

4
My Brother

In December 1921, my brother was born. He was named Louis Charles (and, like my father, nicknamed "P'tit Louis"). When my father returned from the military service, he went back to work at ACAM, where he would remain for another seven years.

My mother with Grand-mère Gauthier and my brother. (1922)

During this period Papa continued to practice sports in his free time, and, in 1926, he decided to enter the Tour de France. He trained every evening after work and on Sundays, but his dreams of victory were squashed after a discouraging mishap in the Tour (which I will explain in more detail later). After that, together with Maurice Joly who, like him, was a well-rounded athlete, he joined the Vincennes Sportif Association, of which their boss (and friend), Pierre Boyer, was a board member. Papa and Maman also belonged to the entertainment section of the club.

As he did not earn much as a toolmaker, Papa thought he might increase his income by driving a taxi. For that, he had to take a difficult test known as *"les papiers taxi,"* which would show that he knew every street in Paris and could go by heart from any given point to another. Though he already knew the city well, he had to study hard until he knew Paris *"comme sa poche"* ("like his own pocket"). He passed the test on the first try, but decided that he did not want to be a taxi-driver after all. However, thanks to this experience, he never ceased to amaze us with his extraordinary knowledge of Paris' intricate topography.

In 1929, my grandfather Cessot recommended my father for a job *dans la presse*. Papa became a newspaper printer, a pressman, specializing as a *clicheur* (plate-maker). It was a profession he would keep for the remainder of his active life, earning at retirement *La Médaille d'Or du Travail* (the Gold Medal of Work) for forty-five years of employment, nine at ACAM and thirty-six as a printer for the same newspaper plant.

My mother. (c. 1925)

My little brother was growing up. In 1925, my parents had moved to the Paris suburb of Fontenay-sous-Bois, rue Roublot, in an apartment next to Tante Valentine and Oncle Baptiste's. During the day when all the adults were working, my brother and his cousin Roger (who was a year and a half older) were cared for by Grand-mère Gauthier in nearby Créteil.

As a little boy my brother used to call my mother *"Mademoiselle maman."* She looked so much like a young girl. My father, proud of his handsome and intelligent son, took him to sports events and practiced sports with him. P'tit Louis was full of energy and mischief, just as my father had been as a child. Tante Yvonne, who was a teenager when my brother was nine years old, told me that her parents took him to spend a vacation by the sea in Criel at my uncle Félix' villa. There, she said, she often had arguments with him because he would not obey and always did "dangerous things."

My cousin Roger had been one of my main sources of information on the family. It was to him that I turned to tell the sad story of how my brother suffered the consequences of one of these "dangerous things":

"1927. I remember very well," Roger wrote in a letter. "I was playing with your brother on the Place de la Mairie in Créteil. Some bigger boys had turned on a faucet located just outside the public urinal enclosure, and they were splashing one another with water. After a while they turned off the faucet and went away. It was then that P'tit Louis wanted to do the same thing, but since he was small he couldn't reach the faucet which was quite high, and so, he hung unto the sheet metal fence surrounding the public urinals and stuck his hand through the metal, in a space cut out in the shape of an ace of spades. By doing that he could reach the faucet. I shouted at him to stop this stupid game, but he was stubborn and wanted to turn on this accursed faucet. He turned it on and water ran out. Satisfied, he turned the water off and jumped down; but as he did that, the little finger of his left hand remained caught in the cut-out metal. His hand was full of blood and he was afraid he was going to be punished. At the same time, he realized he had lost a finger. We ran to Mèmère Gauthier's house, which was close to the Place de la Mairie. Right away, Mèmère took P'tit Louis to the pharmacy. The pharmacist looked at the hand; the finger was gone but the bone was intact, as if a glove had been taken off. Your parents were alerted so they

My brother (right) with his cousin Roger in costumes. (1930)

could take your brother to the Trousseau Children's Hospital in Paris. Mèmère went back to the Place de la Mairie and inside the public urinal she found the little finger which she took and put in alcohol; she thought it could be reattached, but so many years ago it was impossible. Your brother did not suffer too much from the consequences of the amputation because it was the little finger of his left hand."

Roger continued his letter,

"1931. A great sorrow struck the family. Your brother Petit Louis died of tubercular meningitis. If you want, I could give you a detailed account, but it's very painful."

I never had the courage to ask Roger for a detailed account of the death of my brother, who, like my own son, died at the age of ten. I know that his illness lasted less than ten days and that my parents were overwhelmed with grief. I prefer to remember some stories that my father told me about my little brother (who would forever remain my "little brother"). I particularly like this one:

My father and brother were riding in a car my father had just bought. It was his first car, the one that had only three wheels. Looking somewhat

My father's first car. My father, mother and brother.
Woman sitting on car is unidentified. (c. 1929)

like a motorcycle sidecar, it seated two people and had no top. My father, who was driving in the country, found himself at the top of a hill when, suddenly, he realized that his brakes were no longer working. At the bottom of the hill, on one side of the road he could see a big haystack, and on the other, a stone wall. My father, who, of course, knew full well what he was going to do, said to my brother, "P'tit Louis! Quick! Quick! I have no brakes! What should I hit? The haystack or the wall?" "The haystack! The haystack!" my brother shouted. And almost at the same time they ended up in the middle of the haystack, safe and sound. "Ah! Thank You! Thank you! You saved our lives! I'm so glad you didn't pick the stone wall! Now you can tell Maman that you saved our lives!"

My brother, Louis Charles Gauthier. One can still see traces of my mother's lipstick on the photo. (1930)

A year after the death of my brother, Aunt Valentine and Uncle Baptiste moved to their newly-built house, still in Fontenay-sous-Bois, at 12, Villa de l'Ouest. Soon after, my parents bought the house next door at number 10. (It was a wise investment: by 1936 the Franc was devaluated as an after-effect of the Depression, and, while it was a bad thing for people who had savings, it was a good thing for people who had debts; my parents saw their monthly mortgage payments become more and more affordable as their salaries rose to keep up with inflation). After they moved into their new house, my father bought a more substantial car, a Rosengart, and decided to take trips to try to cheer up my mother.

In 1932, my parents went on a vacation to the Côte d'Azur with another couple. While there, they paid a visit to Great-aunt Valentine in Marseilles, and posed for photos with her. With a long pearl necklace and a plume in her hat, my adventurous great-aunt was still chic in her loosely cut summer clothes (see page 36). My mother, up-to-date in the fashion of the thirties, also looked very nice. In these pictures, we see her wearing a small white hat with a black stripe, a black worsted jacket and a black satin skirt. As for my father, he looked slim and sporty as always in his tweedy pullover, golfing pants and peaked cap.

My parents and a friend, posing next to someone's fancy car. Marseilles. (1932)

Meanwhile, in my mother's family, everything was not going well. Since 1920, the year of my parents' marriage, Yvonne had lived with her

Tante Yvonne, Grand-père Cessot, Grand-mère Cessot, a friend. (c. 1928)

Grand-mère Cessot and Tante Yvonne. (c. 1932)

parents. They bought her nice clothes, took her on vacation by the sea to Trouville, Deauville and Criel, but my grandfather's gambling did not cease, and both my grandfather and grandmother's drinking made Yvonne ashamed and resentful. Wanting to be independent, she had first worked as a seamstress, then as a linotype operator. When she turned nineteen, she met Marcel Labbé, and a year later, in 1933, they were married.

Tante Yvonne and Oncle Marcel's wedding. (1933)

About a year later, Grand-père Cessot, looking older than his fifty-eight years, became ill and disillusioned with life. On October 23, 1934, alone in his kitchen, he stuffed towels under the door, turned on the gas and committed suicide. A note he left was found by my father; it accused one of my grandfather's acquaintances of being the cause of his suicide. My father, feeling that nothing good would come out of exposing this bitter note, destroyed it.

Now Grand-mère Cessot at the age of fifty-five had to learn to manage by herself, but it was too late. She had stopped working for some time, and didn't know how to be independent. The only thing she could do was to rely on her two daughters, Germaine and Yvonne. She could not turn to her son Félix (himself a heavy drinker and a lover of the fast life), as he was having problems with his wife Léonie—problems, as we will soon see, that became so severe that Léonie would commit suicide in 1936, and Félix would die of alcoholism two years later. Under the circumstances, it is no wonder that Grand-mère Cessot was incapable of providing any material help or even moral support to Félix' daughters, her granddaughters, Simone, Paulette and Denise, when they became orphaned, something that the two youngest, but especially Denise, greatly resented.

As for my parents, at that point in their life they did not know whether or not they wanted another child. It seemed that they could not have any more children anyway. But, four and a half years after my brother's death, I was born. My birth was a great joy for them, a joy mixed with fear.

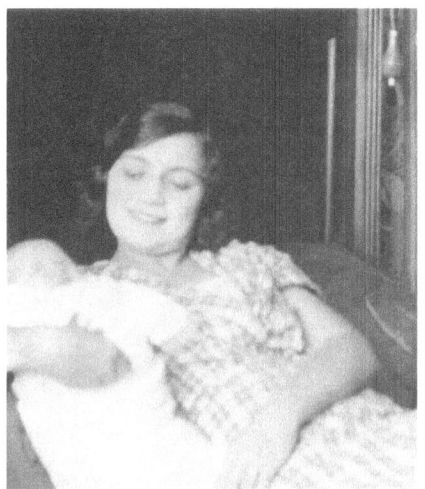

Maman and me in my parents' bedroom. (1935)

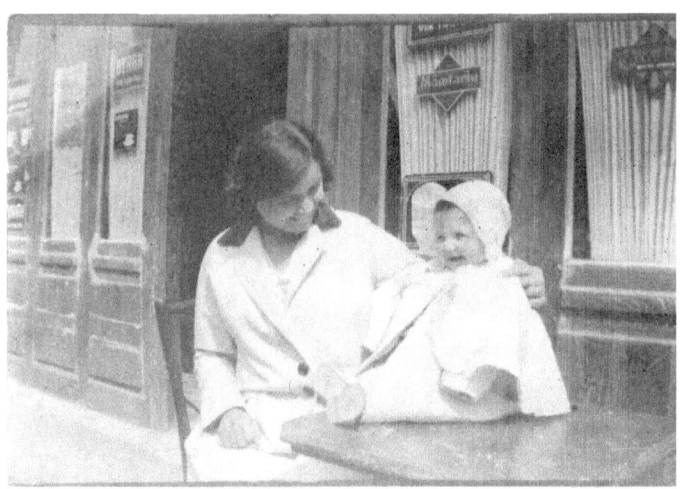

Maman and me in front of the "Chez Brusson" café. (1935)

Maison Penrad: groceries, wines, restaurant. (From left) Grand-mère Cessot, Grand-père Cessot, Yvonne Cessot, Madame Penrad, Félix Cessot, Léonie (Penrad) Cessot, their daughter, Simone, Maman, Papa. (1921)

(From left) Paulette, Simone and Denise with their mother's relatives, the Criez-Bajarts. (c. 1927)

Three

An Interview with my Cousin Denise

It is the right place, I think, to introduce my cousin Denise, whose tale continues my parents' story and gives a glimpse of me as a small child. But, as the threads she holds in her hands are bound to cross some of the family threads already laid out, it is unavoidable that a few passages of her story already have been told. Repetitions? Or perhaps the weft of a stronger cloth?

When, in the summer of 2000, Denise visited me in California, she did not come alone. She came with her troupe: her husband Armand, her son Christian, her daughter Martine, all her grandchildren, her beloved sister Paulette and dear brother-in-law Lulu, her mother-in-law, her friend Carmen, her nieces and nephews, all the people in her club, and of course, Françoise, her terrible ex-daughter-in-law. She brought along her dead parents and mine, Tante Yvonne, our grandmother Cessot (whom she did not like), and her neighbors, and her geraniums. But mostly, she carried with her her Armand and Christian's graves. All this was very cumbersome and heavy, but she was resolute, everything and everyone had to come with us on the bus when we went to San Francisco, in the car when we drove to the vineyards of the Napa Valley, or on foot when we visited the historical buildings of Sonoma. We dragged all her followers everywhere; they rode on the rolling fog engulfing the Golden Gate Bridge; they floated on the San Francisco Bay at sunset; they woke up at six-thirty in the morning and did not go to sleep until we finished watching our French movies at eleven o'clock or midnight. And then, after three weeks, Denise returned to Paris, taking with her all her ghosts.

Denise was seventy-seven at the time she came to see me in 2000 in Sonoma where I live now. She is my first cousin, the daughter of my mother's brother, Félix Cessot. When she was young, the family being quite close, she was in frequent contact with her aunts: my mother and Tante Yvonne. I never really knew my uncle Félix, who died in 1938, when I was three. He and his wife, Léonie (Nini), had three daughters: Simone, Paulette and Denise. Simone passed away some time ago, and I regret not having had the opportunity to know her well; however, her daughter Marie Christine and I became close friends. Marie Christine, who happened to visit me in California at about the same time as Denise, arrived shortly before her (and also left before her). In the five days that their stay overlapped, Marie Christine was able to retrieve a little bit of the plentiful booty that floated every which way on Denise's river of family information. As for me, I managed to formally sit with Denise and write down some of the facts she was strewing about, as we sat for tea, rode the bus, or walked up and down the streets of San Francisco.

My mother's brother, Félix Cessot, his wife, Léonie, and their daughter, Simone. (1918)

Denise was born in Arcueil, near Paris, on October 26th, 1923. Her mother, Léonie Penrad, came from the wealthy Criez-Bajart family, textile mill-owners and tulle manufacturers from the industrial city of Saint-Quentin in northern France. Léonie fell in love with my uncle Félix Cessot, a Parisian newspaper printer, whose father was also a printer. My uncle Félix was very handsome, his dark complexion and burning brown eyes reflecting the (perhaps mythical) gypsy origin of the Cessot family.

In March 1917, Félix and Léonie were married. According to Tante Yvonne, Léonie had been showering Félix with money and expensive presents. Her parents, who had been against her marrying this handsome Cessot boy, relented only when she became pregnant. Proof that the marriage was hasty, Tante Yvonne told me, was that Félix, who was in the army at the time, was granted a short leave and got married in uniform. Tante Yvonne's version of the events is clearly controversial, to say the least, since the couple's first daughter, Simone, was born in May 1918, some fourteen months after the wedding. There will always remain a bit of a mystery there. Anyway, a few years later, the young couple had their second daughter, Paulette, and later, their third, Denise. The girls were very pretty. Simone, a classic beauty, had a soft round face; Paulette had inherited her father's dark eyes and olive complexion; and Denise had delicate features, light brown hair, and beautiful blue eyes.

Denise (right) and her sister Paulette. (c. 1930)

Félix was a hard worker and Léonie was good at managing the household finances. They ran a café-restaurant, as well as the grocery store adjacent to it, both businesses belonging to Leonie's parents, the Penrads. Soon the family was thriving. Léonie was busy tending the store and the café, taking care of her three daughters, and cooking the *plat-du-jour* for the restaurant. She got up at six and went to bed at eleven. Félix held his printer's job, and also helped with the wine cellar. He was doing well, even though he had been gassed by the Germans in World War I. The young

My parents in front of the Penrad café-restaurant. (1921)

73

couple saved money, bought a car, two seaside villas in Criel-sur-Mer on the English Channel, and an apartment building near Paris, collecting rent from seven tenants. Soon, they were able to own the grocery store and the café-restaurant businesses, although the Penrad family retained ownership of the building where the two stores were located. Besides the stores, the building also included two apartments; one of them occupied by Thérèse, Léonie's sister.

And then, things began to deteriorate. Félix started to drink and gamble. Gambling was a family trait; Grandfather Cessot was famous for spending his paycheck on the horses. Félix started dipping in the family savings. Léonie had to rely on herself to pay the mortgages, but the more she saved, the quicker the savings disappeared.

The very Catholic Penrads were hostile to the godless Cessots. They felt that their daughter had married outside her milieu, and despised the Cessot males for their love of partying, drinking, gambling, and chasing women. It was not long before Léonie ceased to be on speaking terms with her in-laws; she became furious every time Félix visited his mother. There were terrible rows. Félix drank more and more; he helped himself to Léonie's secret savings box, and even hit her in front of the children. She tried to commit suicide but was found in time. Soon, they had to sell the café and the grocery store. They also had to move to a smaller apartment. Meanwhile Félix continued to take taxis whenever he was late for work. Léonie could not bear this flagrant waste of money.

"One day," Denise told me, "I came back from school and smelled gas. I opened the door and found my mother lying on the floor, dead. I was the one who found her. It was terrible. I was thirteen and a half. After that I hated my father. I felt it was because of him that my mother committed suicide. People blamed her: 'How could she kill herself when she had three young daughters?' But I don't blame her. I understand. She had no way out. The Cessot family said that my mother was crazy because, after she had my sister Simone, she was locked up for a while in a mental institution, but it was just because of postpartum psychosis. After I lost my mother, I lost everything."

When I asked Denise if she would not mind answering a few questions, she readily complied. As we sat in the kitchen, drinking tea, I conducted an interview and took notes as she spoke.

I heard that your mother was found near the door with her keys in her hand, as if she had second thoughts at the last minute.
No, she did not have the keys in her hand. I think she was holding a handkerchief, but it was true that she was near the door.

What happened after your mother's death?
Right after the funeral (we were all in black and had to wear heavy crepe veils on our heads) we had to turn our attention to Simone. Simone was eighteen then, and educated. She had her *brevet* (a Junior College degree), which was pretty good at the time. Before Maman's death, Simone was engaged and just about to get married. Her wedding dress had been ordered and the restaurant reserved, and then Maman committed suicide, a month or so before the wedding. Even before Maman's death, Papa had wanted to cancel the wedding because Simone's fiancé, Charlot, was sick with tuberculosis. But after Maman died, Simone did not want the wedding to be cancelled, and she got married anyway. Papa did not go to the wedding, and he did not want Paulette and me to go either. But when he was at work, a neighbor lady came to our house. She took us both to the church (but not to the reception), and we hurried back home before Papa came back. He never found out. Charlot died about eighteen months after the wedding, and, if you remember, Simone did contract tuberculosis from him. It took years before she was well again. After my mother's death Papa cried for a week, but I think it was fake because he started partying the same as before. Then he found a woman in Fontenay-sous-Bois who drank also. I couldn't stand her.

What about you and Paulette? Did you go to school? Did you continue to live with your father?
After Maman's death, I just wanted to stay home. I didn't want to go to school anymore, and Paulette didn't either. That's why we don't have a

good education. Paulette, who was about fifteen then, moved in with my mother's sister, but she was not happy. Tante Thérèse was strict, and made her work from morning to night. I remained with my father. I made soup, I cleaned the house, but I didn't want to stay because of his new woman.

Did you go live with my parents then?
No. Not right away. I couldn't go live with Simone who was newly married, and I couldn't go live with Aunt Thérèse, who was such a penny-pincher. At night she made Paulette go to bed early because she didn't want her to turn on the light. My father sent me into service as a maid for a family in Paris, rue Saint-Dominique. I worked hard, cleaned the house and cooked. The people of the house had guests every Saturday and Sunday. I ate well only when they had company, but the rest of the week I had practically nothing but bread and water. I was miserable. I wanted to kill myself.

Wasn't it about that time that your father died?
Yes, he died in 1938, about two years after my mother.

I was told by my parents that your father had fits of delirium tremens. My father always said that Félix saw "black butterflies," and that he had probably committed suicide by poisoning himself with alcohol. Of course, Tante Yvonne denies that, because it doesn't fit with the idea she has of her brother. She claims that Félix died of the effects of having been gassed during World War I. Do you know anything about that?
I know that he died insane.

What happened to you after his death?
When your father, Tonton P'tit Louis, heard that I was so unhappy rue Saint-Dominique, he became very angry and said I couldn't stay there. Through the *Société Laitière Maggi* (pronounced ma-jee) where she worked, your father's sister, Tante Valentine, knew some people who needed a live-in maid, so I was sent to these people's house. They had a beautiful villa at the

edge of the Bois de Vincennes. The people were very nice and treated me well, but they often went out and came back at two o'clock in the morning. While I waited for them, I was afraid to be all alone and I cried. Tante Valentine found out and told Tonton P'tit Louis. He said to Tata Germaine, your mother, "We must do something about Denise. We cannot leave her like that. We have to take her in with us." And that's how I came to live at your parents' house, thanks to Tonton P'tit Louis and Tata Valentine, who were not even my blood relatives. My own family did not volunteer to take me in: my sister Simone did not, my aunt Yvonne, of course, did not want me, and neither did Mémé Cessot, my own grandmother. Mémé was given the opportunity to let Paulette and me live with her in an apartment that your parents had found for us in Fontenay. I saw the apartment; it was very nice. Tante Yvonne and Tante Germaine offered to pay the rent, but Mémé Cessot refused to move in the apartment, just because she did not want to take care of us.

Well, you know, Grand-mère Cessot was not capable of running a household. She was entirely dependent on her daughters Germaine and Yvonne. She never even raised her children herself; she sent them to be boarded in the country. It would have been impossible for her to take care of you, and besides, she had a drinking problem.
Well, maybe, but I know that if it hadn't been for Tonton P'tit Louis, nobody would have wanted to take me in.

I know my father loved you as his own daughter. You were his favorite niece. When he referred to you as "La môme Denise" ("The kid-Denise"), one could feel the affection he had for you. How long did you live at my parents' house?
From 1938 to 1940 (from the age of fifteen to sixteen and a half), I helped take care of you when you were a baby—but I did not spoil you.

Yes! Sure! I heard about that! I was told that when I was a baby and did not want to eat, my mother made little paper dolls to distract me while she slipped a spoonful of food into my mouth, but, with you, there were no paper dolls. You shoved food in my mouth and said: "Eat! And be quiet!" (While you read your teenage love magazine "Confidences.")*

That's right! And I also threw your pacifier away and told you that the dog ate it! I used to take you in your baby stroller to the Bois de Vincennes. I had already meet Armand by then, and we would rendezvous in the Bois. I would warn you not to tell that I met my boyfriend, and you never told on me. Your parents would ask, *"Elle a un amoureux, Denise?"* ("Does she have a sweetheart, Denise?"). And you would answer, *"Pas de reureu, Fanice."* ("No sweetheart, Fanice"). You used to call me Fanice.

You see, I was not a traitor!
That's true.

So you settled in at my parents' house.
Yes, I did. At that time I used to confide in your grandmother Gauthier. She lived in a little cottage behind Tante Valentine's. I didn't tell anyone else about Armand, but Grand-mère Gauthier understood me. She was very nice. At a certain point, I left your parents' house and went to live at the home of your father's best friend, Maurice Joly, and his wife, who was also called Germaine. They needed someone to look after their baby while Germaine worked (she was a clothes designer and a couturier's model), and your father thought I could help them.

Were you happy there?
No. Germaine Joly made me work very hard; she always acted like a *"grande dame."* I cleaned her house, did the laundry, scrubbed Maurice's dirty overalls (he was a mechanic). But, one day, Maurice came home early and saw how hard I was working and he got very angry. When his wife arrived he told her that "the kid" was only supposed to take care of the baby, and not do hard work. He said that I was P'tit Louis' niece, that P'tit Louis was his best friend, and that he had known me since I was a little girl.

He shouted at his wife, and he was so angry that he slapped her. She was lucky he didn't know that she went out every afternoon to visit her lover! Maurice was always nice to me. One time, with the money I earned babysitting, I bought myself a fancy pair of suede shoes "Chez André." I left my new shoes in the box in the living room before going to sleep, and when I woke up, Maurice had tied them up on a string with little ribbons.

Did you stay long at Maurice Joly's?
No, about two months.

Maman, Papa, me, Denise, Paulette, Simone. (c. 1939)

Were you happy at my parent's house?
Yes, it was all right. Your mother was nice, but I helped her around the house and she did not give me any money. It was Tonton P'tit Louis who gave me money behind her back. He would ask me to do little jobs, for instance, I would polish his shoes or pick up the dog's doodoo in the garden. When I was finished, he would tell me, "Look in one of the little drawers by my workbench in the garage." And when I looked, there was always a little change for me.

Did my mother buy things for you? New clothes?
Yes, she did, but sometimes I would borrow her clothes without telling her.

She was taller than me, but I borrowed her silk stockings and folded them up inside my shoes under my feet because they were too long. One day, I also borrowed her green dress and went out with Armand and my sister Paulette and her boyfriend Lulu. And as we were fooling around, Lulu pulled a string from the hem of the dress and accidentally unraveled the whole hem. I had to repair it really fast when I got home, and hang your mother's dress in the closet before she arrived. She never found out.

Why didn't you stay longer at my parents' house? I have heard that it was because you wanted to get married at sixteen. You had decided once for all that you were going to marry Armand, and nobody could make you change your mind.

A picnic at the time Denise lived with my parents. (1938)

That's partially true. I had decided to marry Armand and I was going to leave your parents' house. But just at that time, the war started. Your father was called to the front in 1939, and in 1940 you went to Corbeilles-en-Gâtinais with your aunt Marthe and your grand-mère Gauthier. Shortly after that, Tata Germaine left Fontenay-sous-Bois to join you. At that point, I decided not to go with her. I went to live with my sister Simone who was a widow by then.

So what happened to you after that?

When I was at Simone's house she found work for me right away in a factory where they made bandages for soldiers. I worked all day, and, when I came home, Simone asked me to help her with the laundry and the cooking. On top of this, she kept most of the money I was earning.

Armand and I wanted to get married, but Armand's mother and Simone did not want to let us marry because we were too young. I had an argument with Simone about this, and she slapped me and I slapped her back. My friend Carmen was the one who calmed us down. Finally, everyone consented to the marriage. I was sixteen and a half and Armand was nineteen. Tata Germaine came back from Corbeilles for the wedding, and Tonton P'tit Louis, who was in Toulouse at that time, also came back to Paris. I didn't want to invite Mémé Cessot because I couldn't stand her, but Simone insisted, so I had to invite her, and Mémé Cessot did come. The wedding took place the 18th of May, 1940. I felt that, since I had been so unhappy in my youth, I would be happier married, and it turned out to be true.

Denise and Armand Balordi. (1940)

How long were you and Armand married?

Fifty years, until Armand died of lung cancer in 1990.

Denise and Armand had a son, Christian, born in 1941, and some years later a daughter, Martine. Christian died at the age of fifty-nine, also of lung cancer. Even though both Armand and Christian are dead, they have established themselves comfortably in Denise's life and are content to follow her everywhere. She doesn't do a single thing without involving them. When I talk to her on the telephone, she does mention the trips she takes around the world with her "club" of senior citizens, and she does reminisce about her late sister Paulette, but mostly she talks about Armand and Christian, recalling where they used to go, what they used to do, and what they used to talk about. Everything she sees or hears reminds her either of Armand or Christian. She pays them weekly visits at the cemetery, and tells everyone about the flowers she plants on their graves. However, all this doesn't prevent her from having a life of her own. Now in her eighties, a diminutive woman, she still goes dancing at the senior center in her fetching outfits and gold anklet. Always stylish, she keeps her hair impeccably coiffed and salon-dyed. "I will never let my hair go white. Not me!" *La môme Denise*, the *gamine de Paris*, my father's favorite niece is still going strong.

Grand-mère Cessot, Maman and me, Maurice Joly, Germaine Joly and their son, Jean, Denise. Criel-sur-Mer. (1939)

FOUR

1935 - 1941

1
First Memories

I have few memories of the period before World War II, as I was only four when the war began. One image I can still see clearly is of a road at night in the rain. The tires of our car made swishing sounds on the asphalt; cars coming from the opposite direction passed by us with their double columns of gliding lights. My parents were looking for a room, but the hotels were full. We kept driving into the night. Finally, my father decided to stop at a farm. For a little money the farmer said we could sleep in his barn. The barn smelled of straw and cow manure. Lying on the scratchy straw, I couldn't get comfortable. The cows were close to us; we could see their heads above a low wall. When they began mooing, I was terrified. I snuggled close to my parents and asked, "Are the cows going to eat us?"

I can tell that this memory of monster cows dates from before the war because we still had a car, the Rosengart with yellow wheels. My father was very proud of it. It was the only car in the villa de l'Ouest, the small street on which we lived.

That night, we were probably on our way to Criel where my uncle Félix and his wife Léonie owned their two houses, one named "Villa Dolly," the other "Zig et Puce," after popular comic book heroes.

Now a memory about Grand-mère Gauthier: she had a little cottage in back of Tante Valentine and Oncle Baptiste's house, next door to our house. When I visited Grand-mère, she was often ironing in her kitchen. She did not have an electric iron as we did; she heated her irons on top of her coal-burning stove. To make sure the iron was not too hot, she tried it out on pages of old newspapers. The singed newspapers, yellow and brown, filled her house with their sweet burnt smell. Now, the memory of my grandmother, who died when I was very young, is caught into this smell; it is when I evoke it that I can remember her serious face and unruly chignon, her black housedress almost down to her ankles, and the short purple cape she used to wear, the *pèlerine* that covered her shoulders, and which she crocheted herself. Mèmère used to lend me her *pèlerine* to put around my waist and make a princess dress.

My feet have a memory of their own. Somewhere there was a shadowy place, I cannot tell where, perhaps at La Baule on the Atlantic coast, perhaps on the French Riviera. The ground was covered with pine needles—soft, warm, just slippery enough to elicit a dreamy kind of pleasure. I have often longed for this shadowy place under the pine trees, this dark-green place spattered with spots of sun, this velvety heaven for feet.

Finally: an early memory with the sounds, yellowish lights, and warm air of the Paris métro. When I took the métro with my parents I always seemed to get the window seat. Maman sat next to me, Papa across from us. As soon as the métro left the station and entered the tunnel, I started singing to my reflection in the glass. I could see my mouth opening and closing, but I was convinced nobody could hear me over the noise of the train. I tried to complete a song between two stations, but whenever the song was too short, I repeated it over and over. When the métro stopped, I became quiet and acted like an ordinary little girl traveling with her parents. I wore a beige coat with a brown velvet collar and a matching beige bonnet that tied under my chin; the tie was often undone and a few curls escaped from the bonnet. Around my neck I sometimes wore a little furry animal, the poor beast's mouth clasped unto its tail. I had been told that the animal was *une marte* (a marten), which left me puzzled since I had an aunt called Marthe.

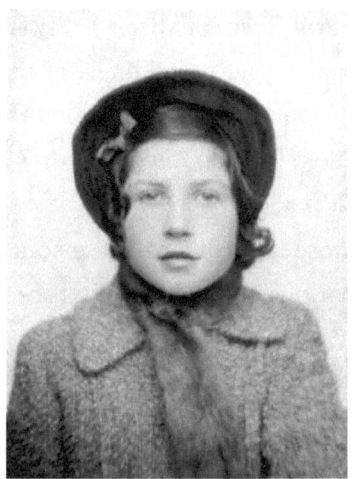

Later photo, but same bonnet
and fur. (c. 1944)

The song I sang most often was *Son joli p'tit chose* (Her Pretty Little Something), which was part of my mother's repertoire when she was asked to sing at family dinners. The adults often sang after a meal when there was a large family reunion, mostly at Christmas or New Year's Eve. They took their turn and stood, holding on to the back of their chairs to give themselves assurance. Some family members knew only one song, but it didn't matter, the other guests were encouraging; everybody joined in to sing the refrains. Oncle Baptiste, who was from Brittany, always sang:

> *Ils ont des chapeaux ronds*
> *Vive la Bretagne!*
> *Ils ont des chapeaux ronds*
> *Vivent les Bretons!*
>
> They wear rounds hats
> Hurrah for Brittany!
> They wear round hats
> Hurrah for the Bretons!

Tante Valentine sang a song about a train disaster: *Roule, roule, train du malheur* (Roll, Roll, Train of Misery). My father and mother had a wide repertoire; they sang either individually or in a duet. At home they sang all kinds of tunes, but at family reunions they usually performed comic songs, some of them with double-entendres, the meaning of which totally escaped the children.

Son joli p'tit chose was one of these songs; it was about a lady whose boyfriend was curious about something she had:

> *Son joli p'tit chose*
> *Tout doublé de rose*
> *Entouré de noir*
> *Entouré de noir*
>
> Her pretty little chose
> With a lining of pink
> And a border of black,
> A border of black

The young man wanted very much to look at that *chose*, but his sweetheart wouldn't let him. The song kept us guessing what the mysterious object was, until the very last verse revealed that it was none other than the lady's *réticule*, her cute little pocketbook.

I thought it was a very nice song and couldn't wait to own a little black pocketbook "with a lining of pink" when I grew up. I can imagine my parents smiling, as they listened to me sing in the métro, so serious, so applied, with my little bonnet, my coat and fur, and the neat white socks on legs that were far from touching the ground.

We lived in Fontenay-sous-Bois, an eastern suburb of Paris, next to Vincennes, less than an hour's walk from Paris. My aunt and uncle, Yvonne and Marcel Labbé, lived in Malakoff, a southern suburb. When we visited them we took the métro, and, by the time we came home, it was dark outside. The métro line was elevated part of the way and passed quite close to tall apartment buildings. If the lights were turned on in the apartments, we could see a little of the interiors through the windows.

Papa would say, "Look! Look! Colette, there is a lady with her slip inside out!"

"Where, Papa?"

"At the window right there! And look at the one over there! I see some people playing cards. One of them is cheating, I can tell!"

"Which window?"

"Oh! Look! Another lady! This one is wearing a necklace. I can see that one pearl is missing!"

"Where? Where?"

But we were too far away by then.

Aunt Yvonne and Uncle Marcel lent a book to my parents. It was a book with black-and-white drawings in comic-strip form, a graphic novel as we would say now. I looked at it, but realized that it was not a children's book; the drawings were stark and frightening. The book was about wolves getting ready to attack sheep. The sheep were the French, and the wolves were the Germans, piling up weapons and preparing for war.

2
The War Begins

Germany invaded Poland on September 1st, 1939. On September 3rd, France and Britain declared war on Germany. World War II had begun.

The onset of the war was difficult and confusing for French families. Under the General Mobilization Order, my father was called into the Army on September 9, 1939. He was assigned to the 778th Company to drive army vehicles and was sent to the front in the north of France. He was thirty-nine at the time. I don't know very much about this period in his life, but I do remember him talking about driving trucks in convoy for hours and hours, taking soldiers to the front. He often had to drive all night. Once, very tired, almost sleeping at the wheel, he suddenly "saw" a cathedral in the middle of the road; he could make out all the details: the sculptures above the tall gothic doors, the rose window, the towers. Then, the illusion was gone, and, in front of him, another truck was slowly making its way through the fog.

In the Paris region, an order came that children were to be evacuated to the country as a precaution should the Germans bomb Paris. In September 1939, my father's younger sister, Tante Marthe, her three children, and my paternal grandmother, Grand-mère Gauthier, were evacuated by convoy by the authorities of the City of Fontenay-sous-Bois to Corbeilles-en-Gâtinais (*département* of the Loiret), a village about one hundred kilometers (sixty-two miles) south of Paris, close to Montargis. For a short while I remained with my mother who, at that time, was working as a linotype operator for the newspaper of the Paris Stock Exchange, *L'Information*. The plan was for me to leave with our neighbor, Madame Mousset, who was going to another village of the Loiret, Beaune-la-Rolande; there, she would leave her daughter Pierrette (my little playmate) with relatives and return to Paris. My parents thought it would be good for me to stay in Beaune, at least until they found out what the situation was in Corbeilles. Although I stayed but a few weeks, I remember being terribly unhappy during my stay in Beaune with people I did not know. Soon, Tante Marthe came to pick me up, and I was reunited with my family in Corbeilles. Needless to say, I was happy to be with my grandmother, my aunt Marthe, and especially my three cousins: Miquette (also called Mimi), who was seven, Jacques, who was four like me, and Claude, who was almost three. And I was happier still when my mother joined us not long after that.

Tante Valentine, her husband Baptiste, and their nineteen-year-old son, Roger, had remained in Fontenay-sous-Bois for fear their house would become prey to looters. At that time, Oncle Baptiste was working in a factory in Bonneuil, a Paris suburb, and Roger was employed by *la Cartoucherie de Vincennes* (the Vincennes Armory), which supplied weapons to the French Army.

Tante Marthe's husband, Yves, had been drafted. He was stationed on the Ligne Maginot, the famous line of defense in eastern France, which was thought to be impenetrable, but would soon be skirted by the Germans.

On October 10, 1939, because of his age, my father was re-classified; he was assigned to the Auxiliary Service, but remained at the front. At that time, nothing was happening at the front. It was what was called *la drôle de guerre* (The Phoney War), which lasted from September 1939 to April 1940, a period during which the Germans and the French observed one another without engaging in battle. There was nothing to do but play cards, one game after the other. My father, bored and homesick, asked to be transferred to the *Cartoucherie*. He was transferred on January 2nd, 1940, and was assigned to work as a toolmaker as he already had training in toolmaking. Now stationed at the *Cartoucherie*, he was happy to be close to my mother: our house in Fontenay-sous-Bois was but a few minutes away from Vincennes. However, before long, my parents felt it would be better for my mother to go to Corbeilles-en-Gâtinais where she would be with me and our female relatives. When my mother left Paris for Corbeilles, my cousin Denise, who at that time lived with us, didn't go with her. She moved in briefly with her older sister, Simone, and then, at sixteen and a half, got married to her sweetheart, Armand.

Although my cousin Roger and my father ended up both working at the *Cartoucherie*, they rarely met, as my father worked days and Roger worked nights.

On May 10, 1940, the Germans attacked France, and on June 14, Paris fell. Millions of French people as well as refugees from Belgium began to flee from north to south. It was *la débâcle, l'exode*, a mass exodus of people fleeing the advancing Germans. They took to the road, often pushing carts heaped with what they could take of their possessions. During this chaotic period, many people were killed, victims of strafing German or Italian airplanes. Meanwhile, thousands of soldiers at the front were taken prisoners, including Yves, Tante Marthe's husband.

When *la Cartoucherie* fell under German control, my father and Roger stopped working there. My father left for the unoccupied zone of southern France, having been informed that his regiment was now in Toulouse, 680 kilometers (420 miles) south of Paris. My cousin Roger decided to go to Toulouse too. The factory near Paris where Oncle Baptiste worked was taken over by the Germans, but continued production from a new location, also in the unoccupied zone, in Marignane, near Marseilles, about 800 kilometers (500 miles) to the south of Paris. Oncle Baptiste left for Marignane using his own transportation: his bicycle.

When he arrived, Oncle Baptiste decided to pay a visit to Great-aunt Valentine, who lived in Marseilles. Elegant as usual, she took him for lunch to a high-class restaurant "Chez Pascal" on the Canebière, the chic boulevard of Marseilles. By that time, her second husband, Monsieur Cuenot, had died. After his death, Great-aunt Valentine, who was in need of money, took in a lodger, Monsieur Garcin, an employee of the Tramway Company, and soon became Madame Garcin. At the time of Uncle Baptiste's visit, she was seventy-one and Monsieur Garcin, fifty. Apparently, he did not know his wife's real age: at the time of their marriage, she had carefully doctored her birth certificate. It is only later, when she died, that Monsieur Garcin realized he had married a woman much older than himself.

With that, I will close the story of my great-aunt Valentine's life. Of her, I only have a few photographs (none, alas, taken during her youth). One of the photos below bears a rhymed inscription in her own handwriting.:

Great-aunt Valentine with her niece Pauline and Pauline's husband. Marseilles. (1937)

Tout ici-bas est éphémère
L'amitié ainsi que les amours
Un souvenir ne dure guère
Mais un portrait reste toujours

Everything here below is ephemeral
Friendship as well as love
A memory barely lasts
But a portrait is forever

Now, let's go back to my father and Roger on their way to Toulouse; Roger left first in a cargo train; soon after, my father decided to drive his own car, his Rosengart. On his way south, he made a stop to see my mother, me and the family in Corbeilles-en-Gâtinais (which was still not occupied by the

Germans). After a short visit, he left for Toulouse, encountering on the way crowds of people fleeing south. On the roads, the confusion was extreme; my father told us that he saw dead people lying by the roadside ditches. He gave lifts to many distressed people who begged him for rides. But the main problem was to get gasoline, something extremely difficult at that time. The roads were full of abandoned cars and discarded possessions.

My parents during my father's visit to Corbeilles-en-Gâtinais. (1940)

In Toulouse my father and Roger reconnected, but my father's regiment was nowhere to be found, and Roger who, at la *Cartoucherie*, had done civilian work for the Army, was left without a position. Both of them were housed and fed by a special unit of the military. Since there was nothing to do, they spent their time visiting the city.

My father thought that this period was an excellent opportunity to give his nephew a little "education," so he took him to a brothel, thinking that Roger, who was shy and awkward, would profit by the experience and become more open to life in general. Afterwards, when he asked Roger how things had gone, Roger only said, "It was all right," but didn't comment any further. My father did not insist.

The village of Corbeilles-en-Gâtinais had been abandoned by its inhabitants who had fled south, leaving their farms, houses and stores vulnerable to looters. Since this was where the authorities of the City of Fontenay-sous-Bois had sent us, we had to try to survive as best as we could. We were lucky to have been assigned to a big house on the main street, complete with furniture, linen and dishes. We also had a vegetable garden, and a well in the backyard.

After a while, we found out that not *all* the inhabitants had left. We were glad to acquaint ourselves with the few who had remained, as well as with the other refugee families. Some farmers had stayed also, but their farms were far from the village. An older Algerian gardener who lived in a nearby cottage gave us Parisians more than one tip on basic survival.

Little by little we settled in, eating vegetables from the garden, going to remote farms for meat or eggs. In spite of her love for animals, Tante Marthe had to learn to kill chickens to feed the family. Soon, she started working at a canteen that had been set up in the village. My cousin Jacques remembers that she used huge pots to cook rice pudding, and that he and his brother Claude would crawl inside in the pots to scrape the leftovers.

One day, Tante Marthe saw an abandoned cow by the side of the road, mooing for need of being milked. Though she never had come that close to a cow before, she started milking it, to the relief of the animal and the gratitude of the family.

However, in this still unoccupied area, our greatest apprehension was about the day when the Germans would arrive, a day we knew was approaching. During the *débâcle*, we had seen hundreds of people pass by our house. We had given them water. I remember them walking slowly, carrying suitcases or pushing wheelbarrows, some of them with their feet wrapped in bloody pieces of cloth.

If I do remember the most vivid scenes, I must admit that, in general, I have few recollections of that period. To write this, I have had to rely on my father's military records, my cousin Roger's memories (which he wrote in long letters to me), my other cousins' occasional reminiscences, and the tales I heard later, when the members of the family sitting around the table after a good meal, a cup of black coffee or tiny glass of liqueur in hand, took turns telling "their war." However, the story of Tante Marthe's sacrifice—which I will share in a moment—was not told around the table. I hold it from a secret source.

Finally the day arrived. Someone came to warn us that the Germans were approaching, but not attacking anyone. With fear in their hearts, our mothers decided that it was better to show ourselves. They dressed us in our

Left to right: my cousin Claude, a friend, me, my cousin Jacques, a friend, my cousin Mimi. In doorway: unidentified woman. Corbeilles-en-Gâtinais. (1940)

best smocks and lined us up in front of the house: first Mimi, the tallest, then Jacques, then me, and last, Claude, my daredevil three-year-old cousin. Next to us children stood my green-eyed, dark-haired mother, frightened but composed, Tante Marthe, fair, full-busted and tightly girdled, apprehensive but in control, and Grand-mère Gauthier, trembling in her black housedress and gray felt slippers.

From afar we saw the German soldiers on the road as they arrived in ranks, stamping their boots and singing "Hei li, hei lo, hei la!" When they came near, they looked at us, but passed our house without stopping. Some time later, we found out that they had established their headquarters at the end of the village and commandeered the café and grocery store. A French-speaking officer came to our house and inspected our backyard. He told us that some soldiers would be coming soon to use our well.

After that, ten or twelve Germans came every day to wash themselves by the well in our yard. I assume it was quite a spectacle to see these blond men, naked but for a cloth wrapped around their waists, splash cold water on their bodies, scrub and rub their muscles, and dry themselves with white towels before exercising in the sun. I was told that at that time French women didn't look at Germans "like that," but I am sure that Tante Marthe (and probably my mother as well) could not help but be fascinated.

Things went on peacefully for weeks. Little by little, we had begun to know the German soldiers personally: Otto would often fix the arms of my celluloid doll with rubber bands (he had a daughter my age). A soldier we called "Chouchou" (I don't know why) spoke French, and talked to us about his village. He was a baker in civilian life and missed his home pathetically.

One day, some of the German soldiers surprised us by cooking lunch for us. They prepared meat balls, potatoes and cabbage, and made a tossed salad. The meal was fine, except that they put sugar in the salad, an aberration that my relatives recalled with disgust for many years!

We were friendly but kept our distance; we never forgot that we stood on opposite sides of the war—and we were often reminded of it.

One day, for instance, one of the Germans sat my cousin Jacques on his lap, patted his head, and said, "Good little soldier for Hitler!"

But time has come to tell the story of Tante Marthe's sacrifice:

One night, we had gone to bed early as usual and were all asleep when we were awakened by a loud knock at the door. A tall German officer and two or three soldiers were standing on our doorstep. The soldiers were drunk and loudly demanded to get in. They wanted "to drink with the women."

Tante Marthe, my mother, and grandmother dressed quickly and told the children to stay in bed and not move. The Germans had brought brandy for the frightened women, who had no choice but to drink with the soldiers. The atmosphere was tense. It was obvious what the men had come for, and, in spite of the presence of my grandmother, they were getting bolder. One put his arms around my mother's waist while another pulled his gun, took aim, and fired at the clock which shattered noisily. We children shuddered in our beds.

It was time for Tante Marthe to take charge. She whispered to the tall officer that she would spend the night with him if he sent his men away.

He gave the word of command, "*RAUS!*" and our lives were saved.

It is this version of Tante Marthe's sacrifice that I hold from my "secret source," who (I might as well reveal it now) was my good Tata Valentine. But who is to tell that she didn't embellish the tale? And what about me? Didn't I innocently scatter a handful of invented details? Doesn't imagination blend a little too well with memory? My cousin Jacques simply remembers being told that his mother "saved the family" when German soldiers came to the house, one of them menacing us with his bayonet.

Whatever the truth was, I would have liked to thank Tante Marthe from the bottom of my heart, but, of course, it was impossible to bring up the subject. I also wanted to tell my aunt that she need not fear that the family had not appreciated her gesture. I can vouch that I never, ever heard anyone whisper a negative word. Tante Marthe was probably alone in wondering: "Maybe they did not understand!" But, dear Tante Marthe, we understood, we did!

If we were worried about the Germans, we had another serious preoccupation. Since the beginning of the war, Grand-mère Gauthier had not felt well; now she was ill most of the time. In April 1940, just before the Germans attacked France, she had gone to Paris to collect her World War I widow's pension and since her return she had hardly been able to leave her bed. Tante Valentine decided to come pick her up in Corbeilles and take her back to Fontenay-sous-Bois where she could put her under a doctor's care. However, by then the exodus was in full swing. They were lucky to find a man willing to give them a ride in exchange for a gasoline coupon. On their way to Paris, they had to stop in Montargis at the *Kommandantur*, the German police station, to apply for their coupon. Since it was clear that a single gasoline coupon would not be sufficient to get them to Paris, the man had to manage to find more passengers in order to get more coupons.

Once in Fontenay-sous-Bois, Grand-mère saw a doctor who told her she was suffering from a liver problem, and gave her medication in little bottles. But the medicine was bitter, so grand-mère emptied the bottles in the sink. She preferred to take a remedy of melissa extract bought at the pharmacy; she put a few drops of it on a lump of sugar and said it made her feel better. Tante Valentine was not surprised by her mother's reluctance to follow doctor's orders. In the past, when Grand-mère had insisted on putting lots of butter on her food (she, after all, was from Normandy, a region famous for its butter), my aunt had tried to admonish her, "That's too much fat! It's bad for your liver!" But Grand-mère had answered, "It's none of your business! Let me do as I please!" She was so obstinate and quick-tempered that there was not much anyone could do.

After the fall of Paris on June 14, 1940, the French government, with Paul Reynaud as its head, retreated to Bordeaux. On the 16th of June, Paul Reynaud abdicated, and Marshal Pétain took command. On the 18th of June, from London, General de Gaulle appealed to the French to organize the resistance.

My father and Roger were still in Toulouse when the armistice (which was in fact a capitulation) was signed on June 22, 1940 between the Pétain government and Germany. France was divided into two zones separated by a demarcation line: an occupied zone covering northern and western France, under German control, and a "free zone" in the south, under control of the Vichy government (when the Allies landed in North Africa in November 1942, the Germans would occupy the free zone). Upon hearing the news of the "armistice," my father and Roger decided to return to Fontenay-sous-Bois. They had to have authorization to cross the demarcation line. By mistake, the clerk who issued Roger's identity card wrote that Roger had blond hair when in reality he had black hair; fortunately this error was of no consequence. My father and Roger left in my father's car, taking two men as passengers, one of them a Belgian refugee who did not have any papers. At Vierzon, they were stopped by the German police, but, luckily, the police only asked to see my father's and Roger's papers. It had been a close call for the Belgian. He and the other man got off at Orléans. My father stopped by Corbeilles-en-Gâtinais to stay with us for a while, and Roger left for Paris, boarding a Red Cross train.

Meanwhile, in Fontenay-sous-Bois, Grand-mère Gauthier was getting worse. Tante Valentine took care of her as well as she could, but between going to work every day at *la Société Laitière Maggi* (a cooperative dairy shop), shopping, cooking, cleaning, and nursing her mother, she had practically no time left. The only thing she couldn't do was the laundry as she had eczema on her hands; she paid someone for that chore, often calling on my cousin Denise. Seeing that Tante Valentine was going through a lot of trouble for her, Grand-mère told her, "I give you too much work, *ma grande*, it would be better if I went to the hospital."

Grand-mère barely stayed in the hospital one week. Tante Valentine went to visit her every evening after work and brought her fruit. Grand-mère couldn't eat anything at all, but pretended she ate the fruit in order not to hurt Tante Valentine's feelings. This went on until the woman in the next bed told Tante Valentine in her country talk, "Your Mom, she don't eat nothing!"

Sick as she was, Grand-mère turned her head and glared at her neighbor. But Tante Valentine had not been fooled. She realized her mother was nearing her end. Grand-mère died that night of pancreatic cancer.

At the time of Grandmother's death, Tante Valentine was alone in Paris. Her husband, Baptiste, was in Marseilles; her son, Roger was on his way from Toulouse; my parents and Tante Marthe were in Corbeilles-en-Gâtinais.

Roger arrived just in time for the funeral, finding Tante Valentine at home with my cousin Denise (now married and living nearby) who was keeping company to Tante Valentine and trying her best to console her. At about the same time, my parents, Tante Marthe and all of us children returned to Paris for good. Oncle Baptiste arrived a few days after the funeral, this time not traveling by bicycle, but by train.

The memory of Grand-mère Gauthier would always be revered by my father and his sisters Valentine and Marthe. They talked about her as a saint, hot-tempered, but admirable. She had been little Louise Jumelin, badly treated by her mother, maid, silk-reeler, married to Arthur Gauthier who died in the First World War, four of her children were dead, her dear grandson P'tit Louis was dead. She had survived hard times, always kind, always loving, always there to take care of other people.

On July 10, 1940, Marshal Pétain, as Head of State, took residence in Vichy. His puppet government, ruled by the Germans, would last through the long years of the occupation.

My family was now back in Paris. My father was officially returned to civilian life on July 3rd, 1940.

3
My Parents' Bedroom

During the war there was a little pink bed for me in my parents' bedroom. I slept there until I was old enough and brave enough to move to my own room, but even then the pink bed was not removed right away, and once in a while I would return to it. For instance, when the Jewish doctor was in hiding at our house, he slept in my room and I went back to the pink bed. The doctor would come at night and go straight to sleep. He didn't eat with us, or even sit with us in the kitchen. He made sure nobody saw him when he came from Madame Haimann's apartment, a short block from our house. He left before daybreak and returned to Madame Haimann's. She hid him during the day until she could secure safe passage for him. Madame Haimann was Hungarian and had a strong accent. My father called her "Elvire Popesco" after the famous actress of the time (who, by the way, was Romanian).

The rose-colored bedspread on my parents' bed was so soft, so satiny that it was hard for me not to roll on it. And I loved the false candles and the little yellow shades of the light fixture. I also loved the big pear-shaped switch at the end of an electric cord that hung over the headboard of my parents' bed, just above my father's pillow, at his hand to turn the light off.

The night stand on the right side of the bed had a square door that opened on a chamber pot. On top of the stand was a little fringed rug made of white, yellow and green silk threads woven, I was told, "in a sanatorium, by people with tuberculosis." The lamp, with its crimped pink celluloid shade, sat next to a round dish with a delicate lid; made of thin opaque red glass, this elegant dish held a few safety pins and three triangular pieces of incense. At the center of the night stand reigned the old-fashioned alarm clock with its yellowish face and Roman numerals. The tick-tock of this old rooster was mighty enough to keep you awake at night, while in the morning its shrieking frightened you to death.

On each side of the bed were two gray and white goatskin rugs, their long hair soft on our feet. When I was born (in the bedroom) the midwife said to my mother, "You must get rid of these rugs; they are dust nests." But the rugs stayed. My mother used to shake them and air them out at the window when the weather was nice. The sheets and all the bedclothes were also regularly draped over the window railing and exposed to the sun.

I was born in my parents' bedroom on September 17th, 1935. It seems that I had passed out from lack of oxygen, the umbilical cord being tied around my neck. The midwife quickly revived me with a slap.

In a heavy oval frame above my parents' bed was a photograph of my brother. It was a posed portrait, taken by a professional photographer. My handsome brother, who seemed to be about nine in the picture, wore a white shirt and a dark sailor suit. His thick black hair fell across his forehead. His eyes, very dark, followed us wherever we were. His expression was serious, his mouth a little pouty. My brother didn't die in this bedroom. My parents already lived in Fontenay-sous-Bois then, but not yet in the villa de l'Ouest.

My brother died of meningitis at the age of ten, in May 1931. He suddenly had a very strong headache, a high fever, and couldn't bear to see the light. There was no cure at the time; he died in a little more than a week.

On the left side of the bed was an armoire with a mirror. The armoire was not of high quality; it had been bought together with the bed and the night table as a "modern mahogany set," but the "mahogany" was just varnish. Everything in the armoire was neatly organized. On the higher shelf were my mother's hats. One of them, deep burgundy, with a turned-down brim was the kind Greta Garbo would have loved to wear. It was so soft you wanted to caress it. On the middle shelves were the ironed sheets, tablecloths, napkins, towels, and handkerchiefs. On the lower shelves were my father's shirts and my mother's cream silk slips and pretty blouses, all perfectly pressed and folded. In the middle of the armoire, a small drawer contained the family's important papers, the savings books, and some money.

There was also an old fashioned vanity table (not part of the "modern" set) which had a marble top and three mirrors, a larger one in the middle and two smaller ones on the sides. Next to each side mirror was placed a small Chinese metal figurine, a man and a woman, sitting cross-legged on pedestals that opened up. When my cousins visited we would go to my parents' bedroom, open up the pedestals and look underneath the little figurines. We could clearly see the man's penis, but we didn't see anything when we opened the woman.

Once, I had a high fever, a strong headache, and light hurt my eyes. This happened during the time the Jewish doctor was coming to our house. He examined me. He said I didn't have meningitis, but told my parents that they should take me to another doctor in the morning, as he couldn't write a prescription. He recommended a doctor in Fontenay-sous-Bois; this other doctor was also Jewish but still practiced in the open. One day, not long after that, Madame Haimann told my father that everything had been settled for the passage. The Jewish doctor didn't need to come back to our house.

The wallpaper, perfectly hung by my father, was not the same on all the walls. The fashion at that time was to have two opposite walls covered with paper of a certain design, and the two other walls papered in a different design. The walls to the right and left of the bed had blue and orange triangles on a light blue background. The walls behind and in front of the bed had stylized orange dahlias on a light yellow background.

The large window was covered by an almost transparent muslin curtain and framed by vertical shades that folded like accordions; it opened on the quiet villa de l'Ouest. The Deco-style window railing, designed and made by my father, consisted of metal triangles and lozenges of different sizes and colors, welded together, and painted muted yellow, rust and blue.

Before I went to sleep in the pink bed, my mother always sang me a song. One of the songs, *Ils sont partis sur la barque légère, les trois p'tits gars* (They left in a light boat, the three young lads) was about three little boys who disobeyed their mother and went out to sea in a small boat; but the boat sank and the boys died. Another song was about a young girl who also disobeyed her mother. Encouraged by her brother, she went to a dance *sur le Pont du Nord* (on the North Bridge):

> *Ma soeur, ma soeur, qu'as-tu donc à pleurer?*
> *Maman n'veut pas que j'aille au bal danser.*
> *Mets ta robe blanche et ta ceinture dorée!*
>
> Sister, sister, why are you crying?
> Mother doesn't want me to go to the ball.
> Put on your white dress and tie your golden belt!

But the bridge collapsed under the weight of the dancers and both the girl and her brother drowned.

> *Les cloches du Nord se sont mises à sonner*
> *La mère demande c'qu'ont les cloches à sonner*
> *C'est votre fille et votre fils noyés.*
>
> The North bells started ringing.
> The mother asks why are the bell ringing.
> It's for your son and daughter, drowned.

There was also a song about a big sister who had tuberculosis. When her little brother heard the doctor say that his sister would die in autumn—when all the leaves had fallen—he tried to tie back the fallen leaves to the trees with pieces of string.

My mother also sang about a woman who was cold in the night and asked a passer-by to take her home.

> *J'ai froid, emmenez-moi*
> *Je n'ai pas de pensées vilaines*
> *Mais voudrais dormir sous un toît*
> *Enveloppée d'un peu de laine.*
>
> I am cold, take me with you
> I do not have bad intentions
> But would like to sleep under a roof,
> Wrapped up in a little wool.

But the song I preferred was the one about the beautiful lady that everyone called "La Madone."

> *On l'a surnommée La Madone*
> *Parce qu'un jour en son vitrail*
> *Un peintre dont le nom résonne*
> *De ses yeux a fixé tout l'émail*
>
> She was called "The Madonna"
> Because, one day, on a stained-glass window
> A painter whose name is well-known
> Captured the enamel of her eyes

I don't remember the ending of this song, but like all the others my mother sang, it was undoubtedly very sad. What I do recall is that I imagined the lady in the song to look just like my mother. My mother had a gentle type of beauty. She had black hair, a pale complexion, and large limpid green eyes that were set wide apart. She was soft and graceful, and I adored her. She died in 1947 when I was twelve years old, at the age of forty-five, in the bedroom.

When I was in the small pink bed, I could hear my parents talk to each other. They talked every night for a long, long time. They talked softly. I didn't try to understand what they said; I was always too tired. They talked on and on until I fell asleep.

4
Tante Marthe

Tante Marthe. (1926)

My parents were not the only ones in the family who hid Jews during the war; as a matter of fact, my aunt Marthe had a much greater role. But before I tell her story, I must draw a portrait of her.

Tante Marthe was a good-looking woman who made heads turn when she entered a room. With her head held high, her coat thrown over her shoulders, she was a star, ready for her public. Her dyed blond hair highlighted both her fair complexion and her hazel eyes, eyes full of spirit under neatly penciled eyebrows. And, while she did try to soften her rather square face with pale powder, she was not afraid to spark it up with cherry-red lipstick. She adored costume jewelry: bangles, heavy brass bracelets, large rings, and sparkling brooches (*des faux bijoux!* commented the family). Her presence was ushered by glints of light and jingling of metal. With her light summer suits, she sported white-rimmed sunglasses; in the winter she draped herself in dark fur coats, heavy with perfume. A real Hollywood lady! But Tante Marthe had a major weakness: she was extremely sensitive about her size. Though shapely, she was a large woman. It was acceptable to describe her as *forte* (strongly built), but one had to make sure that the words *gros or grosse* (fat) were never used in her presence—not even in reference to someone else. These words were totally, absolutely forbidden. As a matter of fact, many things were forbidden when it came to Tante Marthe. She was extremely superstitious: no open umbrellas in the house, never thirteen people around the table, no hats on beds, no heedless champagne corks that may bop somebody. All those things could bring bad luck, perhaps even death! One had to be extremely careful.

She was somewhat theatrical (my father called her Sarah Bernhardt), but she had an excuse. In fact, her life had been full of tragedies. Her first husband had died of intestinal tuberculosis in the same hospital, and at the very same time that she was giving birth to their daughter, my dear cousin Micheline Van Roye (whom we called Mimi or Miquette when she was young, and later called Michèle). Tante Marthe's second husband, Yves, had many faults, some of them she couldn't bear. (I don't know exactly what these faults were, but I am quite sure that violence and laziness were among them.) She was already planning to divorce him when he was drafted into the army and soon taken prisoner by the Germans. At the end of the war, when Yves was liberated, she did ask for a divorce, but a "patriotic" judge granted custody of their two sons, Jacques and Claude, to their father. The reason for the denial of custody was that Tante Marthe (yes, the same Tante Marthe whose commendable "sacrifice" saved us during the evacuation) had hidden a Jewish man in her apartment in Fontenay and that they had become lovers. One just did not cuckold a prisoner of war! However, this love affair did not turn out to be a passing liaison, but ended in marriage after the war. I was too young to remember anything about Yves, so, from the beginning, for me it was always: *Tante Marthe et Oncle Albert*.

Since 1942, the order for Jews in France had been to wear a yellow star sewn on their clothes, or face imprisonment. My uncle Albert had been caught in a raid on persons suspected of being Jews, but not wearing the mandatory yellow star. Held in Nantes by the German police with the collaboration of the French authorities, he and the other prisoners were to be sent to a concentration camp. Miraculously, my uncle succeeded in escaping from Nantes, hiding and avoiding the huge searchlights that swept the ground. Arriving in Paris he found refuge in a brothel where he was kept hidden by prostitutes. Aunt Marthe, who was friendly with the woman who ran the brothel, was asked if she could hide Albert in her apartment in Fontenay-sous-Bois. Having been introduced to Albert, she accepted without hesitation. Sadly, while Albert owed his life to his daring escape and the assistance of strangers, his sister and her husband, who had been caught before him, both perished in Auschwitz. At that time, Albert was married, but separated from his wife. I know that his wife, also Jewish, remained free, but never heard anything else said about her.

Oncle Albert's parents were émigrés, long-time residents of Paris. We called them Monsieur et Madame Schuschmann, but actually, they had never married (Oncle Albert's mother's name was Vatache). They worked in their small apartment, a sort of private sweatshop, assembling cloth caps on their power sewing machines, a backbreaking job for which they were paid by the piece. Both of them wore the yellow star.

My uncle Albert, who did not want to spend the rest of the war in hiding, managed to obtain false papers, and ended up with a new identity under the name of Gaston Roux. We had to learn to call him Gaston, which made my father sometimes jokingly call him "Gasbert." After he got his false papers, Oncle "Gaston" lived out in the open. He and Tante Marthe ran a food cooperative in Paris, and later on started working with Monsieur and Madame Schuschmann, manufacturing work caps for wholesalers. (These dark-blue caps with visors were commonly worn by laborers and farm workers).

Tante Marthe.
(c. 1948)

Oncle Albert Schuschmann.
(c. 1948)

A tall and handsome man, with all-knowing eyes behind glasses à la Woody Allen, Oncle Albert had a terrific sense of humor and was loved by the whole family. My father, especially, appreciated his company. Together they spent many hours talking, playing chess, or going to Chez Brusson to play bridge. I know for a fact that my uncle had a lot of success with women, something that did not fail to provoke Tante Marthe's famous fits of jealousy—another reason for my father to call her "Sarah Bernhardt" (in the privacy of our home, of course).

Oncle Albert and my father. (c. 1950)

During these eventful years, my cousin Miquette didn't always stay with her mother, but was also being cared for by either Grand-mère Gauthier or Tante Valentine in the villa de l'Ouest. Since we lived next door to each other, Miquette and I were practically brought up together. Being three years older, she was like a big sister to me.

Tante Marthe and Oncle Albert did not remain in Fontenay-sous-Bois; they moved to rue Saint-Sébastien, in Paris, where Miquette eventually joined them. The building in which they lived was run-down, but their small apartment was well-decorated and comfortable. In their spare time they liked to go to movies or to concerts, and have friends over for dinner. Tante Marthe was a good cook. I remember that one of her specialties was onion croquettes, the preparation of which included both grating onions and spilling a great flow of tears. Mixing the grated onions with eggs and mashed potatoes, she made small balls that she rolled in flour and deep-fried. A delight not easy to forget! As for my uncle, he made no secret of his propensity for lounging. He spent his Sundays in bed reading modern novels, science fiction, "forbidden" books, such as Henry Miller's *Tropic of Cancer*, or Boris Vian's *J'irai cracher sur vos tombes* (*I Will Spit on Your Graves*), which he passed on to my parents. He also loved to read historical articles in the multiple volumes of *La Grande Encyclopédie Larousse*. As he was reading, he listened to classical music on the radio. The violin he had played when he was younger was now relegated to the top of the armoire.

I liked my aunt and uncle Schuschmann; they were different, unconventional. For instance, when Tante Marthe did not feel like cooking dinner, she made *crêpes* with jam, or just served hot chocolate and buttered bread. She and my uncle didn't think anything of it. The rest of the family thought it was outrageous (except the children, who couldn't have been happier!).

During and after the war I spent quite a bit of time with Tante Marthe, Oncle Albert and Miquette. Reflecting on her past, Miquette once told me, "The first seven years of my life when I lived at Grand-mère Gauthier and Tante Valentine's were my happiest because I really felt loved." And she added, not without bitterness, "Maman was always more wife than mother."

5
Maman

My own mother was not like that, not like that at all. She was wife and mother in the most harmonious way. Her love was not divided, not shared; it was whole, both for my father and me. Memories of her when I was a child delight me to this day.

Until I was perhaps three or four, Maman washed me on the kitchen table. She put a basin of warm water on the table and stood me next to it. She rubbed me with a soapy washcloth (a washcloth in the French style: a little rectangular sack in which you slip your hand). She rubbed me all over. I liked to feel the warm, slippery soap on me, and it felt especially good when the sudsy glove passed between my legs. Then, my mother rinsed me and patted me dry in a big towel. After that, I would lie on the towel, and Maman would kiss me and kiss me; she kissed me all over, my face, my arms, my stomach, she kissed my bottom, and she kissed my little *"mounette,"* saying : "It's mine! It's mine!" And I would protest and say in baby French, *"Non, c'est pas t'à toi! C'est pas t'à toi!"* It's not yours, it's not yours! Then, she rubbed my back and chest with Eau de Cologne, and put clean clothes on me.

Sometimes, Maman took me to the dressmaker who lived near the Bois de Vincennes. First, she and the dressmaker looked at pictures of dresses; afterward, I had to climb on the table to have my measurements taken. I had to be careful not to step on the pin cushions, the scissors, and all the other sewing things, and I had to hold my arms out until the dressmaker finished measuring me with her cold tape. The only thing I liked about her workshop was the smell of new fabric. I didn't really care about dresses. I can't even recall any of the dressmaker's creations, but I do remember walking back home with my mother; we talked and laughed, and I danced and sang and jumped about.

I remember a little story I heard my mother tell my father.

"I was riding my bicycle," Maman said, "when two young fellows, also on bicycles, followed me and called out to me, 'Hey! Beautiful! Stop for a minute!' I was wearing my pleated skirt, and, with the wind blowing, they could see my legs. They kept on, 'You! Pretty girl! Slow down!' I was flattered. They obviously thought I was a young girl. I was not about to disappoint them and let them see my face, so I pedaled and pedaled. I ended up out of breath, but they never caught up with me!"

My parents and me. (1935)

When my mother and my father hugged or kissed, it made me furious. I punched and kicked my father's legs. I hated for my father to hug my mother. She was mine!

I loved to comb my mother's hair. When she sat at the kitchen table, I would stand behind her on her chair, my feet barely fitting between her backside and the back of the chair. I brushed and combed her hair. She had naturally wavy black hair, sometimes a little curly thanks to a permanent. Her hair smelled good. It was a little too short for barrettes, but I clipped some in anyway. Maman would say to me, "You will be a hairdresser when you grow up!" and that made me happy. My mother's eyes were light green and very soft. Once, when I told her that her eyes were beautiful, she said, "No, my eyes used to be beautiful, but they are not anymore: I cried too much when your little brother died."

One day, I had to write a composition about autumn, but I was not inspired. My mother wrote it for me. "I love the Bois de Vincennes in autumn," she said. And she got a pretty good grade! And a few times, when I didn't feel like going to school, she wrote the teacher a note saying that the alarm clock didn't ring. She never wrote that I was sick, for that would have brought bad luck.

Maman. (c. 1943)

At home my father was somewhat of a tyrant. If my mother didn't look at him when he talked, didn't do right away what he asked, or didn't have his medication ready by his plate, he would explode in a rage.

"You don't care a thing about me! I'm good enough to earn the daily bread, but you can't even remember my medicine! You couldn't care less if I died!"

These outbursts frightened me, but my mother was used to them. She would say, "The Gauthiers are *soupe au lait* (milk soup), quiet one minute, boiling over the next." Grand-mère Gauthier and Tante Valentine had the reputation to be *soupe au lait* also. They could be patient, but when something upset them, they became hysterical and started shrieking and stomping their feet. Papa was not like that, but when he got furious, he shouted and banged his fist on the table. When my mother and I knew he was really angry, we remained quiet, but when he was just in a grumbling mood, Maman looked at me and made faces behind his back.

On Thursdays there was no school. Grand-mère Cessot, who lived with Tante Yvonne, came to our house to help my mother with the ironing and mending. She and my mother sat in the kitchen, and I sat with them. The pulley lamp above the table was lowered right over the sewing, and its light made the kitchen cozy, especially in wintertime. On these days, we would talk or listen to the radio. There was a special Thursday program, a talent contest, with little children singing or reciting poetry; just listening to the children made my mother cry. In the middle of the afternoon we would have a snack; it was called le *"quatre heures"* (the "four o'clock"). My mother would grill pieces of sliced baguette in the oven; we'd butter our warm bread and dip it in hot chocolate. Sometimes when she made *crème caramel* for our dinner dessert, she would bake a few extra little pots so we could have a taste beforehand.

Maman had a brown fur coat made of rabbit fur. When I put my nose in it, it felt soft and smelled of her perfume: *Soir de Paris* (Evening in Paris). One day that we were going out, my mother put on her fur coat and took her black patent leather purse, the one with the shiny metal handle. We must have been going to Tante Yvonne's or Tante Marthe's for dinner. I remember that we were on our way home when it happened. My mother, my father, and I were waiting on the métro platform. When the métro arrived many people crowded us as we tried to get through the door. Suddenly my mother shouted, *"Mon sac! Mon sac!"* (My purse! My purse!). We remained on the platform. After the métro left the station, we saw Maman's purse lying on its side on the tracks between the rails, its stiff and shiny patent leather unhurt. Quickly, my father went to find the station agent who arrived carrying a long stick with a hook at the end. He fished for my mother's purse, missing it a few times until he finally grabbed it by the handle. A miraculous rescue!

My mother often told me stories of her childhood. She used to play in the street with some of the neighborhood kids. They liked to go to the public fountain on the main square and pump water to fill their play buckets. Sometimes kids would lie down under the spigot while someone worked the pump with just the right amount of pressure to make water fall into their open mouth. One day my mother returned home crying, *"Maman, Maman! La rouquine m'a marché sur la gorge!"* ("Mummy, Mummy, the red-haired girl stepped on my throat!")

One afternoon, I was playing in the villa de l'Ouest with my friends, totally involved in a game, when my mother came up the rue Jules Ferry and turned into the villa de l'Ouest to go to our house.

"Colette," she called out, "Look!"

I went to her, "What? What should I look at?"

"Me! Don't you see anything different?"

"No! Did you change your lipstick?"

"No! Look again!"

"I can't see anything!"

"My hair!"

And then, I saw that she had dyed her hair blond. Although it was jet black when I had last seen her, I hadn't noticed the change. I have often wondered why. Was it that I was too involved in playing? In a hurry to return to my friends? I don't know. I guess that, for me, it was enough to know that Maman was Maman.

6
Cinema

When I lived in Berkeley, my friend Gisèle, an expatriate like myself, invited me for dinner. She wanted to introduce me to her mother who was visiting from France. During our dinner Madame B., who held strong opinions, told us that in France everyone knows how to appreciate good cooking because the French expect their food to have *"du goût"* (not just "taste," but a "certain quality" of taste). She had traveled widely and had concluded that only the French and the Italians knew anything about *la bonne cuisine*. Other people didn't have this subtle understanding of *"le goût."* She was a nice and vivacious woman, and I very much enjoyed listening to her. After a while, when the conversation turned to our youth, we all were surprised to discover that both Madame B. and I were from Fontenay-sous-Bois.

The parents of Madame B. owned a candy store: *Aux Délices* (The Delights) on rue Mauconseil. I happened to know rue Mauconseil quite well. On that street was found, not only the *Mairie* (City Hall), but also the dairy shop where Tante Valentine worked: *la Société Laitière Maggi*. During the war, cheerfully swinging my aluminum milk canteen by the handle, I went to *"la Maggi"* (" la ma-jee") every week, not because it was particularly close to my house, but because of the special privileges I was granted there: my aunt or her friend-colleague, Madame Abalin, gave me more milk than my ration coupons allowed. After greeting me with, *"Bonjour, ma p'tite poulette,"* their oversized ladles in hand, they dished out the precious milk from one of two deep metal cylinders built into the counter. It was all very nice, but once I got home, the milk often went sour quickly since we had no refrigeration. Whenever that happened, my mother strained the sour milk through a cloth to make *fromage blanc*, which we ate with sugar. Besides milk, the Maggi dairy store carried cheese, eggs, and a few other items such as soap and sweets.

Tante Valentine. (c. 1946)

Madame B. told me that she remembered Tante Valentine's dairy shop. In fact she remembered it very well! *La Société Laitière Maggi*, by selling sweets, was a competitor to the *Aux Délices* candy store.

"My whole family," she said, "wished for the soap to fall in the milk!"

Even though Madame B. is nine years older than me, we shared common memories. We started talking about the movie houses in Fontenay-sous-Bois. There were three of them: *Le Kosmos, Le Celtic* (now remodeled as a supermarket), and *Le Palais-des-Fêtes.*

"When I was young," Madame B. told us, "my brother and sister and I loved to go to the movies, but our father did not like for us to go because he said it would ruin our minds."

Her parents looked with disdain at people "who went to the movies every week." It was not *"comme il faut"* (proper) to go so often. Only once in a while did the whole family go the cinema. It was for Madame B. an extraordinary treat. She, her parents and her siblings always sat in the balcony; it was there that the *bonnes familles* (respectable families) were supposed to sit. (She told us that she would sneak out during the intermission to go say hello to her friends downstairs.) I mentioned the usherettes who showed people to their seats with their flashlights, and sold Eskimo Pies and caramels off the display baskets strapped around their necks.

"Oh, we never bought anything from them," she said. "We had a candy store! We always brought our *petits bonbons*!"

I loved the Palais-des-Fêtes. I asked Madame B. if she remembered the ceiling in the lobby. To my surprise, she did not. Yet, for all the children I knew, the ceiling was an object of wonder. It looked exactly as if cooked spaghetti, flattened and reddish orange had been glued up there. I have never seen a ceiling like that anywhere else.

At the Palais-des-Fêtes the show started at nine p.m. It included a documentary, usually boring, on subjects such as "Rivers of France" or "Melting Iron in Blast Furnaces." Sometimes (to our joy) there was a cartoon, then the newsreel. After that came the *entracte*, the intermission, time for caramels or Eskimo Pies. Once in a while, we were treated to live entertainment, maybe a magician, ballroom dancers, acrobats, or more rarely, a singer. Finally, after the *entracte*, the movie started.

My parents went to the cinema every Saturday evening, fortunately unaware of the fact that a weekly trip to the movies was not considered "proper" (and without the slightest notion that *les bonnes familles* sat in the balcony). They always booked their tickets in advance, requesting orchestra seats, "around the 12th row."

During the war the movies were often interrupted by one or more air alerts. The sirens would sound, and the whole audience had to evacuate the movie house and go to the shelters. I don't remember people being afraid. What everyone wanted was to get back in as fast as possible to see the rest of the film. It was much worse when there was a power shortage: it meant that we would have to return another day to see the end of the movie.

When I was small, before the war, I sat patiently through the first part of the program but often fell asleep shortly after the *entracte*. In that way I saw the beginning of many a great classic such as Marcel Carné, *Quai des brumes* (Port of Shadows), with Jean Gabin; Jacques Feyder's *La Kermesse héroique* (Carnival in Flanders); or my parents' favorite, the trilogy written by Marcel Pagnol: *Marius, Fanny, César*, with the great actor Raimu. When I remained awake, it often was because I was frightened by such films as *Crime and Punishment*, with the dramatic actor Pierre Blanchard and his nightmarish eyes, or by Walt Disney's *Snow White*, with the terrifying witch.

In war time, with film-making being controlled by the Vichy government, movies were heavily censored. Many French directors moved abroad. Some stayed and worked in the German-controlled studio, *Continental*, making light comedies or detective movies such as films based on Simenon's books (starring Albert Préjean as Inspecteur Maigret). Other directors managed to make movies with veiled anti-Nazi messages, the most famous example being Marcel Carné's *Les Visiteurs du soir* (The Devil's Envoys), or treated of subjects removed from the war, as did Jean Cocteau in *L'Eternel retour* (Eternal Return) with Jean Marais, a film based on the legend of Tristan and Isolde.

Movie-goers were given a heavy dose of German propaganda films, something which was not very much appreciated. One of these films, however, *Die Goldene Stadt* (the Golden City), became the greatest success of the occupation, to the surprise of the authorities. It turned out that the movie's message, "Do not move to the sinful city; remain in the wholesome country," got interpreted in a totally different way by French audiences, who liked it for its dreams of freedom and romantic love story. Personally I still remember some scenes in color of the beautiful city of Prague.

At the Palais-des-Fêtes I was fast asleep by the time the movies ended. My parents would wake me up and my father would sit me on his shoulders to carry me home. I felt limp and heavy. It was dark outside, I rested my face against my father's head, and, half awake, looked at the street below, rocked by his steps. My parents always discussed the film; their criteria being mostly whether or not it faithfully represented "reality." I could see the cobblestones gently gliding under my father's feet. I could hear my parents' voices as in a dream. My eyelids were closing against my will.

For a long time after my mother died, I did not go to the movies. Then, I occasionally returned to the Palais-des-Fêtes with my father. When I was about fourteen and innocently in love, Patrick, my sweetheart, always managed to sit next to me. In the dark, we held hands. I had two fears, one that my father would catch us, the other, that he would fall asleep and start snoring.

The Palais-des-Fêtes does not exist any more. Nothing is left of it. There is an apartment building where it once stood. But I can still see it exactly as it was, with its spaghetti ceiling, its usherettes dressed in black, its red velvet seats, and the smoky ray of light coming from the projection room. I can also see Patrick, and my father, and (now that I know they were there), up in the balcony, Madame B. and her brother and sister, eating their petits bonbons.

7
Tante Valentine

My cousins and I called Tante Valentine *Tata Gâteau* (Auntie-cake), not only because she cooked delicious desserts for us, but also because *gâter* means to spoil a child. Miquette, Jacques, Claude and I were her darling nieces and nephews; she adored us, hugged us, called us her *petits poulets, petits lapins, petits cocos chéris,* etc. Roger, her only child, was much older than us. He was an adult, already working.

Tante Valentine's husband, Oncle Baptiste, a thin but strong man with a heart-shaped hairline, protruding ears, a little mustache, and a good-natured smile, was from Brittany. He was not like the rest of the family; he was more innocent, less of an urbanite. My father sometimes said, "Baptiste is a nice fellow, but you can tell he is a country boy!" (I was not to repeat that to anyone.) According to my true Parisian father the way one could tell Oncle Baptiste was a *"paysan"* was that he was always fussing in his garden, and that, with typical country penny-pinching, he only gave us one or two bagfuls of cherries, even though his cherry tree was covered with fruit.

When my cousins came over, we were allowed to play in Oncle Baptiste's garden, but we had to keep on the main path. The exception was when we picked the sweet gooseberries and nose-wrinkling bitter black currants that our uncle grew to make liqueur. As for the mysterious pears that hung in their own little paper sacks on their espaliered trees, we never even caught a glimpse of them.

Oncle Baptiste had an old shed where he kept a few rabbits in cages and five or six hens. Tante Valentine, who stored the eggs in a special basket, penciled each egg with the date on which it was laid. When we went to her house she picked the freshest eggs, soft-boiled them, sat them in fancy little egg cups, and served them with strips of buttered bread that we dipped in the yoke. She made *crème caramel* or rice pudding in individual earthenware pots which she lined on the window ledge to cool. Once, when my cousin Claude dropped one of the pots in the garden (by mistake, I think) she didn't get angry. She was sweet to all of us—she called me *"ma p'tite nénette,"* and let me look at the old family photos and play with her fantastic button collection. But with her husband, she was not so sweet. She often got irritated with him. My parents and I sometimes heard her shout at him from our house when our kitchen window was open. My parents used to say, "Poor Valentine! She'll never be happy!"

Tante Valentine had facial hair; she had to shave, which was very embarrassing to her. When she kissed us, we were never to say *"Ça pique!"* ("It scratches.") My cousins and I never said it, but when a child outside the family pronounced these forbidden words, our heart sank for our auntie. Of course, Papa—who loved his sisters, but couldn't resist poking fun at them in private, called her *"La femme à barbe"* ("The bearded lady").

Tante Valentine was more than ten years older than my father while Tante Marthe was six years younger than him. The only survivors of what had been a large family, they—and especially Tante Valentine and my father—often talked about their dead brothers Émile and Charles, to the point that they became almost like living uncles to me.

From the old photos, it was obvious that Émile and Charles had been good-looking men, my father was still handsome, and Tante Marthe had kept all her charm. Alas, Tante Valentine did not resemble her siblings. It did bother her greatly to be the only plain one in the family. She had a round face, small eyes, a turned-up nose, and she wore glasses. Besides, she was not very shapely: no waistline and a bit overweight. (I guess she had not aged well, for old photographs show her as a fine-looking moon-faced woman, narrow waisted and tightly corseted.) One thing that she often pointed out was that she had beautiful hair. We had to agree: her hair was indeed beautiful: silver-gray, wild and wavy. Even when she wore it in a *chignon*, it could never be completely tamed.

The family sometimes discreetly commented on Tante Valentine's "fashion finds." She often bought her dresses at La Samaritaine, a department store better known for quality housewares than for elegant women's clothing.

"Look at this cute little dress! You'll never guess what a bargain it was!" she would say. (I remember one such dress; it was black and white with big yellow daisies.)

For underclothes she went for black satin, and showed her purchases to my mother and me. Of course, we said that everything was very nice, but at home when we told my father, he commented, "I think poor Baptiste couldn't care less about all this froufrou!"

Tata Valentine had a weakness for kitchen tools; she had several drawers full of them. She just couldn't resist buying the latest implements, often demonstrated and sold by barkers on the Paris Grands Boulevards. She had spoons to cut out melon balls, orange slicers, apple corers, tart cutters, shredders, cherry pitters, corkscrews of every shape and size. Two of her prized possessions were her scale with its shiny copper weights (that we, as children loved to play with), and her "modern" yogurt maker.

When Tante Valentine hung her laundry in the back garden, she sang arias from *Tosca*, *Faust*, or *Manon*. We could see her from our window, among the white sheets, the towels and Oncle Baptiste's work shirts, and hear Marguerite's laughter in the *Jewel Song*:

> *Ah! Je ris de me voir si belle*
> *En ce miroir!*

> Ah! I laugh to see myself so beautiful
> In this mirror!

Or Manon's melancholy goodbye:

> *Adieu, notre petite table!*
> *Qui nous réunit si souvent.*

> Adieu our little table
> Around which we so often met

She loved opera, and often went to the Paris Opera with her friend Madame Abalin, the lady who worked with her at *La Société Laitière Maggi*. She liked to take my cousins and me out, but usually in separate groups because four children at the same time were a little too much to handle. With her and Roger we went to look at the animated Christmas windows of the Paris department stores Le Printemps and Les Galeries Lafayette, or to the children's theater, *Le Théâtre du Petit Monde,* or, exceptionally, to the Opera. When we went to the Opera my cousin Miquette and I had to wear white gloves—and we were reminded not to drag our fingers on the tiled walls of the métro corridors. We brought binoculars and sat in a box. It was absolutely forbidden to talk or cough, which convinced us that, if we had to cough and were forced not to, we would die for sure. One day, when we were watching the ballet *Coppélia,* I leaned over to look at the audience in the orchestra. The spectators were all dressed in green. They were German soldiers and officers, which brought Tante Valentine to remark: "I don't care what people say, but the Germans have culture!"

Our cousin Roger was a great preoccupation for Tante Valentine. He liked to stay home, had no friends, was extremely shy, and had no interest in girls (or in boys, for that matter). He was not handsome; his face was red and often covered with acne. But Roger had marvelous qualities, which I learned to appreciate. Tante Valentine always tried to find "a nice girl" for her son. At first, it was a little laughable, but as time went by, it became almost pathetic. In the end, Tante Valentine never reconciled herself with the fact that Roger never left home, never married, and never led a "normal" life.

I am grateful to Tata Valentine who made the unspoken pledge to take me under her wing after my mother's death. At that time, however, never having tasted disaster, I took her (and most of my family) for granted. Another world absorbed my attention: the villa de l'Ouest. That was where I played with my friends. The life of our small street drew me like a magnet.

8
Villa de l'Ouest

There are numerous *villas* in Fontenay-sous-Bois, but not *villas* in the sense of opulent houses (although there are some of these too). In Fontenay, *villas* are passages that sometimes end in cul-de-sacs, sometimes connect one street to another. They can also be, quite simply, *petites rues*. The villa de l'Ouest, which begins at rue Jules Ferry, ends with a flight of concrete steps leading up to a street at a higher level, the rue Gambetta.

In 1932, a year after my brother's death, the two-story house my parents bought next door to Tante Valentine's was (and still is) the tallest in the villa de l'Ouest. All the houses in the villa have a style of their own. Most of them are built in stone and have a little front garden which can be peeked at through a wrought-iron gate or a wooden fence. Our house stood out among the others, not only because of its height, but also because of the fine ochre color of its façade.

Fontenay-sous-Bois has a long history. Records dating back to the year 847 mention its name, which means fountain (or fountains) under the wood. Originally a hamlet surrounded by meadows, vineyards and woods, it slowly grew into a town. The vineyards are no more and the woods have long disappeared, except for the nearby Bois de Vincennes, once a forest surrounding a royal hunting lodge, now a large park belonging to the city of Paris. In the 12th century the heavily fortified Château de Vincennes, a king's residence, replaced the hunting lodge. At present the *Bois* still harbors this wonderfully preserved feudal castle.

Approximately three miles east of Paris, the town of Fontenay-sous-Bois grew on the side of a hill and on a plateau, later expanding to surrounding flat areas. The villa de l'Ouest is located near the foot of the plateau, close to "Les Rigollots," a busy crossroad which marks the dividing line between Fontenay-sous-Bois and Vincennes. The suburb of Vincennes, bigger and busier than Fontenay, blends into Paris near the district of Porte de Vincennes.

Whenever I go back to France I have the impression that nothing has changed since my childhood. After getting off at métro Château de Vincennes, I catch a bus to Fontenay-sous-Bois. A fifteen-minute ride takes me to the crossroad of Les Rigollots (a strange name since "rigolo" means "funny" but here refers to a brand of poultice, an old-fashioned cold remedy, that used to be manufactured locally). After walking for a couple of blocks on the shop-lined rue Dalayrac, I turn left, go uphill on rue Jules Ferry for two more blocks, and there on the left side, past the primary school, is the villa de l'Ouest. (See map).

The villa de l'Ouest, shaped like an elbow, bends right at a ninety degree angle. The first part, starting at rue Jules Ferry, is very short and looks like an ordinary street with the school wall on the left and two small apartment buildings on the right; by contrast, the part after the bend looks residential and private. This segment, which runs parallel to rue Jules Ferry, ends with a concrete stairway. It is bordered (at least it was in my youth) by eight houses on the left, and five on the right. Since rue Jules Ferry and villa de l'Ouest run close to each other, some houses with front doors on rue Jules Ferry have back gardens that end in the villa de l'Ouest. These gardens run between some of the five houses on the right side of the villa and can be seen through fences.

When I was young, the first part of the villa was paved, or rather, tarred, just like any other street, but the part after the right angle bend was not. This was the subject of constant complaints to City Hall, as the residents wanted the entire villa to be paved. Year after year there was a promise, but never any action. Apparently, one of the difficulties was that, although the villa was wide enough to be regarded as a street, the lots were not aligned, and the fact that some people would have had to give up a few feet of their property created a problem that took a long time to resolve. Then, when the war came and a period of belt-tightening followed, City Hall lost interest. After that, nothing happened for years. When I got married at the age of twenty-two and left my house, the villa was still untouched—although it did get paved not long after that, finally.

I don't have many early memories of the villa before the war or even during the time my cousin Denise lived at my house. However, there are two things I remember vividly. One of them was the horrifying cry of the ragman in his old horse-drawn cart as he drove on rue Gambetta at the

A "banquet" in the villa de l'Ouest. (c. 1942)

top of the villa steps. It started as a blood-curdling howl, and ended with the chant: *Peaux d'lapin, chiffons, ferraille à vendre!* (Rabbit skins, rags, old metal to sell!) The ragman was ugly and deformed, a sort of Quasimodo, and I had nightmares about him. My other memory, very different, is of a lady, sometimes accompanied by a small child, who came to our door to collect food for Spanish children. My mother gave her sugar, a kilo of rectangular sugar lumps packed in their rectangular blue carton. I must have been about three years old then. Later on, I realized that these donations were for the families of partisans fighting in the Spanish Civil War.

As far as I remember, it seems that I always played in the villa de l'Ouest. It was safe; there were no cars (my father, the only car-owner in the villa, had sold his since there was no gasoline). The villa was like an extended front yard for all of us kids to play in. Some of the children didn't live in the villa de l'Ouest itself, but on rue Jules Ferry, and especially *"au trente-six"* (at number 36), in a nice six-story stone building decorated with red bricks (it is still there now) directly facing the entrance to the villa de l'Ouest. On the ground floor, on the left side of the glass and wrought-iron door of the *trente-six* was a café, a bistro (no longer there) where my father and many neighbors spent a lot of time playing cards or billiards, and drinking wine. The café, "Chez Brusson," was a social place where families went for aperitif on Sundays, the children being served *"une petite grenadine,"* water with grenadine syrup in an aperitif glass.

A play wedding in the villa de l'Ouest. From left: me, two friends, Patrick, Lili, Pierrette, Ginette. In back, the 36 rue Jules Ferry building with the Café Brusson. (c. 1942)

At that time there were bistros everywhere, and indeed there was another one, named *"La Madelon,"* down the street at the next corner where rue Jules Ferry crossed rue Roublot, the street on which the entrance of the Jules Ferry primary school and the Roublot market were located.

Fontenay-sous-Bois is famous for two things: one is *"la Belle-de-Fontenay"* ("Fontenay's Beauty"), a variety of potato, grown a long time ago, when Fontenay was still rural; the second is *La Madelon*.

As a child the only thing I knew about *La Madelon* was that it was a song. On the school building across the street from the Madelon café was a brass plate bearing this cryptic inscription: *"La Madelon est partie d'ici pour faire le tour du monde."* ("Madelon left from here to circle the globe".) I knew the words to *La Madelon*, but it was only later that I realized that the song was well-known, both in France and abroad. (Here in the United States, when I happened to meet American veterans of World II, they sometimes sang a few lines of the song for me).

La Madelon, first sung in 1914 by soldiers stationed at the Jules Ferry School, soon became the national World War I song. Its popularity carried over to World War II, and, to this day, it remains a classic among French popular songs:

> Quand Madelon vient nous servir à boire
> Sous la tonnelle on frôle son jupon
> Et chacun lui raconte une histoire
> Une histoire à sa façon.
> La Madelon pour nous n'est pas sévère
> Quand on lui prend la taille ou le menton
> Elle rit, c'est tout l'mal qu'elle sait faire
> Madelon, Madelon, Madelon!

> When, under the pergola, Madelon serves us a drink
> we brush against her petticoat and
> we all have some stories to tell her,
> some stories in our own fashion.
> La Madelon is not upset with us
> when we take her by the chin or the waist.
> She laughs, that's all the harm she can do
> Madelon, Madelon, Madelon!

The pretty waitress was a symbol of hope, of peace. She was a dream; she gave courage to soldiers at the front. Somehow, it makes me proud to know that the town where I was born was made famous by a song—and such a wonderful, warm, and spirited song at that.

The *bande de la villa*, our kids' "gang," consisted of ten regulars: Jacqui Staerck, Patrick Vérité, Pierrette Mousset, Liliane Hareng and her little sister Michou, Ginette Seutet, Claude Gouge, Dédé Anciaux, Robert Chourlay, Jean Grosso, and me, plus some occasional "joiners," such as the two sisters, Marie-Thérèse and Geneviève Quillet, and, a little later, *"La Danseuse."*

Jacqui was the oldest. A strand of his straight blond hair always fell in front of his round face, and, when he chewed food, one of his eyes opened and closed. His parents were from Alsace and both had strong Alsatian/Germanic accents. His father was a chef in a fancy restaurant in Paris.

Since the front of their house was on rue Jules Ferry, it was their back garden and back fence that opened on the villa de l'Ouest. The garden was next to the house of the infamous "Mère Michel" who lived across the street from Tante Valentine, and who, we were convinced, hated all of us.

Because Jacqui had two rather wild dogs we didn't play in his house. Once, however, we were invited for a special lunch (it must have been either during the war or afterwards, in the middle of the rationing period). Madame Staerck asked us children to sit around the dining room table. For a while we marveled at the delicious smells coming from the kitchen. Then Jacqui's father, wrapped in a white apron, came slowly into the dining room bringing the main dish on a beautifully decorated platter. It was *faisan sur canapé* (pheasant on canapé), perfectly roasted, resting on thin slices of white buttered bread, and dripping with shiny sauce. In the back of the pheasant Monsieur Staerck had stuck long tail feathers, and arranged shorter ones into the shape of a fan. Little potatoes, golden and oven-crisp, formed a mouth-watering ring around the beautiful bird. We kids had never seen anything like that in our lives. And I must say that the magnificence of the dish made me forget what the dessert was, though it probably was nearly as grand as the *plat de résistance*. In these times of food shortages, I can imagine how envious our poor parents must have felt when we told them about our feast!

But not all neighbors in the villa de l'Ouest were as tolerant of our gang. I remember one day, when the doorbell rang at my house.

"Colette, go see who it is," my father asked me.

From the open dining room window on the second floor, I looked down at the front yard and called out to my father as he prepared to go downstairs to the gate.

"*C'est la Mère Michel!*"

"I wonder what she wants," he said.

A minute later he was in the yard, ready to open the gate.

"You don't have to come out, Monsieur Gauthier; I can talk to you from here."

As usual la Mère Michel was hanging onto the fence through which we could see a little bit of her wrinkled face, frizzy gray hair, gray smock, and old house slippers.

"Well, Monsieur Gauthier, first I must tell you, I'm not very happy with your daughter calling me 'la Mère Michel.' I know that's what the other kids call me, but such a nice girl! I thought she was different!"

I heard her from the dining room window where I had stayed, and blushed. Yes, she was right! We all called her "la Mère Michel," but not to her face. I had slipped; it was embarrassing.

"Anyway, Monsieur Gauthier, I just came to tell you that I have a complaint about Monsieur and Madame Staerck. Their garden is on the side of my house and it attracts humidity, and, as you well know, humidity attracts spiders. I've seen spiders crawl on the outside of my house and it won't be long before they come inside. Madame Staerck doesn't want to talk to me, but you are very nice, so can you please tell her that her garden attracts spiders, and that she should do something about it?"

"Oui, oui, Madame Michel, we'll see, we'll see. I'm sure Madame Staerck doesn't mean any harm."

"Oh! You just don't know! These people think of nothing but of new ways to bother me. I don't know what they'll come up with next!"

We didn't know her real name, everyone called her "la Mère Michel" because her grandson's name was Michel. He was grown by then, and had moved away. She lived with her daughter, Michel's mother. All the kids in the villa de l'Ouest hated her as much as she hated them, and, of course, the more she bickered, the more she was teased. Nothing really terrible ever happened. The worse thing was perhaps when some kids (I never found out who they were) threw up-

The house of la Mère Michel, viewed from Tante Valentine's dining room window.

rooted tufts of grass on her doorstep, scattering dirt all around. To take her revenge she decided to "close the villa." She brought all kinds of chairs, tables, broomsticks and buckets out into the street and piled them up to make a barricade. It didn't last long; the neighbors convinced her to reconsider.

> *C'est la Mère Michel*
> *qui a perdu son chat*
> *Qui crie par la fenêtre*
> *qui est-ce qui lui rendra*
> *C'est le père Lustucru*
> *Qui lui a répondu*
> *"Donnez-moi un baiser*
> *Vot'chat sera rendu!"*

> Old Mother Michel
> has lost her cat.
> She shouts out of the window
> for someone to bring it back.
> Old Mr. Lustucru
> Answers her call,
> Give me a kiss
> And you'll get your cat back!"

This, of course, is a well-know nursery song about an old hag and an old geezer. Sometimes, to signal la Mère Michel's presence, we didn't have to say her name, we just hummed or whistled the tune.

La Mère Michel's daughter was an attractive and well-dressed woman of about forty. She was always very pale and wore her straight brown hair down. She never smiled or talked to anybody. She walked with a stiff gait and almost looked like a ghost. Every afternoon she left her house and came back at night. My father said that at the beginning of the war she had a Jewish lover (a married man) who came to visit her, but he wasn't coming any more. My parents wondered if he went back to his wife, if he had been deported, or if perhaps he was in hiding. One day, a neighbor told my father that he had seen *la Fille de la Mère Michel* in Paris working as a prostitute. Also, I heard my parents say (I don't know how they found out) that la Mère Michel's daughter sniffed ether, *"Elle respire de l'éther."* I found that extremely odd. I didn't know anything about drug addiction and couldn't imagine anyone sniffing ether, which, at the time, was commonly used to disinfect our sore knees when we fell.

In spite of the fact that I was a member of the kids' gang, la Mère Michel did like me, perhaps because my father was so patient with her. One day, she even invited me to her house. In all the years I lived in the villa de l'Ouest the only houses I ever entered, beside my own and that of Tante Valentine, were my friend Pierrette's, Jacqui's (just a few times), and Monique Thiaumond's, a schoolfriend who was not allowed to play "in the street." Neighbors in the villa were courteous but not overly-friendly, for instance, none of them were on a first name basis (it was "Monsieur et Madame Gauthier," "Monsieur et Madame Éoche," "Monsieur et Madame Mousset"), and they never asked anyone into their homes.

To be invited to la Mère Michel's house was not only unusual, it was downright scary. The outside shutters were always tightly shut; there was no hint of what to expect inside.

"Come in, Colette, I want to show you Michel's albums."

As I had anticipated, the house was very dark. In the front room, the vague shapes of several pieces of furniture revealed themselves here and there under heavy fabric covers. The kitchen was a little more normal but quite messy. It was there that la Mère Michel took me and told me to sit at the table. She cleared some space and deposited three or four big albums. When I opened them I had the surprise of finding them full of wonderful pictures, brightly colored, almost satiny. They were "collectible" pictures from *Chocolat Meunier*, the kind of little cards found in large chocolate bars before the war. One of the albums was of *Blanche Neige et les sept nains* (Snow White and the Seven Dwarves). Suddenly, all these pretty pictures, not a single one missing, pasted with patience and love by la Mère Michel's grandson, lit up the house like sunshine.

9
My Bedroom

At the beginning of the War my friend Pierrette and I were still too young to venture too far in the villa de l'Ouest. Pierrette would come to my house where we played upstairs in my bedroom. When we grew bigger, she still came over, sometimes with our other friends. My bedroom became one of *la bande de la villa*'s favorite playgrounds.

Because the wallpaper was pink, my bedroom was called *la petite chambre rose* (the little pink bedroom). My *"divan"* was a low double bed fitted with a tweedy brown and beige cover and occupying a corner of the room. Above the bed was an encased single-row bookshelf that my father had made. We called it *"le cozy"* (for "cozy corner"). For some reason, he had installed it about three feet above the bed and not closer to it as one would have expected. All the books that were shelved in the long side of the *cozy* were of the same size and identically bound in red. We called them *les gros livres rouges*. I sometimes looked at them; they were movie books, illustrated with scenes from Hollywood movies of the twenties and thirties. I wish I had these books now, although they have probably deteriorated as the paper they were printed on was already turning yellow then. In the part of *le cozy* that ran above the head of my bed were several books including a leather-bound dictionary, *Le Petit Larousse Illustré*, which was a reward Papa got when he received his *Certificat d'Études* (end of school diploma), in 1914. I loved this dictionary, especially its pink second half which was devoted to "proper names" and illustrated with pictures of famous people and drawings of Greek mythological figures. Before going to sleep, I studied all these figures carefully, and I eventually became well versed in the stories of Greek gods and heroes.

In my room, when we looked out the window, beyond the houses and gardens, and between some distant buildings, we could see straight ahead the tip of the Eiffel Tower, and to the right a little bit of the

Sacré-Coeur. To the left, much closer, we could plainly see the dungeon of the Château de Vincennes.

Next to the window was a glass-fronted bookcase with little white lace curtains strung behind the glass. Only the lower shelf contained books; the upper shelves were crowded with pharmacy items such as rolls of bandages, bags of cotton, a specially-designed bowl to inhale medicinal vapors, a dozen *ventouses* ("cupping" glass cups), which, in my grandmother's time, were used to treat colds (the cups were heated and stuck on someone's naked chest or back and left there for about twenty minutes), and two very interesting items: a douche apparatus and a *poire à lavements* (a pear-shaped enema device) which my friends took great delight in taking out to observe, handle and pretend to demonstrate. The books on the lower shelves belonged to my parents and had no pictures. It was there that Papa kept his novels by Pierre Louÿs: *Aphrodite* and *Les Aventures du roi Pausole*, erotic works that I would read much later.

In the middle of the room was a desk, which, when I was young, was never used for writing (there wasn't even a chair to go with it). On top of the desk, resting on a narrow lace throw, were two small bronze figurines of bears. (Later on, my father would make bookends out of the bears figurines and give them to me to take to America.)

The desk was used to store documents such as tax records and official papers. However, hidden under these papers, one could find most interesting things. When my friends or my cousins came, we would dig through the bottom of the drawers and take out a bunch of postcards. One of these was particularly fascinating. It depicted Hitler and Mussolini. Mussolini's pants were open and a gigantic penis stuck out of them. It was so big that it had to rest on a map for support, and it was bright red, with some drops of blood coming out of it. There was a caption on the postcard, but none of us could make any sense of it.

Sometimes when Pierrette came to visit me, we would close the door to my room, open the window wide, and go pipi on the very narrow ledge between the window and the handrail. As we couldn't step on the ledge because it would have been too dangerous, we had to crouch next to the window but close enough to the ledge for the pee to flow down to the garden, as we looked at each other going pipi.

Instead of a closet, my bedroom had a floor-to-ceiling cabinet with pink sliding doors. We could easily go inside. It was one of our favorite spots because, at the bottom of the cabinet, my mother kept a big bag of old clothes and rags in which we always found wonderful things to dress up in or make crazy costumes.

On the cabinet shelf, way up at the top, which we couldn't reach unless we pushed the desk over and climbed on it, was a box filled with souvenirs from my little brother: his black lacquered-wood pencil box (which now sits on my bedside table), some of his old school work, and the piece of veil that covered his face after he died. At the bottom of the wardrobe there was also a box of his old books, one of them a school reader with selections from literary texts. My mother had once pointed out a poem to me, telling me it always made her sad when she read it. It was Goethe's *Le Roi des Aulnes* (*The Erl-King*). Sometimes, when nobody saw me, I sat at the bottom of the cabinet, its sliding doors half-closed and I looked at an illustration showing the Erl-King. Here he was, standing in his black cape in a desolate landscape, and nearby, a man galloped through the night, holding his dying child:

> My son, why cover your face in such fear?
> Don't you see the elf-king, father?
> He's near, the King of the Elves, with his crown and his train!
> My son, it's the mist on the plain.

But these moments were rare; most of the time I thought of nothing but playing in the villa. My friends and I met in the villa after school, then went back to the villa after dinner and stayed there until dark, until our mothers called us from the front of our houses, "Co-lette!" "Pier-rette!" "Jac-qui!"

FIVE

1941 - 1945

1
Life During the War

Back to civilian life, but with no intention of working for the Vichy-controlled newspapers, my father had to find a new way to earn a living. As bicycling had always been his passion, he decided to start a bicycle repair and bicycle parts business. It was a good idea since there was no fuel for cars. Our garage became a bicycle shop, not a store, but a workshop for my father. All the bicycle parts were perfectly organized in drawers or in boxes dutifully labeled, and the bicycles being repaired hung on hooks from the ceiling. I loved to watch my father work; I knew the name of all the parts and played with the ones that looked like toys. My father built a white bicycle for me, sawing off the top of the frame and re-welding it so it would be just right for my height.

My parents became vendors of bicycle parts in open-air markets. Besides food, these markets offered a variety of merchandise such as household goods, clothes, shoes, etc. When the markets were out of town my parents took the train, but when they were close-by, my father carried his wares in a little trailer attached to his bicycle.

Some time later, Tante Marthe and Oncle Albert would also sell in open-air markets. Their merchandise consisted both of the workmen's cloth caps that they or Albert's parents manufactured, and of ladies' handbags, which they purchased wholesale. After the war when my father went back to newspaper printing, my aunt and uncle continued for a time to sell goods in the marketplace.

The towns where my parents most often sold their merchandise were Coulommiers, Nangis and Provins, each a short train ride southeast of Paris. I only went with them a few times and my sparse memories of these expeditions include a sun-bathed street near the quaint Nangis train station, and a street lined with red-flowering trees which looked to me as if they belonged in a fairytale. But what I remember most were the interminable days during which my boredom was only relieved when my mother gave me money to go to the bookstore to buy a children's book. Once (in Provins, I think) there was a country fair with cattle, sheep and goats being led to be sold. It was a big event, full of noise and confusion, with farmers haggling, cows kicking clouds of yellow dust, sheep bleating, and children running everywhere. Since I had rarely been exposed to the country, and even less to a livestock fair, I felt overwhelmed by the scene, which again appeared to me as coming straight out of a story book. For my parents, however, going to the country was a very real affair. During these trips, they always made friends with local people. Papa bartered bicycle parts for a leg of lamb, a chicken, or a sack of potatoes. His best bartering items were rubber tires, hard to find and particularly sought-after.

Most of the time my father went to sell at the markets by himself while my mother and I stayed home. Sometimes, my cousin Miquette and her brothers visited Tante Valentine next door, which made me happy as I loved to play with them. One day, in order to prevent us from getting sore throats in the winter, Tante Marthe and my mother decided it was time for us to have our tonsils removed. They made an appointment at the Trousseau Children's Hospital in Paris.

"Don't worry, it's not going to hurt very much," they told us, and almost filled us with enthusiasm when they added that we would be given ice-cream, a before-the-war treat, the taste of which was all but forgotten.

Our mothers took us to the hospital. After stripping to our undershirts, we were taken to a large room where children were waiting in several lines ending at doctors' stations. We joined one of the lines and waited our turn. As we approached, we saw what the doctors were doing. At that point, it became clear to us why so many children were screaming at the top of their lungs. The doctors, sitting on chairs, wore white smocks stained with blood and held long silver tongs handed to them by nurses. When my turn came, the doctor asked me to sit on his knee and open my mouth wide. Taking only a few seconds, he plunged his tongs deep in my throat, grabbed something inside and pulled. It hurt a lot and tears came to my eyes. The doctor told me to stand up (he was ready for the next child) and the nurse handed me a piece of ice to suck on to dull the pain. When we were finished, we waited until all the other children were taken care of. Then, we had to stand in line all over again in front of the doctors, so they could check if they had "taken everything out." In most cases the first intervention had been sufficient, but when my turn came the doctor found that "something was left." To my chagrin, he had to do the operation once more, after which I got another piece of ice. When the procedures were over, all the children got to spend the night at the hospital. At first we were in pain, but thanks to the arrival of our promised treat of ice-cream, our suffering didn't last long. After a while, we were given comic books to read. And in no time I was able to walk around and go talk to my cousins. Our mothers picked us up the next morning, none the worse for the experience and ready for the winter.

In wartime Fontenay-sous-Bois, life went on more or less normally, except that we were supposed to run to the shelters as soon as the siren sounded an alert. During an alert we sometimes heard airplanes, but most of the time we heard nothing. The closest shelter was in front of my school, two short blocks from our house. When there was an alert during school time, the teachers took all the students to the shelter and made everyone sit on benches. We carried gas masks but we didn't wear them. When we tried them on, they felt tight and smelled of rubber.

When there was an alert and my parents and I were at home, which often was the case, since alerts usually occurred at night, we didn't go to the shelter because my father felt that it was too far. We went downstairs to our garage and stood under the concrete stairway (the stairway which, outside, led to our front door). We remained in the space where we could stand up, which made like a little room close to a storage shelf and the now-empty racks of our former wine cellar. It was impossible to go deeper underneath the steps because coal was stored there. Even low-quality coal (bought with ration coupons) had become an essential commodity. Frequent blackouts had obliged us to replace our kitchen electric range with a coal-burning stove used both to cook and heat the house during the cold Parisian winters. As for the central-heating furnace located at the other end of the garage, it was no longer in use since the high-quality coal on which it once ran was no longer available. Next to our defunct furnace, my father had installed another coal-burning stove, this one needed for heating water for the laundry.

Doing the laundry was not a small enterprise at that time; my parents paid a woman to do it, as my often-ill mother was not very strong. Once a week, in a thick cloud of soap-smelling steam, the white laundry was boiled in a big metal washtub. Leaning over a smaller wooden tub, the laundress scrubbed the clothes on a board with a brush and a bar of soap. The metal washtub used for boiling the laundry had a big lid with a handle.

"No! No! P'tit Louis! Come back, come back! It's too dangerous!" my mother called out to my father.

"Don't worry, I'll be all right!"

During an alert Papa hated to stay in our corner of the garage; he held a washtub lid over his head and went out in the front yard to watch the battles in the sky. Toward the end of the war there were many air raids by the Allied Forces against German positions in France. We could hear the boom-boom of the DCA (the anti-aircraft defense system) trying to hit the raiding planes. When the air raids occurred during the day, the battles were easy to observe: missiles sent by the German-controlled DCA left small clouds of smoke in the sky, and we could see the Allied planes flying between these black puffs. One time we saw a missile hit a plane. A wing fell off and the pilot bailed out in a parachute. My parents assumed that he was an Englishman and theorized that he landed in the Bois de Vincennes, but this was never confirmed.

Sometimes, after an air raid, we found shrapnel in our yard, and collected these jagged pieces of shiny metal. Although Fontenay-sous-Bois was not a strategic town, we were quite close to areas likely to be bombed by the Allies in their efforts to undermine Germany's war plans. The worst bombings in the Paris region were against the Renault factory in Boulogne-Billancourt—the first time, in 1942, when 600 people died and 1500 were wounded, and the second time, in 1943, when 400 people died and 500 were wounded. While we were far enough from Boulogne-Billancourt, west of Paris, we were pretty close to Villeneuve-Saint-Georges, a hub of the French railroad network, southeast of Paris. This site, essential to the Germans for transportation of men and weapons, was bombed in 1944 and totally destroyed by the Allies in an operation that resulted in 200 dead and nearly 200 wounded.

Several times we saw flashes in the sky and heard bombs falling. While the Allies were careful to hit only strategic points, there was always the risk of a stray bomb. One of these did fall in Fontenay-sous-Bois, damaging a building about ten blocks away from our house; I don't know how many victims this bombing claimed.

Papa made a point of not appearing afraid during the air raids; consequently I don't remember feeling afraid myself. He joked, cheered for the Allies, hugged my mother, made gentle fun of her "loose" stomach—all this with the eternal Gauloise at the side of his mouth.

Concealed under empty coal sacks on the storage shelf of our hiding spot, was a box of papers that someone had brought to my father. These papers were tracts: flyers put out by the French Resistance informing the French people of the Allies' progress and of the Resistance's acts of sabotage that hindered Germany's war efforts. Papa distributed these tracts; I don't know where or to whom. I don't remember that he ever instructed me not to talk about the flyers, but somehow I never did.

As we entered the villa de l'Ouest, our house, tall and narrow, stood midway on the left side. A five-foot-tall picket fence (designed and built by my father) was painted ochre to match the color of the house. Looking from the street through the spaces between the slats, one could see the garage and the small cemented yard bordered by two strips of earth where a few bushes grew haphazardly. On the right side of the house, a concrete stairway led to our front door, a wooden door decorated with a wrought-iron motif and topped by a glass and metal canopy.

Houses in which we spent our childhood leave an indelible impression on us; we still see them exactly as they were, and at night we use them as sets for our dreams. I can still see myself opening the front door and stepping into the little entry hall, its floor a geometry of triangles of black, gray, and white tiles. On the right was a coat-rack with a mirror, on the left, two doors that opened, one to the dining-room, the other to the kitchen (the dining-room was on the villa de l'Ouest side, the kitchen faced the back garden). From the entry we could see a carpeted staircase that rose to the two upstairs bedrooms and, at the bottom of the stairs, close to the coat-rack was a little bathroom. Too bad that this bathroom had only a toilet and a sink, because, when we wanted to take a bath, we had to go out of the front door and down the outside stairs to the main bathroom, which for some reason had been built as a separate room inside the garage. Most inconvenient, especially in the winter! During the war, with the central heating turned off and no hot water in the main bathroom, we were obliged to take sponge baths in the kitchen.

Our House at 10 villa de l'Ouest. Tante Valentine and Oncle Baptiste's house is at left.

The backyard, also cemented (my father had laid the cement himself and traced on it perfectly straight crisscross lines), was bordered by a short fence beyond which was our garden. Nothing much grew there. A row of irises produced only a few flowers and half a dozen red-currant bushes faithfully delivered their crop of bitter-sweet fruit. On each side of the central path, Papa had erected thin metal arches on posts connected with wires. These wires were used for hanging the laundry—not such a good idea as the clothes often got caught in the wild rose brambles that grew over the arches. Gardening was not my parents' forte; the irises, red-currants and roses grew all by themselves. It is true that for a while during the war my father attempted (with limited success) to grow potatoes, carrots, and cabbages. And it is true also that at about the same time, setting aside his native Parisian's spurning of "peasants," he was the first to acknowledge Oncle Baptiste's know-how. Indeed, my uncle grew a wonderful vegetable garden and occasionally shared with us his fresh lettuce, radishes, tender peas, string beans, and juicy tomatoes.

At the end of our garden was a hen-house which had remained empty until it became difficult to find food, especially meat. My parents had decided to raise a few hens and a couple of ducks, which, when the time came, would be turned over to Oncle Baptiste to "execute," as Papa and Maman couldn't bear killing animals. One morning when we woke up we found that our two ducks had disappeared. It was obvious that someone had stolen them. But who? Our neighbors were above suspicion. It was winter; a layer of snow covered the roofs and the ground. My father set out to solve the mystery. On the ground in our garden and on the roof of the next-door-neighbor's shed, he could clearly discern boot prints, military-style boot prints.

"The Germans did it! They took our ducks! Our Christmas ducks!"

And Papa wondered who could have informed the Germans about our ducks. He talked it over with Maman. They agreed that the principal suspect had to be Papa's "friend," Patrice.

Every evening, and especially during air raids, we heard the whistle of the *Défense Passive* warning people that light was coming from their windows. We had to close the shutters, hang dark curtains or stick dark-blue paper over our windows so that no light would be visible from the sky—and possibly give a clue to Allied air raid pilots about the city below.

The *Défense Passive* was composed of volunteer French citizens who, together with firemen and the Red Cross, had the mission of helping the population in case of bombardments (in many bombed cities these volunteers turned out to be heroes). While some of the "DP" members were secretly members of the Resistance, others supported the Pétain government. My parents knew a man, Patrice, who worked for the *Défense Passive* and most likely belonged to the second category. Patrice was the lover of a woman named Denise, who lived in a small apartment building at the beginning of the villa de l'Ouest. Denise was a very nice lady, a seamstress, who occasionally made dresses for my mother. But, while she worked hard, her lover slept most of the day. Cheerful and handsome, with a charming Mediterranean accent, he loved to boast about his beautiful Provence.

"It's a paradise," he would say, "a painter's dream. And the land is so wonderful. You just drop a seed, and, *hop!* It grows!"

Listening to him, we could almost smell Provence's mimosa and lavender. Denise adored him, although he sometimes disappeared for months. My parents said he was a gigolo. Since I didn't know what that meant, I assumed that a gigolo was a man who, like Patrice, wore a white tank-top, spoke with a Marseilles accent, and sat among velvet cushions, a cigarette in one hand and a glass of wine in the other. Every evening for a few hours, Patrice worked for the *Défense Passive*. He knew the district well, enough to pass on information about our ducks (and get a tip for it). But nothing was ever mentioned about the duck incident. We had no proof.

We always followed the blackout rules, one of the reasons being that we didn't want to attract trouble when we listened to Radio London, something that was forbidden. From London, General de Gaulle was leading the French Resistance, and every evening a program was broadcast to keep the French informed and united against the occupying forces. The program was *Les Français parlent aux Français* (The French speak to the French).

My parents followed the news closely: August 1940: The London Blitz; June 1941: German invasion of the USSR; December 7, 1941: Pearl

Harbor, followed by the entry of the Americans in the war; 1942: U.S. victories in the Pacific and North Africa; from July 1942 to February 1943: Battle of Stalingrad; September 1943: Allied landing in Italy. Of course, I was too young to understand the significance of such events.

The news from the multiple fronts was always followed by personal messages to units of the French Resistance. These messages, heard through loud scrambling, were often bizarre and sounded like the fairy tales I read: "The sheep will jump three times over the rabbit, I repeat: the sheep will jump three times over the rabbit." "The horse will arrive on time, I repeat: the horse will arrive on time." My parents always wondered what the messages stood for and tried to interpret them. "Could it mean that the Allies are going to bomb the Villeneuve-Saint-Georges railroad hub?"

We also turned on the Vichy-controlled radio, but mostly for the variety programs. As for the "news" broadcasts, they were controlled by the Germans and always ended with the sentence *"L'Angleterre, comme Carthage, sera détruite!"* ("England, like Carthage, will be destroyed!") to which most French people responded, *"Salauds!"* ("Bastards!")

My father had hidden the radio on a shelf in our big kitchen cupboard. He had pierced a hole on the side of the cupboard for the wire, so we could plug in the radio. Should the authorities appear at the door, we could quickly unplug the radio and close the cupboard sliding doors. Many people at that time listened to Radio London, but no one knew who was going to report them, so it was wise to take precautions.

"Here! This is what will happen to you!" My father, with his famous crooked smile, handed my mother a drawing he had just finished. It was of a woman (my mother) hanging onto the bars of a prison while a helmeted Gestapo guard stood nearby.

"Oh! P'tit Louis, arrête tes bêtises!" ("Oh! P'tit Louis, stop this nonsense!")

That was not made to reassure her! She had just returned from buying bread with fake ration coupons, and was afraid that the woman at the *boulangerie* would realize it and denounce her. One could buy false coupons easily enough, but the difficulty was to "pass" them. My mother never sent me to buy bread with fake coupons (some people did send their children, thinking the bakers would never report a child). Always full of apprehension, she preferred to go herself, and only went to bakeries that were supposed to be "safe." It was not easy for the bakers themselves to knowingly accept false coupons, for they had to hand them over to the authorities, but they often took the risk, feeling they could always plead ignorance. And usually, if there was no abuse, nobody said anything. French people love bread; it was no wonder that they tried to do whatever they could to get more; they hated to be deprived of their main staple. I'm happy to say that my mother was never caught.

Something else was illegal, but some people did it anyhow: it was to fell trees in the Bois de Vincennes. The park was protected and guards patrolled it, especially at night. One late afternoon, my father took me on his bicycle for a ride near one of the lakes in the Bois. It was during a very harsh winter when the lake was frozen over. I remember looking (and laughing) at some poor ducks trying to land on the ice and sliding like little kids. The days were short; night would soon fall and we were about to go home. Although I was wrapped up in coat, scarf, wool cap, and mittens, I remember feeling cold. Suddenly, we heard sawing and banging. My father knew that someone was cutting down a tree. We went to watch. Several men were hacking at a big tree with hatchets. Even from a distance we could see them: dark silhouettes against the snow in the dimming light. After a while they called out: *"Attention!"* ("Be careful!") And with a crashing noise, the tall tree fell among other trees, throwing leaves all around. The men rushed with saws and hatchets and started chopping off branches from the trunk. Everywhere we could smell freshly-cut wood. It was dark now, and flashlight beams made spots of light here and there. Obviously the guards had been bribed, but there still was the possibility that the tree-cutters might be caught. Someone called out to my father to come and get an armful of firewood. Several men holding ropes were dragging the big trunk and its branches into the bed of an old truck. Everything was done very fast. I rode back home on my father's bicycle, sitting on the front bike-rack, the wood sticking out of the cloth saddle bags hanging on each side of the rear rack. I will always remember this event, the tree falling, the smell of wood, and a vague fear. My father said that if everyone cut down trees in the Bois de Vincennes there would be none left. I loved the Bois. It was there that we went for walks around the lakes; it was there that our school teachers took us to study nature. In the fall we filled our pockets with shiny-brown horse chestnuts, silky and smooth to the touch, and in the spring we picked *boutons d'or* (buttercups), which we drew in our copy-books and studiously labeled: *genre: ranunculus; famille: renonculacées* (genus: ranunculus, family: ranunculacea).

2
Mother's Day

It was during the occupation that Mother's Day was first observed in France. In 1943, when I was almost eight years old, we celebrated it at home for the first time. My father handed me a "big" bill of ten francs.

"This is to buy flowers for your mother. Go to the garden I showed you the other day, the one near the Boulevard de Verdun. You remember where it is, do you?"

"Yes, Papa, I do. But how will I know what kind of flowers to buy?"

"Don't worry; the dwarf will help you."

On the day my father had shown me the garden, he had also told me about the gardener.

"He is a dwarf," he had said. "He used to be in the circus. He worked with clowns and acrobats and traveled all over the world. He did that for a long time, but after a while he got tired. It's a pretty hard life, you know. Now his passion is his flower garden."

Papa loved the circus and always talked about *les gens du cirque* (circus performers) as if he regretted not having been one of them. His words made a deep impression on me, especially after he told me that the gardener had also played in *Snow White and the Seven Dwarfs*.

"Well, you go now! I'll be *chez Brusson*."

"But what if you are not home when I come back? What will I tell Maman if she sees me with the flowers?"

"Just put them on the dining room table and tell her that they are for a lady."

I set out for the garden. A good fifteen-minute walk from where we lived, it was at the end of several steep streets, on the *Plateau* of Fontenay-sous-Bois. This district, now totally built-up, was still dotted with the last of the orchards and vegetable fields that were once the pride of Fontenay. I knew the area well. Close by, there was a place we called *les carrières* (the quarry), an old gypsum quarry which had been abandoned for a long time. It was now a vast empty lot, bumpy and weedy, part of which was used as a dumping ground for German military refuse. My villa de l'Ouest friends and I went there often. We liked to dig in the debris heaps. We especially looked for "rockets." These "rockets" (cordons Pickford, which were used to start detonations) were thin black tubes filled with a mild explosive. They were dangerous, but we were not fully aware of that. We fired them on the asphalt of the steep rue Jules Ferry and watched, as they smoked and zigzagged noisily uphill.

I also went with my friend Pierrette Mousset and her mother to another part of the quarry, that one more bucolic. There, we picked dandelions for Madame Mousset's poor rabbits whose fate was to grace the table of the Moussets' Sunday dinners.

Although I was familiar with the area, I was afraid I might not be able to find the right garden, as there were many on the same street. The only thing I remembered was that I had seen a lot of flowers through the old wooden fence. I passed a few gardens and then, without a doubt, I knew I had found the right one. Behind the broken fence I easily recognized the garden with its rows of flowers, red, white, yellow, purple, all colors bright in the sunshine. I rang the bell by the gate. The gardener came, looking stern, even a little mean, his body balancing on his hips.

As he opened the gate, I tried to be very polite. "*Excusez-moi, Monsieur*, my father sent me to buy flowers for Mother's Day."

"Oh yes!" he said with a reassuring smile, "your papa told me. Come in, *ma p'tite cocotte*. Tell me what kind of flowers you would like."

"Uh, I don't know." I quickly handed him the ten francs.

"Oh! la la! That's a lot! Let me see what I can do!"

He walked away among the rows of flowers, snipping right and left while I remained standing in the sun. At first, I could see him bending down and examining the flowers, but after a while I lost sight of him. Finally he reappeared, almost entirely hidden behind the biggest bunch of flowers I had even seen. There were gladioli, lilies, sweet peas, tulips, roses of different colors, and many other flowers, all sweet-smelling. He handed me the bouquet and, no taller than him, I also disappeared behind the flowers.

"*Merci beaucoup*," I said, peering through the colors.

"*De rien*," said the dwarf, "and don't forget to say hello to your papa!"

I walked back toward my house, feeling that everyone was looking at me and my enormous bouquet. As my father had told me, I put the flowers on the dining room table.

The dining room, reserved for guests, was always kept spotless. Polished to a shine, the table was partially covered with a lace runner on which was placed a statue of the hunting goddess, *Diane Chasseresse*. Diane, her hair cut *à la garçonne*, her quiver by her side, rested on one knee, embracing her dog. I moved her over a little bit to make room for the bouquet.

My mother, who was in the upstairs bedrooms, came down and asked me, "Who are these flowers for?"

"They are for a lady."

"A lady? What lady? Did Papa tell you that?"

"Yes he did."

At that moment I had a little bit of a doubt. I knew that the flowers were for my mother, but I wondered if there might not be a remote chance that they were for a mysterious lady. What if that lady suddenly arrived at our house? No! That was silly. It couldn't be true!

I went outside to play. Then, in the villa de l'Ouest, I saw Papa walking home.

"Papa! I got the flowers!" I followed him into the house. He quickly placed the bouquet in my arms and (to my relief) told me to call Maman and say "Happy Mother's Day!"

"Maman, Maman," I called, "Happy Mother's Day!"

My mother arrived, acting all surprised.

"Here are some flowers for a lady, a beautiful lady!" Papa said.

3
School and More Villa de l'Ouest

It was something that happened often: The school bell rang while I was still at home having my café au lait and buttered bread. I had to grab my coat and school bag, leave in a hurry, run through the school back gate (it was just a few houses down the way), cross the schoolyard, and join the line in front of my classroom. I was out of luck when the back gate was already locked. Then, I had to turn around the block, run down rue Jules Ferry, speed around the corner to rue Roublot, climb the stairs two-by-two, and enter through the front door—often with a stop at the office of *Madame la Directrice* for a bit of admonition.

My school was a nice stone and brick building whose main entrance had two sets of stairs and two front doors, one for girls, one for boys.

École Jules Ferry. The Boys' school occupies the left of the building, the girls school is on the right. Postcard.

Being on time was not my strong point. My report cards also showed that I talked too much in class. Needless to say my grade in *conduite* (behavior) was less than perfect. In spite of that, I was a good student. The teachers even had me skip grades. As a result, I was almost always the youngest (and shortest) girl in the class.

At school, my closest friend was a girl named Colette Tassel (Colette was a common name at that time—later on, my best friend would also be called Colette). Colette Tassel had an Algerian mother and a Parisian father. Her hair, like mine, was black, but while my hair was thick and wild, Colette's hung in beautiful long English curls that her mother rolled for her every morning and adorned with two firm bows of brightly-colored ribbon. I had bows in my hair too, but unlike Colette's, mine always drooped like two limp butterflies.

Colette and I got along very well. Before the teacher arrived, we made funny drawings on the blackboard or climbed on top of our desks to fight duels with our metal rulers. Luckily we were rarely caught. By the time our teacher opened the door, we were sitting down, arms crossed on our desks, *sages comme des images* (quiet as pictures).

Another good friend of mine was, odd to say, the quietest girl in the class: Micheline Huss, a round-faced girl with a perfect page-boy, the straight line of her bangs reaching just a little above her eyebrows. I still remember her big brown eyes and milk-white complexion. At recess, I also played with Pierrette and other girls from the villa. Pierrette, who was almost two years older than me was in higher grades at first, but I eventually caught up with her.

Every week at school we had a distribution of *bonbons vitaminés* (vitamin-fortified candies). The teacher would put one bright pink chewable pill on each desk. We were told to eat the *bonbons* right away. They were pretty good. They tasted strong and had a special synthetic smell that we all liked.

About once a month there also was a distribution of vitamin-fortified cookies. One of the teachers, Madame Schmidt, loved them. The cookies came in aluminum boxes, each box about one foot square. Madame Schmidt would carry our box, resting it on her fat stomach, and we had to line up in front of her to get our cookies. But we knew she never emptied the box completely; she always kept some cookies for herself; we could see her chewing them in the hallway when the other teachers were not looking.

Nutritious food was always a concern for parents. I ate lunch at home since I lived so close to school, but, at one point my mother had me try *la cantine* (the school cafeteria). That didn't last long since they served rutabaga at every meal. This turnip-like vegetable, plentiful during the war, was hated by French people, who thought it only good to be fed to cattle.

I liked school, even though at times there were embarrassing moments. Twice a year we had a *visite médicale* during which we were examined by a doctor or a nurse, given vaccinations when needed, and screened for tuberculosis. On these days, we had to remove our dresses and undershirts, and stand in line in our panties. One time, the day after such an examination, we were in our classroom when there was a knock at the door.

"Entrez!" the teacher said. A girl came in, holding an undershirt between her index finger and her thumb. Showing it to the class with disgust, she asked, "Did anyone lose THAT?" The undershirt was old, a little frayed, with pale yellow stains on the front. All the pupils, the teacher, and the disgusted girl started to laugh.

"Ha ha ha!" I laughed with everyone "Ha ha ha!" (All the while, thinking that this undershirt might be mine. But was it or wasn't it?) The girl, more and more disgusted, was waving the shirt in the air like a battered flag. "What if someone came forward to claim it? Wouldn't that be too funny?" a student commented. "Enough!" the teacher said. And the girl left for similar scenes in other classes. When I arrived home I was glad to discover that the undershirt wasn't mine. My mother reassured me: there was no underwear missing. To this day I wonder why I had been so worried.

There was a school assignment that we all liked: we were asked to knit (at home) little squares of wool to make blankets for French prisoners. We gathered leftover yarn and knitted squares about 6 by 6 inches that would later be assembled by volunteers. The blankets would then be sent in Red Cross packages.

School was fine but the center of my life was still the villa de l'Ouest. Now that my friends and I were growing up, our games had become more sophisticated. Mostly, we played wartime games.

Up rue Jules Ferry, past "Chez Brusson," there was a house abandoned by its owners who had left Paris during the *débâcle*. The front yard of this house was only partially separated from the street by a little brick wall about three feet high, which, extending less than halfway across the width of the yard, left the property open to anyone. Our gang often met there; we played in the yard and sat on the wall, our feet dangling. We called this place *Le p'tit mur* (The little wall). It was in that yard that we built our war museum. Out of a large cloth supported by sticks, we made a tent and laid an old blanket on the ground to make our tent more comfortable. We declared that it was a "forbidden" museum to small children and sent away those who wanted to get in. Our exhibits consisted of several empty shell cases (some small ones from regular guns, and a couple of big copper ones from heavy weapons, borrowed from someone's World War I collection), a number of sharp pieces of shrapnel, and some old coins and medals; we also had a few of the black "rockets" we had gathered in the old quarry. It was dark in the tent, and, most of the time, I was there alone with Jacqui and Patrick. Patrick was the one I liked, but there was a certain power about Jacqui, especially when night fell. One evening, when I was outside, just about to go home, a heavy rain started falling. It was a big storm with wild flashes of lightning and terrible rolls of thunder. I was never particularly afraid of storms, but I ran inside the tent with my friends, and, at each clap of thunder, I pressed closer to Jacqui for warmth, for comfort, but also for something else, something I didn't quite understand.

"Colette! Colette! I have been looking for you everywhere! You should have been home before dark!" It was my mother, looking for me.

"But it was raining; I didn't want to get wet!"

"Come, come quick then!"

We had school from 9:00 am to 12 noon, and then we went home for lunch from 12 to 1:30. After that, we returned to school from 1:30 to 4:30 pm, and, after a fifteen minute recess during which we ate our own snacks (usually a chunk of baguette with a piece of plain chocolate pushed inside), we went back to class until 6:00 pm to do our homework, supervised by a teacher. There was no school on Thursdays, but there was school on Saturdays. This schedule gave us only limited time to play in the villa, but we caught up on Thursdays and during the vacations. In the summer we often stayed in the villa until 10 pm. Sundays were usually reserved for the family.

We often played a game that we called *la ville* (the town). First, we girls had to bring dolls, toy chairs, toy tables, miniature dishes, and regular-size brooms. Then, on the paved area of the villa, we marked the boundaries of our houses. To do that, we got handfuls of sandy dirt from the non-paved area, and, walking backwards and cupping our hands, we let the sand drop in an hourglass fashion, making lines on the ground. When the limits were well-defined, we swept the houses with the brooms. The regular girls were Lili: short, plump, blond, with laughing blue eyes behind round glasses, already looking like a *petite maman;* Pierrette: a lanky doe, tall, thin, brown-haired, her high cheekbones giving her an air vaguely Asiatic; and me. Always trailing us were the "little ones": Michou, Lili's cute little sister, and Ginette Seutet, a newcomer to the villa. The boys never shared a house with the girls. The idea of "couples" would have been too embarrassing. This didn't mean that the girls didn't have husbands! They did, but their husbands, alas, were all "prisoners of war."

The boys were working guys. They were: the Mayor, Jacqui, who gave us girls news of the front—and generally told us what to do; the mailman, Claude Gouge, alias *le Goujon* (the Gudgeon), a skinny redhead, who distributed letters from our poor husbands; the delivery man, Robert Chourlay, a good-natured boy with a slight limp, who brought us stones and pebbles (our bread and potatoes); and, of course, the singer, Patrick.

Patrick, my closest friend, was a different kind of kid. He was handsome, dark blond, with large green eyes and a slightly aquiline nose. There was a special softness about him coupled with a sometimes wicked sense of humor. His parents lived in a house across from the villa, on the right side of number 36 rue Jules Ferry. He had two sisters, one about my age, the other a year or two younger, but they never played with us; their mother said that it was enough to have one "lost child" in her family, Patrick. She did not allow her daughters to play in the street.

Patrick's mother was not the only mother who felt that way. At the end of the villa, close to the concrete stairs, was a young girl, Denise Lévesque, whose parents also felt that it was not proper for their daughter to play beyond their gate. Denise was always alone in her little cemented yard, behind the high bars of her wrought-iron fence. She sometimes sadly watched us play, and we would talk to her through the fence.

Some of my school friends who lived in my neighborhood didn't play in the street either. One of them, Monique Thiaumond, also looked at us forlornly from behind her fence. At least I was allowed to visit her once in a while. When I reflect on that now, I feel enormously grateful to my parents for having allowed me to play outside. I don't think it ever even entered their minds that I ran the risk of becoming a "lost girl" just because I played in the villa.

Patrick's sisters played the piano, and although Patrick did not take lessons, he played the piano too, and sang. He had a marvelous voice and knew all the words to the latest *chansons* but, unfortunately, he was very shy. So, when we played *à la ville*, and Jacqui announced that a famous singer had come to town, we had to hang a curtain in a corner so Patrick could sing behind it. He accompanied himself by tapping on the lid of a metal washtub (these things had many uses!).

One of the girls' occupations was to prepare the drinks—an important task. We made milk by scraping the whitewashed wall of the school with sharp little pieces of metal, and letting the plaster powder fall into pans from our dolls dish sets. The powder mixed well with water and made very good faux-milk. The other drinks were made by dropping little squares of paint from my paint box into glasses of water, where we let them dissolve for a few seconds. We made lemonade, orangeade, grenadine, a truly life-like mint, and a pretty decent Pernod.

We didn't always have "pretend food" in the villa. Sometimes we had real banquets for which our parents furnished the victuals. Low tables were put end-to-end to make a long banquet table. We covered it with tablecloths, arranged small chairs around it, and ate the treats our mothers made for us. Sometimes my parents hosted an event for *les gosses de la villa* (the kids of the villa). One such event was the christening of our new puppy, a ceremony which Papa initiated and performed.

Since his days as an altar boy my father remembered the rituals as well as a little Latin. Now, the true atheist that he was had no qualms about poking fun at the sacraments. He told us kids he used to be a monk, pointed to the round bald spot on top of his head and said it was his tonsure.

All the children gathered at the foot of the stairs in my house's entry hall, waiting for my father to solemnly descend from the bedroom where he had been getting ready. He came wearing a white silk scarf for a stole, looking very priestly. We formed a circle around him as he made the sign of the cross over the puppy's head and recited: *Paster noster, dominus vobiscum. In nomine patris et filii, et spiritus sancti. Amen.* The designated godparents held the little dog; someone presented a bowl of water; my father dipped his fingers in it and sprinkled a few drops on the puppy's nose. Then came the celebration, which was held in our backyard. We all sat around a table, ate fruit and dessert prepared by my mother with whatever ingredients she was able to gather.

Villa de l'Ouest friends in my backyard. From right: Patrick, Jacqui, Dédé's eyes, me, Ginette with dog, Robert Point, his brother (le petit Point), Pierrette. (c. 1944)

Religion (or the lack of it) was not a real issue in the villa de l'Ouest; some people went to church, some didn't; nobody mixed in other people's business. Among my playmates, although I was one of the few non-Catholics (not that my friends went to mass every Sunday; for them and their parents, Easter and Christmas was generally enough), I was never made to feel "different." There was, however, one exception: it was when the girls celebrated their First Holy Communion at the age of ten or eleven. This event was held on the same day for all the *communiantes* belonging to the parish of Sainte Marguerite, the local church. It was then that I was warned by my friends that I would forever regret not partaking in this glorious event.

My friend Pierrette Mousset. (c. 1945)

Nowadays simplicity has become the rule for celebrating First Holy Communions, but at that time, young girls wore elaborate long white dresses made of organdy and lace, adorned with flowers and bows; they carried dainty little white purses and missals full of holy images to be distributed to family and friends. (Boys wore a suit with an embroidered satin sash fastened on an armband, nothing as fancy as the girls.) The celebrations involved a special mass, a procession, and photographs, and were followed by family banquets. I did feel I was deprived of the chance of wearing a beautiful dress, but my parents consoled me by telling me that I would wear a white dress when I got married. (I didn't—but that's another story.) The worst part came a few days later at school when, unfailingly, the teacher would ask us to write an essay on the theme: "the most beautiful day of your life." Of course, practically all the girls wrote about their Holy Communion. As for me, I never knew what to write about. I didn't even believe there was such a thing as the "most beautiful day" of my life.

Only in one case do I remember becoming aware that religion played an important part in the life of some of my villa de l'Ouest friends, even to the point of sealing their destiny.

Most of us came from families of one or two children. Only Patrick had four siblings (the two oldest ones already on their own). But some of the other kids, those who played with us less often, belonged to one of the only two large families in the neighborhood: a communist family, the Chourlays, and a Catholic one, the Quillets. Both of these families had at least six children each. Of all these kids, only one boy, the very nice Robert Chourlay, played with us more or less regularly; all the others were too young, too old, or too busy helping their parents.

The head of the Chourlay family, Monsieur Chourlay, a strong, handsome man, worked for the Paris métro. He sat in a booth at the Château de Vincennes station and punched holes in métro tickets. (His was an example of a wartime job created by the government to keep people employed.) When my parents or I handed him a ticket, he pretended to punch a hole in it so we could use the ticket again. Even during the war Monsieur Chourlay was not afraid to express his strong political opinions: everyone knew he was an ardent communist. And, to emphasize the fact that he was not Christian, he gave his children (at least the youngest ones) the names of lesser saints. Monsieur Chourlay also had the reputation of drinking too much; he was a regular at the Brusson café.

Monsieur Quillet, on the other hand, was a pale red-haired man who never went to the café. He was a police inspector. In his family, religion was all-important. Sometimes, two of his daughters, the eldest, Marie-Thérèse, a handsome, lively, bosomy girl, and her sister Geneviève, a tall, quiet, narrow-faced girl, joined us in the villa, not to play, since they were already teenagers, but to talk. That was how I learned that Monsieur Quillet, who had suffered a serious illness, had promised his eldest daughter to God if he recovered. And he did recover. Marie-Thérèse knew she was fated to become a nun—not only that, but a cloistered nun! I couldn't believe it. I asked Marie-Thérèse if she agreed to it.

"I have no choice," she answered, "it was a promise made to God."

Indeed, a few years later, she entered a convent and we never heard of her again.

Meanwhile, at about the same time, her sister, Geneviève, became pregnant out-of-wedlock and was made to move to the country. We never saw her again either. The Quillet sisters' fate was the first example I encountered of the power religion can have over people's lives.

But religious subjects were hardly ever part of our conversations. Far from it! The latest *chansons*, together with jokes and innuendos about who liked whom, were our favorite topics. Sex was on our minds, but precise words about it were taboo. I vaguely heard it whispered that people did "this and that" in bed but I didn't believe it. It was just too disgusting. Kissing was the naughtiest act I allowed myself to think about. The boys made fun of my girlfriends and me when they found out we hugged and kissed my bedroom *traversin*, the long, column-shaped bolster that supported my two square bed pillows. The boys said we were "dirty," which made us giggle and blush.

An unfortunate event put a temporary stop to my kissing fantasies. While combing my hair, my mother found the unmistakable traces of lice. She gave me a good shampooing while speculating that it was at school that I had fallen victim to this dreaded invasion. Several days passed during which I received the traditional fine-tooth-comb treatment and saw lice and nits fall on a newspaper laid out on the kitchen table. More shampooing, more fine-tooth combing. I scratched and scratched to the point that I had sores on my head. Maman took me to the doctor.

"The only remedy," he said, "is to shave off her hair."

"No, no!" I cried, but there was nothing I could do. Maman took me to the hairdresser and in a matter of minutes all my beautiful thick black curls were all over the floor. I cried some more. Now we had to go outside. I saw my reflection in a shop window: an egg! Maman and I went to a clothing store.

"I would like to buy a cap for my daughter."

"I'm sorry, *Madame*, we don't sell caps for little boys!"

"She is not a boy!" my mother protested. I said 'my daughter.' She is a girl! She just had her head shaven."

"Oh! *Pardon*! Here is a cute cap. It will cover her head and ears and she can tie the ribbon under her chin."

Except at home, I didn't want to take off my cap. At school I tried to keep it on, but the teacher didn't let me. At least, there, I was not the only girl with a shaved head. The lice problem had been going around.

For days I didn't dare to go out and play. But staying home was just too painful. The call of the villa was impossible to resist. Finally I ventured halfway out of my gate. My friends saw me and invited me to play. I went, but it was not the same; I was not myself. I felt ugly and different, and with both hands, I clung to my bonnet. But little by little my hair grew back and my self-confidence returned. Now when I look at the one picture I have of myself *sans cheveux*, wearing a béret, I can see it wasn't so bad after all.

And so, although it was wartime, life for us children went on more or less normally. In fact, it was the life of these five years of war that seemed normal to us. We were too young to clearly remember the period before the war. And when people talked—as they often did—of what they would do *après la guerre* (after the war), we vaguely felt that they were dreaming of something far off in the future, something that might never happen at all.

An outing with Madame Mousset and her friends. Behind Pierrette, her mother, Madame Mousset. (c. 1943)

4
Flashes of Awareness and Papa's Ideas

Brightly coloring the world of my childhood were the songs my mother sang, the funny sports stories my father invented, and the countless fairy tales I read. It was a limited world, peopled only by my parents, my family and playmates. I existed in it without wondering much about things around me, and even less about my own identity and the rest of the universe. I suppose all children are like that—I suspect some adults are like that too. A few times, however, I did have revelations that pulled me for a brief instant out of my day-to-day reality and somehow gave me an inkling about who I was. They were nothing serious, no "Hand of God," or anything like that, just ordinary little incidents.

One day, my mother sent me to buy bread at the Boulangerie Pâtisserie Émorine, a bakery-pastry shop well-known for the luscious pastries displayed in the window. I went there almost every day. It was just two blocks away from my house, at the corner of rue Jules Ferry and rue Dalayrac. Often, when I came back with my baguette, I would balance it on two fingers and walk with it for a few steps. All the kids did that: palm up, balance the tip of the baguette on the extended index and middle finger. Sometimes the baguette would fall, but it was no catastrophe; we would just pick it up and brush it off. That day, I was coming back from the bakery, walking on rue Jules Ferry's wide sidewalk with my baguette properly held in my arms when I began to pay particular attention to people walking in both directions on the sidewalk. I suddenly realized that all these people had minds of their own, minds filled with thoughts, memories and dreams, just like my own. I had been so absorbed in my life that I believed my world was the only world, but it became clear to me that everybody else also had a private, unique personal world.

Another day, I was playing, standing up next to a little wall. I had found perhaps a button and two little stones, and I was saying aloud, "This is the mommy, this is the daddy, and this is the little child," and, of course,

I was doing the different voices: the big daddy was saying something in his baritone, the mommy was answering in her sweet voice, and the little kid was either whining or yelling for joy in his high pointy voice. All of a sudden I stopped and literally saw myself doing that—and realized that I did it every time I came upon a few little dolls, or three or four spools of thread, or some leaves, or some stones and buttons. I heard myself imitating all these voices and creating a family drama, a little *guignol*, and I wondered about it, as if suddenly I had become an adult and was looking at a kid playing.

My third "flash of awareness" was slightly different. It happened while I was sitting at the table with my parents, at the time our radio was hidden in the kitchen cabinet. After the Vichy-controlled news, there was often music—nothing extraordinary, just popular French songs with a certain rhythm to them. Whenever I heard the songs, I tapped my foot or moved my head or my shoulders; sometimes it was my whole body that bopped along with the rhythm. I couldn't help it. I did it every single time. Suddenly, perhaps because someone made a remark that "woke me up," I became acutely aware of having been "taken over by the music," as it were. That time, however, I didn't see myself as an adult looking at a child, but more as a judge looking at a repeat offender. And I asked myself: Why do I do that? Why does music make me do that?

During the war my father did his best to follow his conscience. For instance, while practically everyone called the Germans *les Boches*, he never used that term. It was not that Papa had sympathy for the enemy, but, as he said: "We cannot generalize, there are good Germans and there are bad Germans; most of them are family men just like me, who went to war through no will of their own." His ideas about war had nothing to do with patriotism. For him, wars were decided by politicians and carried out by generals. The soldiers and the populations were the victims. He used to say (and for me it played like a scene in an old black and white war movie): "If I were caught man-to-man with a German and he had his gun pointed at me, I would drop my gun and ask him, 'Why do you want to shoot me? Don't you have a mother, a father? Don't you have a wife, children? Kill me if you want, but I will not kill you. I couldn't live with myself if I had killed a man, a man just like me,'" and he added, "If the German soldier didn't speak French, I would go like this." Upon which, he would draw curvy lines in the air to suggest a shapely wife, and, with his hand going from high to low, he would imply the height of his hypothetical children: *"Kinder, Kinder,"* he would say (one of the few German words he knew).

As a child I visualized my father's "story" as it if were a real occurrence, while of course his unlikely scenario was but the illustration of an idea: whether or not to kill, even in war. It took me a long time to understand my father and admire him for his respect of mankind and his lack of prejudices.

In spite of the story about the German and the gun, one shouldn't assume that my father was against fighting the occupiers. His love of freedom, his hatred of fascism, and the realization that the Nazis wouldn't be suppressed by peaceful means compelled him to resign himself to the necessity of this particular war. He respected the sacrifice of the Allies and of the Resistance fighters, and, when he was called to war, he went. Fortunately, he never found himself in a situation where he had to kill or be killed, so it is impossible to know whether he would have sacrificed his life in order not to kill another human being. But such are wars. Should killing someone under orders (or for a cause) be equated with the murderous taking of a life? I don't think my father clearly resolved this dilemma. But one thing is certain: He hadn't made up his mind to be a conscientious objector, but he decidedly was a pacifist. He believed every effort had to be made by peaceful means in order not to let conflicts escalate.

Before the war, until the last minute, he had hoped for a peaceful solution. Even during the war, he hoped for some voices to be raised. More than once, I heard him say, "Only one man can stop the war: the Pope." Of course, the Pope alone couldn't have stopped the war, but he could have used his influence to at least denounce Nazi atrocities. In this case my father was not altogether wrong in criticizing the silence of the church.

Always thinking for himself, questioning, analyzing, and staying true to his own values, my father provided an example I would later strive to follow. But at that time it was too early for me to reflect much on the world around me. In spite of a few "flashes of consciousness," I didn't yet have ideas of my own. I relied entirely on my father's opinions and adopted them, unaware that they often differed from accepted ways of thinking. I was still too young to understand the circumstances and repercussions of the war, too young to be aware of the large canvas on which it was played. Mine was a protected day-to-day existence. In the dream of childhood where I lived, my experiences, although vivid, never reached the point of being traumatic. It was only later, when my mother became ill and my heart started to tear, that I began to think for myself.

6
The Kitchen

It was in the kitchen that we settled down, ate, read the newspapers, listened to the radio, and received our friends. By today's standards our kitchen would be considered small, but then it felt just right. A cheerful room with a bright tiled floor, it was on the second floor, off our little entry. The blue and white oilcloth, faded through years of scrubbing, which covered the rectangular table, didn't hang down as one might picture it. Papa trimmed it a little bigger than the table and tacked the edges underneath the tabletop, neatly hiding them behind molding strips (he loved to do things like that).

When people sat around the table there was just enough room behind their chairs to squeeze by. It was at the end of the table that Papa piled up his *cahiers* (notebooks). Every day, he wrote in them, either the records of the household budget or his "inventions," or even his mysterious "calculations." As for me, I often used the table as a stage for my paper dolls; I made them and their clothes myself, and endlessly acted out little scenes. My grandmother did her mending in the kitchen; her sewing, threads, scissors, boxes of supplies were often spread all over the table. When all of us were busy with different projects, Maman would say, *"Quel fouillis! Un cochon n'y r'trouverait pas ses p'tits."* ("What a mess! A pig would not be able to find its little ones!") And I imagined a mother pig in the kitchen, looking in every corner and digging in our *fouillis,* trying to find her little piglets.

The kitchen walls were ivory white and the sliding doors of the cupboard light gray. The area around the sink was lined with blue and white ceramic tiles. I can still see the colors of the kitchen as they appeared to me, soft and vague, through oblique beams of yellow summer light, filled with thousands of flying particles of dust shining and doing their dance.

Above the sink was a mirror. We needed it as, during the war, the kitchen also served as our washroom. On a glass shelf under the mirror were bars of soap, toothbrushes, combs, eau de Cologne, Maman's perfume *Soir de Paris* in its night blue bottle, and Papa's Brilliantine.

As we looked to the right through the large kitchen window we could see the neighbor's garden with nothing on it but a shed (a house would be built there later). It was on the roof of that shed that Papa had once discovered the duck thieves' boot prints. To the left was Tante Valentine and Oncle Baptiste's house. It was easy for me to go from our backyard to my aunt and uncle's backyard since the gate between the two houses was always left unlocked. Next to the gate, on Tante Valentine's side, a white lilac tree grew, and on our side, a purple one. In the spring, when both trees mingled their blossoms, we made big bouquets, filling our houses with the sweet smell of lilac.

In my aunt and uncle's backyard, we could see Oncle Baptiste tending his garden or feeding his chickens. In the summer, when the window was open, we could hear Tante Valentine sing her opera arias or arguing with Oncle Baptiste. She often got irritated with him, but whenever she shouted, he remained calm. We rarely heard him say anything except, *"Bien sûr, tu le défends toujours!"* ("Of course, you always take his side!") and we knew they were arguing about Roger.

It was in the big kitchen cupboard that we stored our food—not many people had refrigerators in those days. Also stored in the cupboard were some glasses and plates. One of these plates (it was hardly ever used) was hand-painted with a naive landscape; it was a gift from Thomas, one of Papa's acquaintances, who had painted it himself. In the past, Thomas, an older man with a gravelly voice and a pock-marked face, had been a clown and had traveled with the circus.

"I wished I had been a clown myself," my father sometimes said. "I think clowns are true artists. They are acrobats, jugglers, musicians; they communicate in every language and play practically every instrument."

My father adored the circus. His heroes were the legendary Fratellini, the clown brothers, famous all over the world. He was a friend and admirer of Albert Fratellini whom he had met long before the war. Papa sometimes ran into Albert Fratellini (or one of his numerous performing relatives) at the market of the nearby town of Le Perreux-sur-Marne where he sold bicycle parts. Perhaps in exchange for providing the Fratellini family with bicycle tires, my father was invited to go (with me) to the Fratellini's dressing room at the Cirque Médrano, a famous dressing room which was often visited by celebrities; Picasso, for one, loved to go there.

I realize now that I was too young to appreciate the favor. The visit disappointed me and even left me a bit frightened. The dressing room was dark, cavernous, and dusty. Albert Fratellini opened one of his large trunks and showed us some props, one of them a giant spider. But outside the ring, these objects were lifeless. Our host, who was not in his clown costume, looked old and wrinkled. He sat next to a mirror by a cluttered make-up table, talked to my father, smoked Gauloises with him, and joked a little with me. I was glad to leave the circus and find myself in the bright sunshine.

But, let's return to the kitchen for a moment. In the lower part of the cupboard my parents kept several bottles of table wine. My father, who was a social drinker, never touched those bottles, except at meal time. It was Grand-mère Cessot whom we had to watch around the wine bottles, especially the ones that were already opened. But I'll talk about that later.

It was probably because of his drinking that my father suffered from stomach ulcers which became so painful that he had to have surgery. According to what the doctors told him, his entire stomach was removed. I don't know whether or not it is possible to remove the entire stomach, but it may very well be. When he came home from the hospital and sat down in the kitchen, I jumped on his lap. But it was too much for my once-athletic daddy who told me I could not do that just yet. I remember feeling extremely embarrassed.

During his period of recuperation at home, my father learned how to make cookies, something totally out of character for him since he didn't know anything about baking - or cooking, for that matter. His cookies were delicious, but, when his convalescence ended so did his culinary prowess. He recovered fast and in no time was able to eat his habitual *"biftek frites"* and drink as though he had never been ill. Soon, when my cousins Jacques, Claude and Miquette visited, Papa was well enough to tell us stories of P'tit Louis, the invincible bicycle champion, as we all sat around him in the kitchen. Entranced and laughing at the jokes, we would sometimes without thinking put our hand on his arm. Then Papa would say, *"Attention! Ne fais jamais ça!"* ("Careful, don't ever do that!") pretending that if he suddenly folded his arm, our fingers would be crushed between his muscles.

After the stories, when Maman gave us our *goûter* (afternoon snack), the kitchen filled with the smell of grilled bread, mixing happily with the aroma of hot chocolate. Chocolate, of course, was severely rationed, but being a "J2," I got a small allotment each month. Children were divided in three categories: J1: toddlers, J2: young children, and J3: teens. Food coupons were assigned accordingly.

It was not impossible to get food, but we had to stand in long lines and be content with the meager choice that was available in the Paris Region, or else we had to go to the country. Whenever my mother could gather the proper ingredients, she prepared wonderful dishes. Sometimes she made roast beef, done on the outside, rare inside, surrounded by *pommes château* (small round crisp potatoes), sometimes she baked salt cod (de-salted by overnight soaking) mixed with thinly sliced potatoes and topped with a layer of white sauce, or once in a while, she cooked *pot-au-feu*, which we ate in three courses: the first, a rich broth; the second, slices of tender boiled beef; and the third, a vegetable dish of leek, carrots and turnips. My mother, who would have preferred to cook fancier dishes, always complained that my father was no gourmet. *"Ni gourmet, ni gourmand"* ("neither gourmet nor sweet-toothed"), he said of himself, admitting that he only liked "plain" food. He also had certain dislikes, which reduced our menu choices even further. For instance, he hated cheese of any kind, whether raw or cooked. To have a dislike for a specific dish seems to be a trait common among Frenchmen, but a dislike of cheese is a rare thing. No one in the family ever dared to question Papa about it. In spite of the difficulties caused both by rationing and by my father's imposed limitations, I have to admire my mother for her talent at creating memorable dishes.

In the kitchen, we sometimes prepared packages for Tante Marthe's husband, Yves, the prisoner of war. We put in whatever we could spare: cans of food, chocolate taken from our rations, dried meats. I understand that in the stalags, the prisoners shared all their goods.

It was not only food that was a problem: soap, for one, was difficult to find. In the kitchen cabinets under the sink Maman stored all the ingredients necessary for soap-making, an operation akin to a chemical experiment that she conducted among a great jumble of paper sacks, bottles, and pails, with the help of my grandmother. Besides soap, French people tried to make all sorts of things; for instance my father attempted to "make" tobacco. Tobacco was so scarce that many people tried to create substitutes. The ersatz tobacco made from linden leaves was a total disaster. The ersatz coffee made from various roasted grains was no big success either. But in the cabinets under the sink, it was not the soap-making supplies that interested me; it was something else, of which no trace remained.

"This is where I used to keep my white mice," my father told me. I imagined the mice, loose in the cabinets, waiting all day for my father to come back from work and play with them.

Animals were always part of our household. When I was very young my parents had a German shepherd, Cora. Everyone loved Cora in spite of her one fault: her hatred of cats. However, although Cora was a terror to neighborhood cats (once, she returned with a poor cat in her teeth, dead—my father surreptitiously buried it), she adored our white cat, Blanchette, and even helped her move her kittens around by delicately carrying them in her mouth. After Cora died, we had a black dog, Dick, my darling, and later, a little brown mutt, Surcouf, who, as a puppy, was honored with a christening ceremony. During the war, Minouche, a neighborhood cat of indistinct gender adopted us, and later, a beautiful gray cat, Mizou, became an inspiration for my childhood poems. Our old photos show a variety of pets, happy to pose with the family.

After dinner when I did my homework on the kitchen table, the warm glow of the pulley lamp seemed to bring me closer to my parents. Once, my assignment was to draw a familiar object. I looked around, but couldn't come up with an idea. My father suggested the wall coffee-grinder. "It's too hard!" I protested. Then Papa volunteered to draw it (Maman had written an essay on autumn for me, now it was time for Papa to take his turn). The coffee grinder, in Dutch style, was made of white porcelain decorated with a blue windmill; it had a little wooden handle and a glass drawer to receive the ground coffee. Not an easy object to draw! But my father gave it his best. I didn't think his drawing was child-like enough but the teacher never had a clue that I didn't do it myself. (To our great disappointment, Papa only got an average grade!) My father loved to draw; he was always creating little characters and cartoon animals, and, when my cousins visited, he made flip books of Charlie Chaplin and of P'tit Louis, the bicycle champion.

Cora, Blanchette and kittens. (c. 1938)

The kitchen door was usually left open but when we were inside the kitchen and closed the door, we could see, tacked behind it, the large black-and-white portrait of Franklin D. Roosevelt. My parents admired President Roosevelt. Later, when he died, they pinned a black ribbon across the upper corner of his photo.

7
The War Ends

The Allies' raids became more frequent and the Resistance increased its efforts. Everywhere we went, we heard rumors: "The Allies have landed! The Allies have landed!" A Vichy anti-rumor campaign, with posters of a big ear next to a wall, warned, *"Les murs ont des oreilles"* ("Walls have ears"). These posters could be seen in all the local stores.

Finally it was not a rumor anymore. The news of D-Day spread like wildfire. The Allies had landed in Normandy on June 6, 1944. The Germans were retreating. Radio London kept us abreast of the latest news. The Allies sent airborne divisions to protect their positions along the beaches, while their forces fought behind the German lines. But the Germans did not give up easily. Deaths numbered in the thousands.

Dungeon of the Vincennes Castle. (postcard)

The Germans were retreating, but Paris was still occupied. In August 1944, the French resistance started an insurrection against the remaining Germans. There was fighting all over Paris and many French people were killed. In Vincennes, twenty-six members of the Resistance were brought to the castle, lined up against a wall, and shot.

From my bedroom I could see the dungeon of the Vincennes Castle. Since June 14, 1940, the Château de Vincennes, a former French military post, had been used by the Germans as a military stronghold. On the night of August 24, 1944, we heard an explosion followed by another. My parents ran upstairs and we all looked out of my bedroom window to try to see what had happened. The Château de Vincennes was on fire! For the first time I was really afraid. I asked my father, "Papa, is the fire going to come to our house?"

"No, it's too far away," my father reassured me.

It was a large fire, but it only burnt a tree-planted area and a fortified wall alongside the moat; it did not destroy any of the main structures of the castle. What we did not know as we were looking at the fire was that the Germans were leaving. It was the liberation.

General de Gaulle, with the agreement of General Eisenhower, had planned for French troops to be the first to enter Paris. On August 25, 1944, the tanks of General Leclerc liberated Paris. General de Gaulle, now President of the Provisional Government of the Republic, arrived in Paris the same day. The first newspapers of a free France were printed. On August 26, de Gaulle, the members of the insurrection, and the military commanders marched on the Champs-Elysées and attended a solemn mass at Notre Dame Cathedral.

Paris was liberated, but the war in Europe continued. It wouldn't be over until May 8, 1945, when Germany capitulated. I was four years old when the war began, almost ten when it ended. Too young to follow the developing events, I was nevertheless struck by a scene my father described. During the last days of the Paris insurrection, riding around on his bicycle to see what was happening, he witnessed something that left him bitter and disgusted: a group of French people beating up a single German soldier they had found hiding. They were dragging him, spitting on him; one of his eyes hung out of its socket, blood running down his face. The civilians let go of him only when the police arrived.

"Now, I bet they will brag that they were in the resistance!" my father said. "A whole crowd against one! And I wouldn't be surprised if some of them were collaborators!"

Suddenly many people were walking around with armbands marked "FFI" (*Forces Françaises de l'Intérieur*—French Forces of the Interior). These armbands were supposed to identify their wearers as combatants of the Resistance. And, sure enough, who came to visit my father, wearing a "FFI" armband? None other than Patrice, Monsieur Défense Passive! My father was given one of these armbands for his role in distributing *tracts* but he refused to wear it, feeling that only the men and women involved in direct action, the ones who put their lives on the line, deserved such recognition.

The Americans went on parade everywhere in Paris, acclaimed by the people they had liberated. They tossed candies and chewing gum to children. French women ran to kiss them. The mood was of celebration. Everyone talked about what they were going to do now that they were free. But it was not over yet. In many areas the Germans managed to regroup and major battles were still to be fought.

With little understanding of what was happening around me, I developed an intense curiosity for chewing gum—we called it *chwing* (pronounced: shwing). I had never heard of such a thing before, and now, at school everyone talked about it and how wonderful it was.

"You put it in your mouth, chew and chew, and it never disappears." I couldn't wait to have some. I dreamt about it. A girl in my class told me that an American soldier had given a pack of chewing gum to her big sister and that she would bring me some. I waited, asking her every day. "Do you have my *chwing*?"

But she always said, "Tomorrow, tomorrow." Then, one day, she told me, "I have some *chwing* for you at home . . . but . . . do you mind if it's a little bit chewed?"

I wasn't too sure, but I had waited long enough, so I said, "No, it's all right!"

However, the next day, she told me that she had stuck the *chwing* under the table and that her little brother had stolen it and swallowed it. She was sorry, but she did not have any more.

Then, we were told the Americans would come to Fontenay-sous-Bois. And indeed they came. They rode in "caterpillars," in jeeps, in trucks. People lined up the streets to greet them. When they drove up rue Jules Ferry, right by the villa de l'Ouest, I rushed out to see them. But I did not forget what I had heard my father say to my mother a little earlier, "What are the Americans going to think? That all French women are whores and all French children beggars?"

My friends and I waved, hoping, but not begging. But at that spot, at the corner of rue Jules Ferry and villa de l'Ouest, the Americans didn't throw any candies or chewing gum. They just waved in return!

The liberation of Paris didn't mean a return to normalcy. Food was still rationed and would remain so for several years; it was difficult to find anything in the stores; people had to stand in line for hours. By some mix-up in translation, the Americans sent tons of corn to the French, who had asked for wheat but had used the British term "corn," which in England means wheat. So, with all the corn flour around, bakers tried to make bread using their regular methods of baking. Corn baguettes, heavy as lead and hard as rock, tasted awful but we ate them anyway. The stores also sold corned beef (we called it *"cornet d'boeuf"*) which we ate although we found it strange-tasting and not very good. The black market continued.

We listened to the news on the radio. The information was no longer distorted as it had been under the Vichy government. Now that freedom of the press had been restored, a number of newspapers became available. Again Papa could buy *Le Parisien* every day. (It was now called *Le Parisien Libéré*). He closely followed the events on the remaining fronts, as the war was coming to an end.

Then the death camp newsreels arrived. We watched them at the Palais-des-Fêtes cinema. They showed the liberation of the camps in April 1945: Auschwitz, Büchenwald, Dachau, exposing the reality of the Holocaust with images of dead bodies piled up, survivors looking like skeletons. We had known that thousands of Jews and resistance members were sent to concentration camps, but no one had imagined such horror.

Around that time we learned that Adolphe Schtoel, who as a little boy had been raised by my grandmother Gauthier, had been killed early in the war. A French Jew who had served in the air force, he must have been about twenty-five when he died. Adding to their pain, his parents had received a photo of their son as he lay, shot dead.

Germany surrendered on May 8, 1945. The war in Europe had finally ended. It was a great mixture of emotions at that time: atrocities committed, whole cities bombed and destroyed, dead and wounded everywhere, but at the same time, the knowledge that we were free.

The war was soon to be over on the Pacific front also. In August 1945, we saw newsreels of Hiroshima and Nagasaki. Giant mushroom clouds in the sky, cities reduced to ashes, people reduced to ghosts. On August 14, 1945, Japan surrendered. World War II had ended.

Now it was time for retribution against the collaborators who had denounced Jews or members of the resistance to the Gestapo. They had to be found and exposed. The easiest ones to identify were the women who had slept with the Germans in exchange for favors. In each town of France, in each district of Paris, there were such women, and, of course, some were found in Fontenay-sous-Bois—one of them just a few blocks away from where we lived.

As was done throughout France, people in our neighborhood went to the woman's house and dragged her out, shaved off her hair and painted a swastika on her head.

"The whore, the bitch," they said. "She slept with the Germans. She gave them names in exchange for food and silk stockings. Now, she must pay!" They spat at her and marched her in the streets of Fontenay, shouting, *"La Tondue! La Tondue!"* ("The Shaven One! The Shaven One!" Words which took on the meaning of "The Traitor!")

I saw this woman as she was taken up the steep rue Jules Ferry. There was not a big crowd marching her, six or seven people at most and very few spectators. My parents did not go to what they called a "spectacle." They felt that the really guilty people, if they were powerful enough, would manage to escape retribution. They also wondered if there was any proof that this woman had indeed collaborated, or if it was just hearsay - something we never found out. But from then on, she would always be known as *La Tondue*. She defiantly did not move away from Fontenay-sous-Bois, but stayed in the same house all her life, grew her hair very long, below the waist, and dyed it blond.

In the villa de l'Ouest, of course, there was an echo to this: my friends and I played the game of "La Tondue." Lili was "it." She didn't seem to mind. Her hair was tied up in a tight bun, and all of us kids walked her up rue Jules Ferry, turned left on rue Gambetta, walked down the steps of the villa de l'Ouest, and back to rue Jules Ferry (it was what we called *"faire le tour de la villa"*). And all the way we shouted: *"La Tondue! La Tondue!"*

Little by little things became more normal. Although there was a lot to reorganize and rebuild, at least we could live without fear. The war prisoners returned, among them my friends Lili and Michou's father, and Yves, my aunt Marthe's husband. Since Tante Marthe was then living with my uncle Albert Schuschmann in an apartment of their own, the returning prisoner went to live with his sister, soon taking his sons Jacques and Claude with him. For my cousins this was the start of a tug-of-war between parents, and for my aunt the onset of a divorce suit that would go on for several years.

General de Gaulle, as head of the nation, made speeches for the rebirth of France. I particularly remember one of these speeches, which was read to us in school. *"Écoliers de France, vous pouvez marcher la tête haute!"* ("Schoolchildren of France, you can walk with your head held up high.") I have to confess that I took *le Général* quite literally and started walking straight as a picket with my nose up in the air.

To celebrate the end of the war the entire family had always planned to have *"un grand gueuleton"* (a big feast) in a restaurant in the country where food was available. The family had talked about it at length, enumerating the glorious dishes they would order and already tasting the fine wines they would drink. My cousins and I were left under the care of Mémé Cessot (a bit upset at not being able to partake in the festivities). All dressed up and ready for a good time, the adults gathered at our house. Sad to be left behind, we said good-bye to everybody: my father, my mother, Tante Valentine, Oncle Baptiste, Roger, Tante Marthe, Oncle Albert, Tante Yvonne, Oncle Marcel, my cousins Paulette and Denise, and their husbands Lulu and Armand. For months after that, they all talked about this *"grande bouffe,"* recalling every single dish and laughing at how some of them got so drunk they had to be pushed from the restaurant to the waiting cars in a wheelbarrow. *"En brouette, en brouette!"*

SIX

1945 - 1946

1

Lost Love and Still More Villa de l'Ouest

In 1945, when my father began to work again for the newspapers, my parents decided to send me to a *colonie de vacances* (summer camp) in the French Alps, under the sponsorship of *la Presse*. They thought a change of air would do me good me since we had not left the Paris region (except during the *Exode*) through the four years of war. I wasn't so sure I wanted to go, but when my mother told me about mountains that were so tall and air that was so pure, I felt that something wonderful was about to happen to me.

The fact that I had never been away from my family for any length of time was something no one expected to be a problem. I was sent to Vizille, a small town outside Grenoble, with the prospect of spending two months there. The children were housed in a very nice residence and had all the necessary comfort. However, with no experience of group life, I now found myself in regimented company, having to eat in a refectory, sleep in a dormitory, walk two-by-two, play organized games, etc. Unable to adapt, I cried every single day. The counselors thought I would start having fun after a while, but I did not—I kept on crying. The only times I enjoyed myself was when we took trips, especially once when we waded in an ice-cold torrent at the foot of snow-covered mountains, and when we were taken to the Grenoble museum and saw charcoal-black Egyptian mummies.

The counselors nicknamed me "Toura, Goddess of the Jungle" because of my green eyes and wild-looking hair. They were nice to me but it was not enough. I missed my parents too much. Mostly, I missed my dog. I pictured myself going home and hugging and kissing him, and I imagined him jumping for joy at seeing me again.

Dick, the dog my parents got after the war was a groendael, a very handsome breed. He looked like a German shepherd, but his coat was shiny black. He was young, playful and strong. My father, who had owned several dogs before, had assumed Dick would be easy to train, but it turned out differently. Dick was an escape artist: the minute we opened the gate just a little, he would run away; after that, it was almost impossible to get him to come back. He just loved his freedom; he ran wildly until he was out of sight. However, as much as he loved running, he hated to see any other creature run, especially children. He would chase after them and try to snap at their legs or buttocks—and succeeded a few times. I knew he just wanted to play: he didn't mean to hurt anybody; the damage would be limited to pants or skirts. But who was to believe that? In the villa de l'Ouest the boys said that he liked to make "triangles" on their pants. But the day he bit a "triangle" off the mailman's pants, it wasn't taken lightly. We had to be extremely careful not to let him out, so we kept him either inside the house, in the garage, or in the yard where he had a roomy doghouse that my father had made for him. That didn't last long. Dick soon taught himself to jump over the fence. At that point my father decided to tie him to a long rope. It worked well until the day Dick jumped anyway, still tied to the rope, dragging it after him, together with its post. My father found him after he saw traces left by the rope and post on a sandy area near the covered market. But Dick was a lovely dog, and inside the house he was well-behaved and obedient. He could sit with a lump of sugar on his nose and throw it in the air and catch it when my father gave him the order. I played with him, rode him like a horse. I adored him—and he adored me.

At summer camp things didn't improve. I was miserable. After two weeks or so, the director wrote my parents and told them I would have to be sent home (I wasn't the only one, a couple of other kids had to leave also). I was never so glad to see my parents as they waited for me at the train station. My first words to them were: "How is Dick?" Then they broke the news. Dick wasn't there any more; they had to give him away. They said (as many parents have said before) that they gave him to "some people in the country." He would be fine there, with a lot of room to run around.

"Can we go see him?"

"No, we don't know exactly where he is. We can't get in touch with the people."

I was crushed. I came home and cried and cried.

During the day I would crawl into Dick's doghouse and gather tufts of his hair, and kiss them, and cry. I can truly say that Dick was my first love and my first *chagrin d'amour*. To this day I still think of him, and still remember the feel of his long black nose under my kiss.

Meanwhile, in the villa de l'Ouest, I had admirers of the human kind, although my feelings for them were never so strong. There was Jacqui (a little older than me; I was ten, he was thirteen), who did not hide his interest in me—he even once held my hand for a few seconds when nobody was looking; there was Claude Gouge, whose grandparents owned the little corner store which sold threads, ribbons, newspapers and candies and which we called *la petite boutique bleue*; and there was Robert. But it was Patrick I liked best. He was closer to me in age than the others, only a year older. We were soul mates; we didn't have to say we liked each other, we just knew it. A little incident was a proof of that.

"What are you drawing?" Patrick asked me.

"A girl."

"Can I have your drawing?" said Jacqui.

"No!"

"Can I have it?" said Claude Gouge.

"No!"

"Please, can I have it?" Claude Gouge begged.

"No, I told you, you can't!" I tore the drawing in little pieces and threw the pieces on the ground.

The boys picked up the little pieces of paper.

"I have the feet," Jacqui said, brushing a blond strand of hair off his face.

"I have the head," Patrick said, smiling knowingly.

"I have the heart!" said Claude Gouge, a.k.a. The Gudgeon, casting an amorous look toward me, his red-hair shining in the sun, his mouth pursed for a kiss.

Whap! I gave him a hard slap across the face. He had insulted me in front of my friends, especially Patrick!

Now when I think of this scene, I feel embarrassed at having been such a shameless coquette, and sorry for the poor kid. But it was an era of easy slapping. Offended women did it in the movies all the time.

While the cinema had a strong influence on our lives, music was even more important We all bought *"chansons"*—by which we meant the printed and illustrated scores that contained the lyrics of *chansons*—and traded them among ourselves. Our taste was different from our parents'. They liked Edith Piaf, Georges Guétary, or Luis Mariano (although Papa still stuck to his 1930s and 1940s' favorites), but we preferred the more modern songs we heard on the radio, such as *Les Feuilles mortes* (Autumn Leaves) sung by Yves Montand. In the domain of music, Patrick was our leader. He always knew the best new singers and their latest hits. Once he gave me a *chanson* that was called *Mademoiselle Swing*. I liked it a lot, but it was difficult to sing; we had to say the words very fast while shaking our index finger in rhythm.

Posing at the piano, but not practicing very much. (1946)

When I was about eleven I started taking music lessons. My father, who as a boy had played in the Créteil Communal Marching Band, was able to read music and play popular tunes on his mandolin or his banjo. He dreamed of having me play the accordion, but since I didn't like the idea I asked to learn how to play the piano instead. I started taking lessons with a piano teacher whose house was on rue Jules Ferry. Her back garden ended at the villa de l'Ouest, directly across from our house. This meant that the teacher could easily hear me practice (or not practice) my scales. She had a passion for music theory; I don't think she ever taught me an actual piece of music. This, together with the fact that I was neither enthusiastic nor gifted, did not help in my initiation to serious music. I kept trading *chansons* with my friends and sharing their enthusiasm for popular music.

On Thursday afternoons my friends and I often went to the movies at the Palais-des-Fêtes or the Celtic. I remember being particularly enchanted by *The Adventures of Robin Hood* with Errol Flynn, a romantic action film still admired today. Patrick, always a leader in the arts, suggested that we show movies in my garage—and charge admission. His family had a projector; my parents supplied a sheet for the screen and chairs for the audience. We showed cartoons. The best ones (we all agreed) were of Felix the Cat. But soon we wanted to have a more active role in the entertainment field. It wasn't long before we decided to set up our own theater in the villa de l'Ouest.

First we had to write a play. Patrick was the principal playwright, but our oeuvre was really a joint creation: Jacqui, Pierrette and I were contributors. The actors included the gang regulars, plus Robert Point, a younger kid. The play, titled *Le Mystère du Deuxième Palier* (The Mystery of the Second Landing), was a drama with elements of comedy. A mystery had to be solved. The action took place in an apartment building where a young ballerina (Ginette Seutet) had been found murdered on the stairs landing. Every tenant was a suspect, including the gangster (Robert Point), who left every evening, a cap pulled down to his eyes, and the annoying old maid (Pierrette), detested by everybody. But the concierge

(Jacqui in women's clothes) with "her" fancy hair, big chest, broom, and ugly shoes, was beyond suspicion; and so was her meek and dominated husband (me, in a boy's suit, and with a painted-on mustache). The Inspector (Patrick) had to gather the clues and find the murderer. The end revealed that it was the concierge who did it. As "she" was roughly taken to the police station, her bra stuffing escaped from her dress and scattered all over the place, to the delight of the spectators.

Back row: The concierge (Jaqui); the detective (Patrick); the old maid (Pierrette), the singer Laurette Daysi (me). Front row: The gangster (Robert Point); the ballerina victim (Ginette Seutet). (c. 1943)

We had rehearsed carefully, made posters, distributed programs, and given a nearly flawless performance. Actually, the play was not the only billing of the day. We had first offered a variety show, then the play, as *pièce de résistance*. I still have the program:

FIRST PART
1. Orchestra
2. Musical entertainment with Le Trio de la Villa
3. The voluptuous and graceful dances of Miss Ginette Seutet
4. You will laugh with Patrick Vérité and Jacqui Staerck in *The Green Hat*
5. The singer Rigolero (Patrick)
6. The singer Laurette Daysi (Colette)
7. From French Cancan to Swing with Pierrette, Ginette and Colette.
8. Big Bill, singer (Jacqui)
9. Intermission. Surprises.

SECOND PART
10. Dance "Uranium."
11. The Mechanical Dolls
12. The (girl) singer Ermado Pâquitera
13. The Mystery of the Second Landing: Police drama in two acts. 1st act.
14. The Mystery of the Second Landing. 2nd act
15. Intermission
16. The two gossips
17. The singer Lise Mignonette
18. The Fakir, by the clowns

It was a big success; the audience was sizeable; our parents took photos (I changed into my Laurette Daysi costume for the picture). This encouraged us to try other endeavors, and, under the guidance of Patrick, our cultural leader, we "published" our first newspapers: *Echo Villa* and *Le Canard de la Villa* (all written by hand, with headers, columns, etc.). Reading these pocket-size "newspapers" now, I find them truly amazing in their imitation of grown-up versions. They contained ads for real products: "*Soir de Paris*—The Best Perfume!" as well as imaginary ones: "The electric razorblade Fulgur," "Timor, *Insecticide de France*" (in one issue), and "Timor, *Insecticide d'Amérique*" (in another). They also included film announcements for our local movie houses, as well as Patrick's original crossword puzzles and film reviews such as:

"The best Walt Disney animated pictures are *Pinocchio* and *Fantasia*; *le plus moche* (the most terrible) is *Saludos Amigos*."

There were also comic strips, lottery results, and serialized novels:
"During a fashionable soirée, high-society people elbowed one another. Suddenly the light went off. A woman cried for help, 'Au secours!' An uproar followed. The light came back on. What happened? (To be continued)."

And, of course, topical articles such as this one:
"Serious Crime!" (said the header in fancy letters). "Who is guilty? Was it the man in the bathing suit or the man in the jumper? Yesterday afternoon a sinister-looking individual going under the name of Joseph Quillet (seven years old) met another individual, Jean-Claude Seutet, in the villa de l'Ouest. They began to trample beautiful flowers in a garden, reducing them to a mush of flesh, petals, sap, and pollen. After this abominable carnage Madame Seutet arrived on the scene of the crime. A first-class interrogation ended with the culprits being condemned to a spanking."

Or this one:
"This morning, Mr. Patrick Vérité trained on his bicycle in the streets of Fontenay-sous-Bois with his manager, Jacqui Staerck, a renowned swimmer. Vérité is planning to enter the Tour de France; he has an excellent chance."

And in the "Marriage column," my friends didn't fail to poke fun at me:
"Monsieur et Madame Gauthier have the honor of announcing the engagement of their daughter Colette to Monsieur Claude Gouge. The cause of the engagement was a postcard."

(In spite of the slap incident, Claude Gouge had sent me a sweet vacation postcard.)

For me it was not only in the villa that art and literature were brewing. Exposure had also begun at school. Our teacher introduced us to the intricacies of the sonnet, and made us memorize some worthy examples. I was fascinated. When the assignment came for us to write our own sonnet, I put my heart into it. I wrote on the terrible occurrence of war and the desire for peace (in awfully pompous verse). Somehow my work earned the honor of being included in the "Teacher's Poem Notebook," where only one poem per year merited this distinction.

But soon a real artist was about to enter our midst: the daughter of a middle-aged couple who had just moved into the apartment building at 36 rue Jules Ferry. The newcomer immediately became known as *La Danseuse*. An actual ballerina (not like Ginette Seutet, who improvised her dances in a crepe paper tutu), La Danseuse belonged to a ballet troupe and performed professionally. We were impressed—and of course a little jealous. To make things worse, La Danseuse (whose name was Josette) happened to be pretty. She had huge expressive eyes that dominated her rather flat face, a pink mouth and a snowy complexion. She looked like a girl straight out of a turn-of-the-century picture book.

When I told Josette that I intended to become an actress and a singer when I grew up (I hadn't yet realized that I couldn't sing), she said that I should ask my parents to register me in a performing arts school.

"The teachers will have you do children's skits and sing children's songs," she said.

But that was not what I had in mind. What I was planning to do was to act in love scenes and sing adult songs. I wasn't about to follow her advice.

La Danseuse filled me with envy when she told us she had met my movie idol, Jean Marais. I absolutely adored him. Even if I had been aware of the fact that he was a well-known homosexual and the lover of artist-writer Jean Cocteau, it would have been totally irrelevant to me and to the "love" I felt for him. I could hardly believe that Josette had seen Jean Marais in the flesh. She had been in the same room! Close enough to touch him!

"How was he?" I asked. "Was he as handsome as in the movies? Did he talk to you? What did he say?"

Josette wouldn't tell. Finally she had to admit, "I saw him in his dressing room. He did not say anything. I couldn't see his face. He was in his beast costume for the film *La Belle et la Bête*" (*Beauty and the Beast*).

It was quite a disappointment!

Jean Marais and Madeleine Sologne in *L'Eternel Retour* based on the story of Tristan and Isolde. (1943)

Jean Marais in his Beast costume.

2
Nasty Events

Innocent as I was when I was nine or ten, it is no wonder I did not know how to act in unseemly situations. The first time I found myself in one of these situations, it was in our own villa de l'Ouest, our beloved playground. There was a new kid in the villa. He must have been temporarily staying with relatives because we saw him only for a few months and then he was gone. He was about thirteen, tall and skinny with a plain face. His name was Fernand. At that time, young girls used to make little dolls out of yarn, some simple, some elaborate, with heads, hands and feet of different colors. My friends and I thought they were very cute and collected them. One day, Fernand said to me and one of my friends, "I've got a lot of pretty yarn dolls at home. I'll give two of them to each of you if you do something for me."

"What? What?" we asked.

For several days he didn't want to say. Finally he told us, "Just let me take a look at your you-know-what."

It was a daring request! The regular boys in the Villa would never have asked anything like that. But the dolls were tempting. I consulted with my friend. She was not against it. We would just go like that: Lower our panties real fast. Plop! And it would be over.

"Have you decided yet?" Fernand asked us every day. He had already picked the spot, a doorway, and the time, nightfall, when all the other kids had gone home. He insisted and insisted. Finally we agreed.

It was a summer evening; the villa de l'Ouest was deserted, and, in the shadow of the doorway, nobody could see us. Fernand was ready, "Now let me see!" My friend and I did our "plop" real fast.

"No, no! I didn't see anything! You each take a turn, and let me see better."

"All right!" We held our panties down for a minute. Fernand conducted his inspection; first my friend's turn, then mine.

"Okay, now I want to touch!"

"You did not say that!"

"Then, no yarn dolls!"

Since we had already gone that far we decided to go along with the new demand. Fernand caressed the outside of our hairless private parts with his index finger. The examination lasted a few seconds and our panties went right back up.

"Now, give us our dolls!"

"Don't worry! I'll give them to you tomorrow!"

The next day we asked for our dolls . . . and the day after . . . and the day after. They never came. Fernand never gave them to us. I felt cheated. My friend and I never told anybody, but obviously Fernand did. One day Jacqui chanted, "Pretty yarn dolls! Pretty yarn dolls!"

We pretended we didn't know what he meant.

"You are blushing, you are blushing!"

All my life I have hated the name Fernand.

The second disturbing event took place in the Bois de Vincennes. This beautiful park was so close that, as children, we often walked there with our friends. Before we left, our mothers always warned us to stay in a group and never wander alone because, hiding in the bushes, behind the trees, and around the lakes, there might be *satyres* ("satyrs," dirty old men).

"They follow little children. You must never go near them."
Satyrs were easy to identify: they were shabbily dressed, always alone, and usually wore dark overcoats. We were also told that we could recognize them by their shifty eyes when they looked at children.

One day my cousin Miquette, her brothers Jacques and Claude, and I went to the Bois. As we walked across a large clearing dotted with kids and their families, we saw a man sitting in the middle of the grass, and we heard him call my name.

"Colette, Colette, come here for a minute!"

"Don't go," my cousin Miquette said. "He could be a satyr."

"But," I said, "how would he know my name? Maybe he knows Papa, and has seen me with him." And so, I went.

"Sit here, Colette," the man said.

I sat on the grass. Immediately he seized my wrists. "Look," he said, showing me his exposed genitals. I tried to break loose. He led one of my hands against his penis. "Touch it. Isn't it soft?" It was disgusting—a sack of flesh, wrinkled, pink and flabby. I wriggled away and ran.

"Miquette, Miquette! It *was* a satyr!"

"I told you so!"

"But how did he know my name?"

"Maybe he followed us when we were playing and he heard us calling you."

I did not mention any of this at home, but Miquette told her mother and Tante Marthe, in turn, told my mother. That night, when Maman put me to bed, she said, "I heard what happened in the Bois. You should have told me. You must always tell Maman when things like that happen. And never, ever go near these men. They are always trying to do bad things to little children."

While I never had any other encounters with the Bois-de-Vincennes satyrs, I had other encounters with other satyrs—as all young girls did at the time. Whenever we took the métro, there were always shadowy men who, when the trains were full, often succeeded in groping us, knowing full well that we would quickly move away from them and that we were too shy to make a scandal.

3
Cemetery

Not only did my family follow the French tradition of going to the cemetery every first of November on the day of la Toussaint (All Saints' Day), but my mother and my grandmother Cessot took me with them to visit the cemetery about once a month. We called these visits "monter au cimetière" (go up to the cemetery) because it was uphill most of the way.

On the first part of our walk (the flat part) we passed the Palais-des-Fêtes movie house. A bit further, as we walked by *la Maggi*, rue Mauconseil, we waived at Tante Valentine through the store window. Then, just before reaching the classic building of City Hall, we made a left turn on a street that was suddenly very steep. We had entered *le Vieux Fontenay*, a historical area now restored and renamed *"Fontenay Village"* as a reminder of the times when Fontenay, perched on a hill and overlooking its renowned vineyards, was indeed a village. The only monument remaining from this pastoral past, which lasted from the Middle Ages to the nineteenth century, is the thirteenth-century church, Saint-Germain-l'Auxerrois, well-proportioned and harmonious in spite of the numerous modifications and additions in diverse styles made to it through the years.

Église Saint-Germain-l'Auxerrois.
Postcard. (c. 1980)

As we slowly walked past the church on the hilly cobbled street, we passed an old stone wall covered with brown moss, weeds steadfastly clinging to cracks between the stones. Behind the wall, a jungle of trees and shrubs grew unattended. My mother called that walled garden "the monastery." I expected to see monks sweeping along the walls, but the old monastery had long been abandoned.

In the fall or winter, it was often cold and windy when we reached the cemetery, and, from the top of the hill, the view was most of the time shrouded in fog. Our first stop was at the flower shop at the entrance, where we bought white flowers for my brother's grave and bright flowers for our other dead. Throughout the year flowers adorned the cemetery but never so much as on All Saints' Day, when everyone brought chrysanthemums, hundreds of them, in pots or bouquets. Then, under the white sky or through a veil of rain, all these chrysanthemums spilled their soft colors onto the gray tombstones.

My brother's grave was near the center of the cemetery. Since we reached it by taking the same paths every time, we were familiar with the graves along the way. They were either rectangular monuments about two or three feet high, made of stone or marble, or they looked like little framed gardens. Large stone crosses usually stood at the head of the graves with, embedded in them, enameled photographs of the deceased. Important people were honored with bronze or marble busts, but it was porcelain angels or open books made of bisque that graced the rest of the graves as testimonials of love and remembrance.

Fontenay-sous-Bois cemetery with grave of the writer Hector Malot.

For me the cemetery was not a sad place. I walked around or kept busy by filling a watering can at the fountain or reading the inscriptions on the tombs. On both sides of the central alley, paved and as wide as a street, family crypts in the shape of small gothic chapels stood in a row. They looked respectable, if slightly dilapidated. Their doors were always locked. It was obvious that most of them had not been opened in years. When I peered through the half-broken windows, I could see narrow altars with holy figures, frayed lace, dried flowers, and dusty vases—all that remained of ancient devotions. Some of the vases were made of cobalt-blue glass that looked almost black in the obscurity of the crypts; but a shard that I once found and held up to the sun took on a magic blue color, a color that, later, I would recognize in the glass windows of medieval cathedrals.

The most fascinating grave of the cemetery was "the grotto." Built of gray-brown concrete and made to look like a real grotto, it was about six feet high. A tomb lay inside, and, at the entrance, the rocky walls were inlaid with enameled photographs of the beautiful young woman who was buried there. We could see her playing tennis, looking healthy, happy. I never failed to look at the photos of this young woman who, according to the engraved dates, died at the age of twenty. Sometimes, when I went to the cemetery with Madame Mousset and Pierrette, we made a stop to look at the grotto. Once there, Madame Mousset felt sad, as she was reminded of Pierrette's big sister who also had died in her twenties.

There was nothing monumental about my little brother's grave. Narrow strips of white stone rimmed a rectangular area of plain earth covered with white pebbles. It was in that earthen area that we planted flowers or arranged them in vases. At the head of the grave stood, not a cross since my parents were not Christian, but a truncated column symbolizing my brother's too-short life. A sepia photo of him was inlaid in the stone marker and set in an oval frame. It was an enameled reproduction of the portrait that hung in my parents' bedroom, the portrait with the eyes that followed us. My mother kneeled to arrange the flowers she had brought, and, after fussing for a while with the little garden, stood up and remained there. She wore a scarf on her head to keep her hair from blowing in the wind. I remember her in her dark coat, silhouetted against the sky, silent and sad.

Next to my brother's grave was a gray marble tomb adorned with a large cross cut in relief into the marble. There was no marker, no name. My mother and grandmother said it must be a priest buried there, for they believed that priests were supposed to be anonymous in death.

During the war, and for some time after, we visited my grandmother Gauthier's grave. But one day it was no longer there. It had been removed. The lease for her plot had expired and had not been renewed.

It is the rule in Fontenay-sous-Bois that tombs are only retained for a specific length of time, depending on the contract signed by the survivors. This does not apply to the chapel-like crypts or to the graves of officials since these are secured "in perpetuity." However, when I recently visited the cemetery, there was talk of removing the chapels because of their deterioration.

My grandfather Cessot had also been buried in Fontenay-sous-Bois, but like Grand-mère Gauthier's, his tomb had been removed after a few years. As for my uncle Félix, I was told that he was buried in a common grave, like a pauper. One can understand that, at the time of his death, his three orphaned daughters were too young to secure a place for him in the cemetery. But why had not Grand-mère Cessot, my mother and Tante Yvonne shared the expense of granting their son and brother his own resting spot?

As we walked across the cemetery Maman and Grand-mère Cessot chatted while I looked at things around me. On the way to Grand-mère Gauthier's grave there was an area between two tombs where a few wild poppies grew. I was familiar with the red poppies we see everywhere in the French countryside, especially in wheat fields, but these poppies seemed enormous, and they were mauve or purple. My mother and grandmother told me they were opium poppies. As I reflect on that now, I can't help wondering how opium poppies found their way to the Fontenay-sous-Bois cemetery—or was it perhaps that my mother and grandmother's botanical knowledge was a bit unchecked. In any case, they both explained to me that opium was made from the pods of the poppies, and added, "When people smoke opium they have beautiful dreams, but opium is dangerous and sometimes those people die." And with their hands they made big round gestures against the sky to show me the beautiful dreams. This sounded strange to me. How could a flower make you dream and make you die?

4
Tante Yvonne

Before letting this story follow the course of time, I will pause a while to introduce Tante Yvonne, dear now, but not always dear.

At the beginning of the war, Tante Yvonne was a young woman of twenty-six, beautiful, desirable and self-assured. She and Oncle Marcel married in 1933 and had a son, Bernard, born, like me, in 1935.

Oncle Marcel, who was from Brittany, had come to Paris in his youth. He worked for a major radio and electrical equipment company. Although he had but a primary education, he rose through the ranks with training and became a manager. He had his own office where he presided over other employees and where everyone (himself included) took him for an engineer. This reinforced his and Tante Yvonne's opinion that they were more "bourgeois" than the rest of the family. Their apartment, in the Paris southern suburb of Malakoff, was stylish and modern, and was decorated with tasteful artwork. Tante Yvonne delighted in elegant dress and good manners. Very particular about cleanliness, she constantly warned us about *les microbes* (which prompted my father to call her *"La mère microbe"*). She also insisted that Bernard and I speak and write proper French, correcting us (like it or not) every time we made grammatical or spelling mistakes.

Bernard and me. (1938)

When she was young she had learned dressmaking. Soon realizing she would not earn a good living as a seamstress, she had joined her parents in the field of newspaper printing, and, like my mother, had become a linotype operator. She stopped working in that field when the war broke out, changed careers to become an insurance agent, and retained this occupation (on a part-time basis) until her retirement.

There was a basic flaw in Tante Yvonne's character: she could not help making nasty little remarks that resulted in hurting people's feelings. I do not think she was mean-spirited, but she was one of those people who say what's on their mind, priding themselves on their candor, while showing no regard for the feelings of the recipients of their supposedly innocent forthrightness. My father said of her, *"Elle jette des pierres dans notre jardin"* ("She throws stones in our garden"), an expression which, I think, describes very well her modus operandi.

From left: Oncle Marcel, Bernard, the housekeeper, me, Tante Yvonne, Grand-mère Cessot. (1937)

Tante Yvonne also had the habit of complaining about her marital problems, describing Oncle Marcel as someone very nice in public, but "a monster" in private (actually there must have been some truth to that; Grand-mère Cessot was ready to corroborate her claim). My father did not understand Tante Yvonne's constant complaining.

"Why doesn't she leave him if she is so unhappy?" he would say.

But Oncle Marcel had many good qualities: he was sensitive,

generous—and tender when he wanted to be. He was also a good provider and it was obvious to all (including Tante Yvonne herself), that he adored his wife and son. So, in spite of all, she stayed.

Oncle Marcel was a good-looking man, always impeccably dressed. He was tall, athletic, with intelligent eyes and a dimple when he smiled. In the family he was famous for exaggerating. My father said that everything Marcel talked about had to be "divided by two, if not by ten." For instance, during the war, when he got somewhat involved in the black market, he claimed that he had an "industrial" quantity of goods to sell: wagonloads of metal, tons of electric parts, dozens of bolts of fabric, and so on. I don't think any of these goods ever materialized, except perhaps the fabric. I do remember a few bolts of rayon standing in a corner of our dining room. The bolts soon disappeared; the only thing left of them was a piece of fabric big enough to make a dress for me.

Tante Yvonne was exotic and classy. She dressed in a way the family called "eccentric," but her clothes were well-cut designer models, often in bright colors to contrast with her olive complexion, black hair and brown eyes. If the family truly descended from Gypsies, she certainly had inherited from these ancestors her almost East Indian features. She had, besides, a shapely body of which she was very proud. I remember that toward the end of our seemingly interminable Sunday lunches during which the family sat all afternoon around the dining room table, she often found an excuse to briefly lift up her elegant dress to show us how tanned her legs were, revealing them almost all the way to the thighs. Privately, my father had another nickname for her: *"La Belle-en-Cuisses"("Beauty-in-the-Thighs")*. Already naturally dark, she could not resist exposing herself to the sun. I still can see her, shiny with suntan lotion in a chaise-longue at the Molitor swimming pool, or in her bikini, lying on the polished parquet floor of her Malakoff apartment, doubly framed by a towel and a rectangle of sun.

It is thanks to both Tante Yvonne and Tante Valentine that I secured a lot of information on the family history, although, I am sorry to say, Tante Yvonne's input was not always reliable. She unswervingly defended her side of the family, the Cessots, refusing to see their dark sides, sprinkling her memories with gold powder, as it were. In spite of this, I made a point of including her recollections, even when I found that they clashed with the chronology of events or with what others remembered of the past. As an example, she once told me about my mother's supposed "liaison."

After the war my parents often listened to the radio. When the sports commentator, Raymond Marcillac, came on the air, my father sometimes said to me, "Here comes your mother's boyfriend!" and my mother would smile. But in fact it is possible that she knew Raymond Marcillac. Tante Yvonne told me that, some years before I was born, a scion of the de Marcillac family had fallen in love with my mother. This scion, however, was certainly not Raymond Marcillac, a hero of the resistance and sixteen years younger than my mother. Who the suitor was, I have no idea. And if or how he was connected to Raymond Marcillac, I don't know.

"He met her at work," she said. "His family owned the printing house where she worked." It is true that the de Marcillacs (their name with the "de" particle) were newspaper magnates.

"Your mother was so pretty," Tante Yvonne continued, "all the men wanted to flirt with her. One day this man slipped a ring on her finger. It was a ring with his family crest. He was from the nobility, you know. If your mother had wanted, she could have married him. But at least, *il lui a mis la bague au doigt* (he put the ring on her finger). *Il aurait pu être ton père!* (He could have been your father!). But she chose to stay with her husband . . ."

Whatever Tante Yvonne told me about this story (including her assertion that there was more to it than a ring on a finger) I have a hard time believing. The same goes for what Tante Yvonne told me about my father.

"He was *un coureur de jupons* (a petticoat chaser). He broke your mother's heart many times. Even when they were newlyweds he ran around with his sister Marthe's girlfriends. Your mother was very jealous."

But when Papa got married, he was twenty and Marthe fourteen. I imagine her girlfriends were about the same age. A little too young for Papa, I think!

Every time my aunt volunteered her questionable recollections, I felt like saying: Hush, Tante Yvonne, hush! Keep your secrets, *ma tante*, I don't want to hear them.

But about Tante Yvonne I will say no more right now as she will appear many times during the rest of my story.

Tante Yvonne at the Molitor swimming pool. (c. 1948)

5
Brittany

A vacation spent in Brittany in 1945 made the greatest impression on me, probably because it was my first real contact with the country. My cousin Bernard and I went with our grandmother Cessot to spend a vacation at the house of Bernard's other grandmother, Grand-mère Labbé, who lived in Brittany in the very village where she had raised Bernard's father, Oncle Marcel.

The two grandmothers were very different. While Grand-mère Cessot, thin and pale, wore gray clothes and forever complained about being cold, Grand-mère Labbé, a robust woman with a round face and red cheeks, wore gaily printed smocks over her ample black dresses and cheered us up with her sunny disposition. Mémé Labbé did not live in a farm, but in a trim white house in the middle of the village of Guer, in the Morbihan département, at the very heart of Brittany. From the back rooms of her house we could see a bit of her garden with its tall red flowers that seemed to want to dash in whenever we opened the windows. At the end of the village she had another garden, a larger one, where she grew vegetables and still more flowers in great patches of bright colors.

In the morning when we got up, Grand-mère Labbé prepared big bowls of hot chocolate and slices of fresh country bread spread with salt butter. During the day, Grand-mère Cessot stayed home with Grand-mère Labbé, while Bernard and I were free to wander wherever we wanted in the village or its vicinity. One of our favorite places was *Le Four* (The Oven), which was an actual stone oven, set in the front yard of a house. We crossed the yard, knocked at the door, and for a few coins, the lady of the house made buckwheat crêpes (*galettes,* as they are called in Brittany). The only thing required of us was that we bring our own plates and butter. We could order our *galettes* with or without eggs. The lady poured the thin gray dough straight on the hot flat stone, and when the crêpe was almost done, she turned it over and melted a piece of butter on it. If we had ordered an egg, she broke it right on top of the crêpe. The *galette*, the butter and the egg fried at the same time, their tastes blending in delicious togetherness. Our mouths watering from the smell, we watched, fascinated, as the border of the crêpe turned into lace. Then, the lady picked up our crêpe with her wooden paddle, fanned it for a couple of minutes, rolled it and served it to us, burning hot on our plates.

Bernard and I sometimes took walks away from the village. Once, after stopping under the walnut trees that marked the boundaries of a meadow, we decided to pick some walnuts. We were busy admitting that they were still too green, when a small snake darted out from under some leaves and startled us. Immediately, Bernard declared that he had recognized it as being of the most poisonous kind and warned me that hundreds of snakes were hiding everywhere, ready to bite us. It was typical of Bernard. I wasn't particularly worried.

It was the end of the summer, time for *la moisson* (the wheat harvest), an event which, up to then, I had only associated with boring school poems. I didn't quite know what to expect when Grand-mère Labbé told us we were going to her cousin's farm to help prepare the end feast of that year's *moisson*. We walked and walked, first on wide paths along hedges framing green meadows, then on narrower lanes between still uncut fields of golden rye or oats. We walked a very long time, wondering if we would ever arrive. But Mémé Labbé, wiping her forehead with her big white handkerchief and keeping a good pace in her sturdy shoes, kept telling us that we would soon be there.

Finally we arrived at the farm. A lot of women were already there, working in a huge kitchen, preparing great quantities of meat and vegetables or slicing hams with sharp knives. Outside, in the backyard, boards had been laid end-to-end on trestles to form a long table. We were asked to help. A woman dropped several big onions in front of me and told me to peel them. I had never peeled onions in my life; in fact, I didn't have the slightest idea how to peel onions. But I did my best, tears flowing on the table and all over the onions. We worked very hard until everything was ready. Then the men came back from harvest. They sat around the tables, poured themselves bowls of fermented cider, and "attacked" the food. Everyone talked, laughed, ate and drank until the sun went down.

We were to stay at the farm for the night. In the evening, Bernard and I sat in front of an enormous fireplace in the company of a girl our age who told us stories of ghosts and fairies, of lights appearing at the ends of beds, and of will-o'-the-wisps flickering over swamps. She also told us stories of the saints, and of a little boy's miraculous rescue. This boy had fallen in quicksand, and, as he sank deeper and deeper, only his finger remained visible above the surface. When good Saint Gabriel saw the finger, he pulled the boy out, and saved him. "It's a true story!" the girl assured us.

Before we went to bed, we found some yellowing magazines. All of them were about Jesus, Mary, Joseph, and the saints and their miracles.

At that time, Brittany was still traditional; many people spoke the Celtic Breton language, and women, especially older women, wore *coiffes*, caps made of fine lace, and starched to look like tall white tubes or dainty little wings.

One day, with our two grandmothers, we rode in a horse-drawn cart (a treat!) to a faraway farm. At the farm, Bernard and I, happy at first to have a try at turning the handle of the butter churner, quickly gave up when we realized how much effort it took to produce the renowned Brittany butter. It was more fun to watch the yellow salt butter being shaped into rectangular blocks and "stamped" with a design specific to the farm.

While the smallest children played outside, the oldest ones were called in by women who had gathered in the kitchen to make jam. They cooked red plums in huge copper cauldrons. When the jam was ready, they ladled it with big spoons and poured it into, what seemed to me, hundreds of glass jars lined up on two long tables. At the end, when the children were allowed to dish out the leftover jam from the big cauldrons, there was much pushing, shoving, spoon licking, jammy faces and sticky fingers.

During this vacation everything was so different from my life in Fontenay-sous-Bois that, once more, I had the impression of having been transported into a story from one of my books. I read a lot and took books with me wherever I went. I had brought several to Brittany with me, one of these a translation of the tales of Edgar Allan Poe. In the evening after dinner, when the two grandmothers had gone to bed, Bernard and I stayed in the dining room to read stories. We sat on opposite sides of the heavy wooden table, polished to a high shine by the meticulous Mémé Labbé. Around us were the traditional pieces of Britton furniture: a large hutch used to display Mémé's good dishes, and a massive carved sideboard. To better feel the atmosphere of the stories, we turned off the light and lit the kerosene lamp. Using my most frightening voice, I read to Bernard from *The Pit and the Pendulum*:

> "Down—steadily it crept . . . Down—certainly, relentlessly down . Down—still unceasingly—still inevitably down."

And Bernard begged, "No! No! Please stop!"
But I wouldn't stop. From *The Telltale Heart* I read

> "Yet the sound increased—and what could I do? It was a low, dull, quick sound . . . the officers heard it not . . . It grew louder—louder—louder."

And Bernard pleaded, "No! No! Stop!"

But I kept on reading until he ran out of the room. That made me happy! Bernard was afraid, this naughty, teasing boy. Good! I had succeeded in frightening him—except that in the process, I had also succeeded in frightening myself!

6
The Dining Room

Our dining room was mostly used for guests. Its wallpaper, studded with geometrical marine-blue flowers and brightened at regular intervals by petals of yellow gold, made us feel as if we were inside a beautifully-lined gift box. The hardwood floor was highly polished. For a while we used *patins*, rectangles of felt or other soft fabric a little bigger than the size of a foot; we slid on them, walking and polishing at the same time. But the use of *patins* didn't last long; my parents disliked the concept.

We could see a little bit of the villa de l'Ouest through the floating muslin curtain that covered the large window. Across the street were my piano teacher's garden and the house of the old bachelor, Monsieur Finaud. Next to his house was la Mère Michel's house, which itself was next to Jacqui Staerck's backyard fence.

The dining room furniture, in the Renaissance style popular in the 1930s, consisted of a dark walnut table, chairs with leather seats, and an ornate Henri II two-level sideboard buffet. The space between the top and bottom sections of the buffet made a niche that served as a curio area. It was there that my parents displayed an Art Nouveau metal plaque, twin open-tailed bronze pigeons, a leather box containing the pipes my father occasionally smoked, and two oversized 1930s Bakelite cigarette lighters. The doors to the top cabinet were carved with motifs of three-masted sailing ships and their sailors; the lower cabinet's doors were plainer, with medallion carvings.

It was in the upper cabinet that my mother stored the pale-pink dishes used for company and the light blue-and-gold Japanese coffee set made of porcelain so fine we could almost see through the cups when we held them to the light. Squeezed in a corner was Papa's collection of books by Alexandre Dumas. *The Three Musketeers* was one of his favorites. Having learned and taught fencing in the army, he must have loved to fancy himself as the swashbuckling hero.

Personally, I was much more interested in the things that could be found in the lower cabinet of the buffet. There, Papa kept his mandolin and his banjo. Listening to him play his repertoire of French songs, I was determined to try to play also. When he wasn't home, I sometimes took out the instruments and fumbled with the strings, but to my disappointment, I was never able to produce any recognizable tune.

Stored flat underneath the banjo and mandolin were four or five thick blue albums containing wax phonograph records, each one slipped in its own paper pocket on which my father had inscribed a number referring to an index he had created. Most of the popular songs on these records dated from before the war and were already pretty much out of date.

In a corner was a little box containing my mother's tarot cards and her book on palm-reading. As far as I can tell, these were the only items that could be connected to our alleged Gypsy roots. Though it seems that in the past she had consulted fortune-tellers (together with other women in the family), I don't think she really believed in anyone's power to predict the future. However, I remember her saying that she would never again have her cards read because she did not want to know if anything bad was going to happen. There was sadness in her voice when she said this; it made me think a card reader must have predicted the death of my brother. As for my father, he was vehemently opposed to anything having to do with the occult.

Not far from the tarot card box, my father stored a notebook with diagrams of his "inventions" (one of these looked like a forerunner of the helicopter). There was another notebook with newspaper clippings of his Tour de France, and a box of souvenirs of his voyage to America. It's too bad the invention notebook has been lost, but I'm happy to say that the other mementos are in my possession.

In the family, my father was much admired for having ridden in the Tour de France. The fact that he did not complete the Tour was barely acknowledged, and in no way diminished everyone's admiration. Recently I was talking to my cousin Jacques. Remembering my father, he said, "Didn't Tonton Louis ride in the Tour de France three times?" No!

My father rode only once, in 1926, and for no more than three *étapes* (stages), but it was already quite an achievement. He entered as an individual, without a trainer, without a team to support him, after having practiced alone, everyday, his mind fixed on winning. At that time, bicycles were heavy, the *étapes* were long, and the race was merciless (the Tour is still considered the most grueling of all sports events). My father kept a scrapbook titled *"Souvenirs sportifs."* In it, he noted all the sports events he participated in, and pasted newspaper clippings in which his name appeared. Of all the souvenirs preserved in the scrapbook, the most moving is the cloth number he wore while riding in the Tour de France. His number was 142. The rectangle of stiff cloth is now yellowish, showing a few black spots that most likely are bicycle grease.

My father's number in the Tour de France. (1926)

In 1926, the Tour de France was still in its beginnings although it was not exactly a new event. The first Tour, organized in 1903 by the sports newspaper *L'Auto*, had taken place every year after that, except for an interruption during World War One. In 1924, a journalist coined the expression *"Les prisonniers de la route"* ("The convicts of the road") to describe the riders. It was exactly that: the Tour participants were expected to suffer during seventeen long and arduous *étapes*.

My father had been involved in sports since the age of sixteen. He had run in speed races and marathons, entered numerous bicycle competitions, and, in 1925, had scored high in a multi-sports event that included bicycling, swimming, weight-lifting, and cross-country racing. He was as prepared as he could be to compete in the Tour de France (which, in 1926, turned out to be the longest of all time, covering a total distance of 5,745 kilometers, or 3,570 miles). During the first three stages, under the rain, he held his own, though the terrain was difficult. For the first time the Tour had not started in Paris. The first stage began in the Alp Mountains at Evian, took a northern direction across the Jura Mountains and ended in Mulhouse. The second stage stretched from Mulhouse to Metz, crossing the provinces of Alsace Lorraine. And the third stage, starting at Metz, ended in the northern city of Dunkerque, on the English Channel. It was during this third stage that bad luck struck: on the road, a horse too close to the runners panicked and ran into my father, damaging his bicycle. Papa spent precious time fixing his bike, and when he finally succeeded, he started again, alone on the road, determined to finish. But by the time he reached Dunkerque, night had fallen. It was too late. The control gate was closed. Defeated and sad, he had to step out of the Tour.

The scrapbook, however, does not stop there. It shows that my father soon joined the club Vincennes-Sportif and continued to participate in bicycle races, together with friends— including his best pals, Maurice Joly and Pierre Boyer (Pierre was at that time vice-president of Vincennes-Sportif). The club not only organized sporting events but also

Tour de France registration card.

My father. (1932)

held banquets and soirees, utilizing the talent of its members. After the club banquets, when the participants had already offered their numbers of classical piano or operatic singing, my parents were probably the favorite stars as they arrived on stage with their double-entendre songs and their comic duets, including their classic *Faites-ça pour moi!* (Do that for me!), a tune by Vincent Scotto with lyrics by G. Roger and E. Audiffred.

Excusez ma franchise
Cher monsieur, entre nous
Il faut que je vous l'dise
J'ai le béguin pour vous.

Mademoiselle quel language!
Vous m'suivez jusqu'ici
Mais j'suis un jeune homme sage
J'n'aime pas qu'on m'parle ainsi

Allons j'vous en prie soyez gentil
Je suis folle de vous, j'en rêve la nuit
Je n'ai qu'un désir, c'est insensé
Laissez-moi seulement vous embrasser
Faites ça pour moi, j'vous en supplie

J'regrette beaucoup,
J'peux pas faire ça pour vous!

Excuse my directness
Dear sir, between you and me,
I must tell you
I have a crush on you.

Mademoiselle, what language!
You have followed me all the way here
But I am a proper young man
I do not like to be spoken to like this!

Come on, I beg you, please be nice
I'm crazy about you,
I dream of you all night
I have only one desire, it's maddening,
Just let me kiss you,
Do that for me, I beseech you!

I am very sorry
I can't do that for you!

And the song went on with the aggressive demoiselle demanding more and more until she expressed the desire to see the prudish young man *tout nu* (all naked). After having repeated for two refrains "I can't do that for you," her companion finally gave in and was only too happy to comply with whatever his naughty companion requested.

What else was in the dining room? The buffet also held my father's mementos of his voyage to New York aboard the Normandie. The Normandie may not be as well-known as the Titanic but, like it, it was a luxury liner. In fact, it was perhaps the most magnificent vessel ever built. Called "The Ship of Lights," the Normandie was a showcase of France's art

The Normandie. (1935)

and technology, and the pride of the Compagnie Générale Transatlantique. The decor was a fantastic Art Deco creation. At the end of the promenade, close to the popular Café Grill, the descending grand staircase led to the first class smoking room beyond which was the grand salon, which was often transformed into a glamorous nightclub. Two decks down from the promenade was the ship's extraordinary first class dining room which could sit seven hundred guests. The dining room was illuminated by twelve pillars of Lalique glass, thirty-eight bright columns along the walls, and two chandeliers which hung at each side of the room. Christened in 1932, the Normandie took off for her maiden voyage on May 29, 1935 and set sail for New York.

My father's entrepreneur friend, Pierre Boyer, who had a contract with the Compagnie Générale Transatlantique, offered Papa a free trip on the Normandie in exchange for some work. Three or four workers were needed to do last minute additions and repairs, such as fixing locks on cabin doors and other minor things. Since my father was very skillful at this type of work, his friend Pierre "hired" him temporarily, long enough to go to New York and back.

In December 1936, my father left the port of Le Havre. As a member of the working crew he was able to go anywhere he wanted on the great ship (had he been a regular third class passenger, he would not have been authorized to enter the first class areas). He brought back newspapers from aboard ship, menus of fancy dinners—some of them autographed by personalities on board—a Normandie deck of cards, and a large foldout showing a "slice" of the ship with detailed color drawings of the upper and lower decks, the cabins, the luxurious dining rooms, the Grand Salon, the large swimming pool, the theater, and all the ship's interior below deck including the boiler rooms, which he also had the privilege of visiting. I loved to look at this foldout, carefully opening it and examining it in all its details.

The voyage on the Normandie was a fantastic opportunity for my father. It gave him a lot of prestige, not only in the family, but also at work where his friends nicknamed him *"P'tit Louis l'Américain."* I am glad he had the good idea of taking an eight-millimeter movie camera with him, as I still have the film that both he and a friend shot. Unfortunately something went wrong with the camera for much of the filming, but the existing footage I have of my father shows him walking on the promenade deck with a big cigar in his mouth and arriving in the port of New York, still smoking his cigar like an American millionaire. The last two minutes of the movie were taken in Fontenay-sous-Bois, when Papa returned. They show my mother, pretty and graceful, opening her arms to a baby (me) who had just learned to walk.

My father arrives in New York (movie still). (1936)

And what did my father do during the two or three days that he spent in New York? He visited the city, went up the Empire State Building (a landmark just four years old then), enjoyed a strip-tease show at the Burlesque, shopped at Macy's for presents (using gestures), and went to a "private club." He explained to us how he had to knock on a door and say the password (provided by a fellow-worker on the ship) to a woman who appeared at a little window. It was obvious to him that, since he was in America, he had to get close to American women (I don't know how close he got). I wonder what my mother thought of that, but I have the feeling she was not too upset. It seems to be an accepted fact that my father was unfaithful. He had the reputation of being a bon vivant, lover of wine, food, laughter, parties, and of course, women. Providing the marriage was not hurt, I don't think Papa's infidelities were cause for really deep trouble—although I don't know for sure, as I was too young to understand much of this.

Beside the *souvenirs sportifs* and the Normandie mementos, there was another captivating item in the lower cupboard. It was a box filled with my father's tricks and puzzles, mostly objects he had designed and constructed himself. He loved three-dimensional puzzles, interlocking pieces of wood or metal which were almost impossible to re-assemble once they were taken apart. He often distributed them at the end of a family meal, and the guests tried to figure them out. He also made little games to amuse children: small boxes that contained smaller boxes that contained even smaller boxes that contained tiny little boxes. All my young cousins loved Tonton P'tit Louis. They were fascinated by him. He told jokes, did card tricks, folded napkins in the shape of pigeons, told scary stories such as *La Main noire* (The Black Hand), which made one shudder at the beginning, but turned out to be funny at the end. My father was always thinking of ways to entertain people and, in doing so, obviously entertained himself.

In a corner of the dining room, near the window, was a phonograph. It was called (in French) "*un pickup.*" It was not a table-top phonograph but a regular piece of furniture, tall and square. When I was small, one of the things I loved most was to be carried in my father's arms and dance. Papa would put on a record and we would turn around the dining room table; following the rhythm of the music, we danced waltzes, tangos, rumbas, fox-trots ... I remember that I fell into a sort of ecstasy: my eyes closed and my mouth opened a little. My mother used to say, "*Elle se pâme! Elle se pâme!*" ("She is swooning!")

School picture. (1945)

Later on, there would be an addition to the dining room, a piano, set against the wall directly across from the sideboard. It was an upright piano, black and serious looking. On top of it my mother put a frame with my school picture. I looked kind of cute with a missing tooth, but my detachable collar was all crooked, and my hair went every which way; a couple of barrettes did not seem to help.

It was only when we had guests that we ate in the dining room; then, everything became very lively. We pulled out the sides of the table, inserted one or two extensions, and Maman laid out a white tablecloth. We set the table with the fancy pink dishes and the good silverware. Maman brought from the kitchen several platters of well-presented hors d'oeuvres that she placed on the table. Then we waited for our guests to arrive. In their wine glass, the adults would find a white napkin, accordion-folded, opening like a fan, and the children would be happy to play with the pigeon-napkins nestled on their plate. Our guests, of course, always brought a bouquet of flowers, *a* cake from the pastry shop *chez Émorine*, or a *bonne bouteille* of wine. The lunch easily lasted for three hours. Toward the end, when everyone was drinking coffee from the pretty Japanese cups, my cousin Miquette and I sometimes were asked to sing a duet that we performed in costume (and which, I realized later, was the French version of *Buttons and Bows*):

> *J'ai quitté mon vieux rancho*
> *Je suis à San Francisco*
> *Je fréquente en élégante*
> *Pomponnée de la tête aux talons*
> *Les bars chics et les grands salons*
> *J'allais pieds nus dans la rosée*
> *Me voilà métamorphosée*
> *En toilette avec voilette*
> *Mon ombrelle et mon petit manchon*
> *Ma guépière et mes longs jupons*

> I have left my old rancho
> I am in San Francisco.
> Now, a woman of fashion,
> All done-up from head to toe, I frequent
> The chic bars and the grand salons.
> I used to walk barefoot in the dew
> Here I am, metamorphosed!
> All dressed up, with my hat-veil,
> My parasol, my little muff
> My bustier and my long petticoats.

Needless to say, we were a big success.

7
Peaceful Days

Le Premier Mai (May first) was officially Workers' Day, but for my parents it was *La Fête du Muguet,* the Lily of the Valley Festival. The custom was to give relatives and friends a few sprigs of *muguet* as a guarantee of good luck for the year. We could easily have bought the luck-giving white bells from the *muguet* vendors, who suddenly appeared at every corner, but on that day, we didn't buy our lily of the valley, we went to the country to pick it.

My parents woke me up early. We got ready and loaded our bicycles with our picnic provisions. Usually, after meeting with the few relatives not afraid of the long-distance ride, we left for the Forêt d'Armainvilliers, outside Ozoir-la-Ferrière, about thirty miles away. Pedaling at good speed, we crossed several of the small towns to the east of Paris, and soon we were in the country. Papa set the pace, slowing down when someone got tired, which didn't happen often as the roads were flat and the ride easy.

When we arrived in the woods, the first thing we did was to find a good place to rest for a while and have our picnic later. We took out the wine and lemonade, and the men smoked cigarettes. I listened to my father, a natural organizer.

"We'll go pick *muguet* for a couple of hours, and then we'll eat. After that we can either rest or pick more flowers, but by four o'clock, everyone should meet at this spot. We'll tie the bouquets and go home."

We looked both for *jonquilles* (daffodils) and lily of the valley. The *jonquilles* were easy to find as their bright yellow color betrayed them, but the lily of the valley liked to hide in the shade, behind bushes, under trees. But we did find it! Enjoying the earthen smell of the woods, we stepped on spring grass or soft moss, encountering a few mushrooms and perhaps one or two *violettes des bois* (wild violets), survivors of their early spring bloom. There were other people picking flowers, but everyone found enough to gather a good harvest. Now we were ready for our picnic. We opened the bags and took out baguette, *jambon, saucisson sec,* camembert, boiled eggs, cold chicken with mustard, fruit, and, for the adults, plenty of red wine. We talked and laughed and fought the mosquitoes. Some of us went back to pick flowers until it was time to prepare the bouquets.

The daffodils were simply tied with a string, but the lily of the valley was bound according to tradition: the sprigs of delicate white bells were stripped of their long pointed leaves and gathered together in an all-white bouquet around which several layers of leaves were arranged, making each bunch look like a big white flower protected by a green crown, somewhat like a bride's posy. In that way, we tied many lily of the valley bunches, leaving enough free string to fasten them across our backs or attach them to our bikes, suspending them from the handlebars, the frames, and the front and back bike-racks. Finally it was time to go home. Laden with flowers, we rode carefully and crossed the same small towns, this time under the appreciative looks of passers-by.

After we arrived home we still had time to distribute a few sprigs of sweet-smelling *muguet*. "Here you are, Tante Valentine, Oncle Baptiste and Cousin Roger, good luck for the whole year!"

"Here, Monsieur and Madame Mousset and Pierrette, we brought you some *muguet*. And good luck in everything you do!"

It was night now, time to go to bed. I had mosquito bites and my legs were tired. When I closed my eyes, I saw green grass, earth, and pointed *muguet* leaves. Goodnight everyone! Good luck for the whole year!

Long or short bike rides were never a problem for me; they were part of my life as were sports in general. Papa, who was a *sportif*—both an athlete and a sports fan, took me to all sorts of events. On Sundays, we often went to the *vélodrome* to see bicycle speed races, or to various rings to watch boxing or wrestling matches. But it was the cross-country bicycle races that I liked best, especially after the rain when the terrain was muddy and slippery. It made it difficult for the racers to keep their balance; they often slipped and fell. They never seemed to get hurt but ended up covered in mud, which made the race more exciting. My father and I hurried up and down the hills of the racing area. Papa knew all the shortcuts that allowed us to see the racers as they arrived at different points, but we had to run so we wouldn't miss them. We had our favorites, we cheered, *"Vas-y! Courage!"* It was a bit chilly. I could feel my nose getting red.

"Make an effort! You are almost there!"

"He won, Papa, he won! I told you he would win!"

My father held my hand and we went down the hills making sure we didn't slip in the mud. After that we went to a bistro. Papa had one or two glasses of wine, sometimes three, and I was given *une petite grenadine*. Perhaps I would have preferred a nice cup of hot chocolate, but I don't think it came to the mind of either my father or the bistro people.

My father and Maurice Joly.
Nogent. (c. 1946)

Papa also took me fishing. He had a rowboat on the Marne River, near Nogent, a few miles away from Fontenay-sous-Bois. It was a small fishing boat with one pair of oars, just big enough for two people. We left in the morning. I either bicycled alongside my father or we rode on the small motorcycle he had bought at the end of the war. We went to Nogent, a place well-known for its *guinguettes*, dance halls with live bands and accordion music where young men and pretty *midinettes* went on Sundays to have a good time. (The Renoir painting *Les Canotiers* picturing a lunch by the Seine shows that, at the end of the 19th century, the *guinguettes* were already celebrated as places to have fun, places where is was easy for the well-to-do to mix with boatmen and friendly working women.)

Papa rowed his boat away from the dance halls and the restaurants which lined the river bank, their geranium-decorated terraces soon to be filled with chatting customers. Stopping when he found the right spot, he threw his bait, prepared his line, hooked a worm to the hook and began fishing. We talked softly so as not to frighten the fish. Eyes fixed on the floater, I fished too but since I never caught anything I soon got bored. Papa's specialty was small-sized fish, especially *gougeons* (gudgeons); he would throw his line and catch at least two dozens gudgeons in a couple of hours. When he finally rowed back to the shore, I dragged my hand in the green water and felt happy at the prospect of going home. But Papa was not ready yet. He stopped to have two or three glasses of wine or a couple of Pernods at the café owned by the man who looked after his boat. When we arrived home Maman cleaned Papa's catch, rolled the gudgeons in flour and deep fried them. They were small and crunchy; we ate everything, even the bones.

It is also near Nogent, in the calm river Marne, that Papa taught me how to swim. I remember his patience as he held me and gave me confidence. Although the water was not cold, I often felt chilly. Papa, seeing me shivering, was careful not to prolong the lessons. A lot of people swam in that area, especially in a big outdoor swimming pool whose limits were marked by colorful buoys. Children and adults lay on the grass, played in the water or jumped from the tall diving board. A 1929 documentary, *Nogent, Eldorado du dimanche*, by the director of *Children of Paradise*, Marcel Carné, fully captured the spirit of Nogent. Though anterior by at least fifteen years to the time I went there with my father, it shows the same joie de vivre that was (and in a certain measure still is) associated with Nogent.

When I went out with Maman, the outings were different, mostly utilitarian. We went shopping, or to the dress-maker, or the local health clinic. Only once Maman took me to the Musée de l'Orangerie which housed the Impressionist paintings; she had been there before and knew her way around the museum. We stayed a long time in front of her favorite, *La Loge* (The Theater Box), by Renoir.

"J'adore ce tableau, c'est comme si c'était moi dans la loge" ("I adore this painting, it's as if I were there myself in the theater box"), she said, pointing to the beautifully dressed and bejeweled woman with wistful eyes sitting by her companion absorbed in looking through his binoculars. Now I wonder if Maman was nostalgic for another life she might have dreamt of. Was there perhaps some truth to her supposed "friendship" with the aristocrat who "put the ring on her finger?" But we were there to look at art. There was another Renoir that Maman loved: *La Balançoire*. Taking a long look at it, we marveled at the way the painter captured the spots of light shining through the shade of the trees.

My parents and I sometimes went to visit Tante Marthe and Oncle Albert rue Saint Sébastien in the 11th arrondissement, near Boulevard Voltaire. Their apartment, in a run-down building with creaky wooden stairs, was small but cozy. I liked to go there, mostly to be with my cousin Miquette. When I was eleven, she was fourteen, looking older already, tall and shapely, with a special radiance. With her soft chestnut hair, light complexion, deep-blue almond-shaped eyes, high cheekbones and fleshy mouth, she was a true beauty. It was not surprising she was starting to have admirers. I loved listening to her stories. I sometimes stayed over at her house and slept with her in her tiny room that looked more like a closet than a bedroom. It was there, when the two of us were alone in her bed, the door closed, that she told me *"ses amours,"* (her loves), innocent, but to me fascinating.

Miquette's parents were friendly with a married couple who lived in the same apartment building, on the floor below theirs, and with whom they sometimes partied. On a day when my parents and I were invited for dinner, this couple was also there, together with a few more of my uncle and aunt's friends, all sitting elbow-to-elbow around the table in the small apartment. After a while, it became obvious to me that these guests did not behave the way our relatives did at family reunions. The women were fashionable and perfumed. Everyone drank a lot, first wine with the meal, then champagne. Both men and women made loud jokes and laughed at things I didn't understand. The friend from downstairs, Roger (who bore the same name as my cousin but was nothing like him), was particularly rowdy. He suddenly disappeared and Oncle Albert warned us, "Get ready for a surprise when he returns!"

After a while, Roger reappeared, but he was no longer Roger. He was a woman. And what a woman! She had a blond wig, tight clothes and a lot of makeup—eye shadow and bright-red lipstick. This Roger-woman was applauded by all. There was laughter and songs as she began to dance. She soon climbed on the table (a corner of it had quickly been cleared off) to continue her hip-twisting and fake-breasts holding. Everyone laughed and clapped until she lifted her skirts showing her silk slip and panties, her black stockings and garter belt. And she yelled oohs and aahs as people pretended to pinch her bottom. More laughter and more champagne! I had never seen anything like that!

On the way home my father and mother talked in the métro (we had been lucky to catch the last one).

"I understand dressing as a woman for fun," said my father, "but don't you think Roger went a little too far?" My mother agreed.

Christmas and New Year

Although they were a lot of fun, our family parties were never so wild. The best ones were for Christmas or the New Year's when, soon after the war, we resumed the tradition of the two *réveillons* (dinners that lasted most of the night).

Christmas for the children was exciting, although it barely resembled Christmas as we know it now: we didn't have a tree, we didn't have a fireplace (so, there were no stockings hanging from the mantelpiece—we did not even know about that custom), and nobody dressed as *le Père Noël*. We sat for a late dinner, eating course after course, waiting for midnight. For us children, the hard part was to wait for the dinner to be over and for the adults to stop their interminable conversations about the war. Finally when Papa looked at his watch and announced: *"Minuit!"* (Midnight), we all started singing *Minuit Chrétien*—which was a little funny since hardly anyone in my family was Christian. Anyway, we only knew the beginning:

> *Minuit Chrétien, c'est l'heure solennelle*
> *Où l'Homme-Dieu descendit jusqu'à nous*
>
> Christian Midnight! It's the solemn hour
> When the Man-God came down to us.

We did sing another carol, of which at least we knew the first verses:

> *Il est né le divin enfant*
> *Jouez hautbois, résonnez musettes!*
> *Il est né le divin enfant*
> *Chantons tous son avènement*
>
> He is born, the divine child
> Play oboes, ring *musettes*!
> He is born, the divine child
> Let all of us sing His Advent

After that, there was a mysterious signal among the adults. When the Christmas dinner was at Tante Yvonne's house, Papa or Oncle Marcel would get up, go to one of the bedrooms and tap very hard on the inside wall of the bedroom, several times, boom, boom, boom. At that, everyone turned to my cousin Bernard and me, and said, *"Le Père Noël est arrivé!"*

Happy that the moment had finally come, Bernard and I rushed to the bedroom and there, we would find our presents, all laid out on the bed, unwrapped. There were board games and a Meccano erector set for Bernard, a doll or a paint box for me, and children's books for both of us.

When the Christmas celebration was held at Tante Valentine's it was the same routine: a long meal, and then... Boom, Boom, Boom on the other side of the wall... "Le Père Noël est arrivé!" The only difference was that, after we opened our presents, my cousin Miquette, her brothers Jacques and Claude, and I held each other by the hand and gathered around the *salamandre*, the little round charcoal stove in the dining room. After counting *"Un, deux, trois,"* we shouted together: *"Merci Père Noël!"*

It was not elaborate but we were happy.

The *réveillons* were held either at my parents or my relatives' houses, but in 1945, when the war ended and we could at last celebrate with much fancier meals, Papa, Maman, Tante Valentine, Madame Mousset, and Monsieur and Madame Brusson got together to organize a memorable New Year's Eve *Réveillon* to be held after hours "Chez Brusson." Since we were still in the rationing period, everyone pooled their food coupons together. Besides that, and thanks to prized connections with farmers in the country, the black market, and every possible kind of barter, everyone managed to gather all the food necessary for the celebration.

After a day of preparations, dishes cooked at home were taken to the café (if need be they would be re-heated at the last minute in the bistro's tiny kitchen). The dinner party was to start around 9 p.m. The billiard table was pushed into a corner, tables were placed end-to-end to fill the whole length of the café, and crepe paper garlands with hanging lanterns were stretched across the ceiling. There were white tablecloths and nice sets of dishes borrowed from various households. Places were marked for each guest, the children sitting among the adults. First, aperitif was served at the café counter: a choice of Dubonnet, Cinzano, Ricard, pastis, etc. It made people feel relaxed and already slightly dizzy.

Everyone found their seats. First the oysters on the half-shell were brought out (several men had worked hard at opening them). Fresh and appetizing, resting on crushed ice, and served with a vinegar and shallot sauce on the side, they were accompanied by *bonnes bouteilles* of white wine from Monsieur Brusson's cellar. Then came the hors-d'oeuvre platters, some of these with *charcuterie*, such as *pâté truffé, rillettes du*

Périgord, saucisson de Lyon, andouillette, some with *crudités*: radishes cut in the shape of roses, grated carrots next to grated celery roots *à la moutarde,* and others still with *oeufs Mimosa,* shrimp and vegetable macédoine served with home-made mayonnaise.

The guests numbered about thirty, the men in shirts and ties, the women lovely, made up and perfumed, their hair nicely curled, sometimes pouffed above the forehead as was the fashion of the time. Everyone was in a happy mood, talking and laughing, smoking while waiting for the next dish. No one was in a hurry. Maman, Tante Valentine, Madame Mousset, my cousins Paulette and Denise were the cooks. The plats de résistance appeared: fish in white wine sauce, roasted ducks with fresh peas, and, of course, the traditional *gigots* (leg of lamb) spiked with garlic, served with dishes of creamy *mousseline* mashed potatoes and *flageolets verts* with country butter. After that, bowls of fresh lettuce, and, of course, trays with all kinds of cheese, from special Camemberts, to Bries, to Roqueforts, all from various provinces. The bottles of wine kept appearing, Burgundies, Bordeaux, a very special Châteauneuf-du-Pape and other such treats. Suddenly the guests realized that it was almost twelve. They counted down the minutes and . . . "Happy New Year!" Kisses all around. *"Bonne année! Bonne santé!"* Even grumpy Oncle Marcel, who had complained about the oysters, even dear Tante Valentine who had worried so much that the *gigots* would be overcooked (they were not) smiled and kissed everyone. Happy New Year! And no more wars! No more wars! Serve the dessert and the champagne! Raising his glass, Papa offered fancy toasts and all the guests raised their glasses and sang along with him:

> *Chic à l'amour à la mignonette*
> *Chic à l'amour à la mignona*
> *Ah! Ah! Ah! Mignonette*
> *Ah! Ah! Ah! Mignona*

> Here is to love and a little cutie
> Here is to love and a cutie-Ah
> Ah! Ah! Ah! Little cutie
> Ah! Ah! Ah! Cutie-Ah

Then came the *bombe glacée* (an ice-cream dessert), and finally the *pièce montée,* a tall cake made of *choux à la crème* (cream puffs), and more champagne, still more champagne, then the baskets of fruit, then the coffee, then the liqueurs. The guests were now quite dizzy, the voices higher, the laughter easier. Beautiful Tante Yvonne showed how tanned her legs were, even in the middle of winter. Madame Mousset told stories about her youth, when she worked at the Folies Bergères or the Casino de Paris as a wardrobe lady for Mistinguett and Maurice Chevalier (penny pinchers, both of them!). The children ran around throwing confetti, until the adults decided it was time to entertain them with a game of musical chairs.

After the game everyone danced to Papa's records. Young and old danced with the small children, and I danced with my cousins and my friend Pierrette. Then, forming a line, each person holding on to the waist of the person in front, the guests did a chain dance, a *farandole* and snaked around the café, past the wooden bar with its zinc counter, past the billiard table, around the big table still laden with desserts, singing, following the leader, walk-dancing, kicking their legs on command. Soon everyone was tired. Out of breath, blowing air through their cheeks and wiping their forehead, the *farandoleurs* plopped back into their chairs.

Then, after everyone had rested a little, Papa announced: "Time for chansons!" And he was the first to sing to put all the guests in the mood. His repertoire was comic; he often sang songs made famous by singers of the thirties such as Georgius or (more rarely) Maurice Chevalier.

Meanwhile, just before it was her turn to sing, Maman disappeared for a while and came back transformed: she had blackened several of her front teeth to make it look as if she had some teeth missing. She wore a scarf tied under her chin, and an apron over her dress (she didn't mind looking ugly if it was needed for the stage). She sang about a naive peasant woman, who, at the end of the song, turned out to be not so naive after all. My parents had a lot of success and were often asked for encores. Papa sang another Georgius number and Maman my favorite song, *Son joli p'tit chose.* She had reappeared, pretty again, and, as a grand finale, she was the daring demoiselle as she sang in duet with Papa, *Faites ça pour moi*

(Please do that for me). Then it was time for Oncle Baptiste to sing *Ils ont des chapeaux ronds,* his usual couplet from Brittany. Now Tante Valentine was ready to move us all with her *Train of Misery*: "Roule, roule, train du malheur!" Grand-mère Cessot had a classy number about *La Païva*, a famous cocotte who broke men's hearts and emptied their wallets:

> *Jadis vivait sous l'Empire*
> *Une superbe étaïre*
> *Belle comme tout*
> *En grand tralala*
> *On l'appelait "La Païva."*

> Long ago under the Empire
> Lived a superb courtesan
> Pretty as they come
> Dressed in grand tralala
> She was called "La Païva."

Another of my Grand-mère's big successes (which I understand used to be in Grand-père Cessot's repertoire) was the ballad of two bandits sharing their thoughts on the difficulties of their trade, and the sad possibility they might end up under the guillotine:

> *Vous êtes gras, joufflu, bien bâti*
> *Et"couic!" v'la qu'on vous raccourcit*
> *Après, vous êtes méconnaissable.*
> *On n'a pas d'chance dans c'métier-là!*

> You are plump, chubby-faced, well-built
> and "zap!" you are suddenly shortened.
> After that, you are unrecognizable.
> There is no luck in this blasted trade!

Tante Yvonne couldn't hold a tune but was very willing to sing *"avec les gestes"* (with all the gestures). One of her songs was *Le Vagabond*, the frightening story of a sinister beggar going from place to place, carrying his dreadful knife. The end went like this:

Il sortit son couteau de sa poche
Et planta sa terrible lame

He pulled his knife from his pocket
And stuck his terrible blade

(Here, we expected the worst, but Tante Yvonne sang on)

Dans la miche de pain!

In the loaf of bread!
What a relief!

Tante Marthe's beautiful voice never failed to send a shiver down our spines. Too bad she was shy and rarely consented to sing, but when she did, we were all moved by her melodious voice rising and falling with the tune, quivering a little from stage fright. Her repertoire was quite romantic:

Mon coeur est un violon
Sur lequel ton archet joue
Et qui vibre tout du long
Appuyé contre ta joue

My heart is a violin
Upon which your bow is playing
And which vibrates throughout
Cradled against your cheek.

After a while Monsieur Brusson led all the guests in singing along with him:

Joyeux enfants de la Bourgogne
Je suis fier d'être Bourguignon
Quand je vois rougir ma trogne
Je suis fier d'être Bourguignon

> Happy children of Burgundy
> I'm proud to be a Bourguignon
> When I see my mug turn red
> I'm proud to be a Bourguignon.

Then all the guests sitting around the table put their arms around one another's shoulders and, swaying like a wave, sang all together:

> *Ah! Ah! Ah! Ah! Ah, mon amour*
> *Ah! Ah! Ah! Ah! À toi toujours!*
>
> Ah! Ah! Ah! Ah! Ah, my love
> Ah! Ah! Ah! Ah! Yours forever!

And

> *Ah! Le petit vin blanc*
> *Qu'on boit sous la tonnelle*
> *Quand les filles sont belles*
> *Du côté de Nogent.*
>
> Ah! The good little white wine
> We drink under the pergola
> When the girls are pretty
> Round about Nogent

It was two o'clock in the morning, maybe three, maybe four, the children were falling asleep everywhere, but the adults were still going, some happy, some sleepy, some philosophical, some crying, some laughing. Happy New Year my friends! And no more wars! No more wars!

SEVEN

1946 - 1948

1
Papa's Songs and a Trip to Le Havre

Whenever someone got ready to take a picture, my father turned his head a little to the side, fixed his eyes on a distant point, and assumed a serious, even stern, expression. When I look at these pictures, I know he didn't really look like that. Fortunately, when the camera happened to catch him before he struck his usual pose, I can see him just the way he was, with a spark in his eyes and a hint of mischief in his little crooked smile.

This is the image I have of my father. I can still see him at his workbench in our garage, building or repairing something, while at the same time singing and imitating Joséphine Baker's "exotic" accent in her famous hit:

> *J'ai deux amours*
> *Mon pays et Paris*
>
> I have two loves
> My country and Paris

Or, with a good dose of drama, striking up the old standby:

> *C'est la Femme aux Bijoux*
> *Celle qui rend fou*
> *C'est une enjoleuse*
> *L'homme n'est qu'un joujou*
> *Pour la Femme aux Bijoux*

> She is the Jewel Woman,
> the one who drives you insane.
> She is a vamp, a deceiver.
> A man is nothing but a toy
> in the hands of the Jewel Woman.

Papa was a good-looking man with green-brown eyes, a big straight Norman nose, a squarish chin with a masculine cleft, and exquisitely-drawn lips. Too bad a combination of sun, wine and Pernod had succeeded in making his complexion a little too florid, too bad also the thick curly hair of his youth was no more, replaced by a wavy crown encircling the bald spot he liked to refer to as his *"tonsure."*

Of medium height, well-built, Papa retained for a long time the agility acquired during his many years of practicing sports. He liked to go swimming, thought nothing of jumping on his bicycle for short or long rides, and, in his profession as a printer, used a great deal of strength. He was especially proud of his wide shoulders and muscular arms. I remember my feelings as a young girl: to walk at his side was to be protected.

Papa was not exactly a model of elegance and was even known for following fashions already fallen by the wayside. For instance, he was one to keep wearing "golf pants" (like those of the famous Tintin) after everyone had abandoned them. He also remained faithful to his dear *casquettes*—these flat tweedy caps with a visor, popular in the thirties, but less so thereafter. However, as he grew older, he dressed not only in the fashion of the day, but even with a certain *cachet*. When he rode the métro to and from work, he always wore shirt and tie under his sports jacket. In the winter, with his fedora, his tweed overcoat or his trench coat, he saw himself as a Jean Gabin-type, or perhaps as Simenon's *Inspecteur Maigret*. He sometimes told us with a smile that, when he sat at a café counter, he could tell that people took him for a police *inspecteur* by the side looks they gave him and the way they had of behaving properly.

In fact, it was Papa himself who had a certain fear of the police, and that in spite of the fact he was honest to a fault. He told me that it all started when he was a child. His mother had sent him to the *boulangerie* to buy bread. While the *boulangère* was in the back of her store, he snatched a small fruitcake (which, in French, is called "*un cake*") from the counter display.

"*Petit Voleur!*" (Little thief!), the *boulangère* shouted as she returned just in time to catch him in the act. Papa was so ashamed that he never again laid a hand on anything that wasn't his. The fear of the *boulangère* remained forever in his heart. Nonetheless, that very day he swore to himself that when he grew up he would eat *cake* for breakfast, lunch and dinner.

My father was very proud; he had an almost obsessive preoccupation with not "losing face," as we put it now. Whatever happened to him that was slightly negative or embarrassing was "rewritten" in his head before he told other people about it. However, with my mother and me, he was open about these unhappy occurrences and occasionally asked for our help in concocting a more presentable version of the truth.

His reluctance to appear ridiculous sometimes pushed him to do impractical things. Once when he was riding his motorcycle one of the tires blew out. As he walked his bike up the rue Jules Ferry just before turning off at the villa de l'Ouest, he happened to run into Madame Brusson who was standing outside her café.

"*Ah! Monsieur Gauthier, vous avez crevé!*" ("Ah! Monsieur Gauthier, you have a flat tire!")

Probably because of the bad quality of the tires, it happened a second time. Again he had to walk his motorcycle up the rue Jules Ferry, and again he ran into Madame Brusson. Her half-amused, half-mocking smile put even more lines on her crumpled little face, and, in her high-pitched voice, she said, "*Ah! Monsieur Gauthier vous avez encore crevé!*" ("Ah! Monsieur Gauthier, you have another flat tire!")

As bad luck would have it, it happened once more. That time, my father couldn't take the chance of running into Madame Brusson. To avoid passing in front of the café, he walked his motorbike up several back streets until he arrived rue Gambetta, and then, carried it all the way down the cement steps of the villa de l'Ouest.

But these were only quirks in Papa's personality. Other things were more important. Next to his warmth, his good-spirit, what was immediately noticeable about him was his intelligence. To me, it was also his language. He didn't speak in the trailing nasal intonations characteristic of Parisians blue-collar workers, but in a rather refined tone, and expressed himself in a truly unique fashion. Although he was a master of argot, the French slang that is a language in itself, he used it sparsely, and at appropriate times. From it, he borrowed newly introduced terms, revived older ones, or picked some that were specific to the printing world. He integrated this into his colorful French already dotted with colloquial expressions, popular catch-phrases, proverbs, and even poetic terms. All this wordplay produced in me an early awareness of language. I especially liked the strange words that crept up in some of the mysterious-sounding songs that Papa used to sing:

> Dans les montagnes du Hoggar
> Une reine au méchant regard
> Au coeur félon
> Règne, dit-on,
> Antinéa, c'est son nom.

> In the Hoggar Mountains
> A queen with an evil look
> And a felonious heart
> Reigns, it is said.
> Antinea is her name.

What distinguished my father from many other people around us was the number of *chansons* he had memorized and the pleasure he had in singing them. Whether he was getting ready in the morning, busy in his workshop, driving his car, or entertaining guests, he always found some songs to pick from his repertoire. These songs, part of the weft of French popular culture, are still celebrated today, and are being reissued into *"albums de chansons rétro."* Maman and I listened to my father sing as an everyday matter. His songs, the words more important than the tunes, were part of our life as were the names of the singers popular in the thirties:

Tino Rossi, Damia, Rina Ketty, Germaine Sablon and her brother Jean Sablon, Lys Gauty, Lucienne Boyer, Mireille or Marie Dubas.

Un souvenir, c'est l'image d'un rêve
D'une heure brêve
Qui ne veut pas finir

A memory is the shadow of a dream
Of a brief hour
That doesn't want to end

J'attendrai le jour et la nuit
J'attendrai toujours
Ton retour

I will wait day and night
I will wait always
For your return

Un amour comme le nôtre
Il n'en existe pas deux
Ce n'est pas celui des autres
C'est quelque chose de mieux

A love such as ours
There is not another like it,
It is not like the love of other people
It is something much better

My parents' musical taste was not limited to popular songs. Unfamiliar as they were with what they called *"la grande musique,"* they did not listen to Bach or Beethoven, but loved Johann Strauss' Viennese waltzes, Franz Lehár's *The Merry Widow*, and other such favorites. Before the war they often went to see operettas, and now they looked forward to being able to see again *L'Auberge du Cheval Blanc, Violettes imperiales*, and all the big successes of the time. Once, for a special treat they took me to the Théâtre du Châtelet to see Hammerstein and Harbach's *Rosemary*. I am sorry to say that, except for the songs, I remember practically nothing of it; too short to see the stage, I could only catch a few glimpses of the spectacle.

And so, life was normal again. Papa filled the house with songs; I did my homework under my mother's loving eyes in the glow of the kitchen's pulley lamp. I was eleven, happy. My mind was simple. I knew nothing of the outside world and had only a vague idea of what had really happened during the war. However, all that was soon to change.

In the summer of 1946, my parents decided to visit their good friends, Jeannette and André, in Le Havre, a major French port on the English Channel. We took the train. Our friends waited for us at the station and drove us directly to their apartment building, which by chance had not been bombed. The day after our arrival Jeannette and André took us to see what remained of their city. Block after block, everything had been reduced to rubble. Now almost two years after the bombings, the streets were cleared off and the stones from the downed buildings neatly piled up, but the whole city remained a sight of destruction I will never forget. One

Remnants of war damages on the beach. In front, at right: my mother. In back: I am standing with friends. Le Havre. (1946)

could see far in all directions, and there was nothing left. On some streets, little wooden cabin-like stores had been built and people were shopping. We couldn't get close to the port, still off-limits to the public. In one district razed by Allied bombings, only one structure had remained standing: the World War I monument to the dead.

In the days that followed, we went to the beach. Off-shore we could see the half-sunken remains of several warships. On the beach itself (a beach of pebbles, not of sand) there were patches from an oil spill; we had to be careful not to sit on the sticky black stuff. Our friends' daughter, Ginette, took me to visit a blockhaus, one of the concrete bunkers erected

Sunken warships. My father, me, my mother, a friend. Le Havre. (1946)

along the Normandy coast by the Germans. It was dark and empty inside and smelled of urine because people now used it as a toilet.

In spite of these reminders of the war, we all shared happy moments. After a long separation my parents and their friends were glad to see one another. There were walks in the country, jokes, good food and wine. André had a great sense of humor and Jeannette was extremely nice, but the person who captured my attention was their beautiful daughter Ginette, who at that time must have been about nineteen or twenty. In the morning when she got up, she walked around in her nightgown or her slip and made little comments about this and that. One day she peeked down into her slip and took a look at her breasts.

"You poor little bumpkins," she said, "you woke up all crumpled this morning!"

Nobody in my family would ever have dared say anything like that! I was filled with admiration.

I remember this vacation with nostalgia since it was the last time I would see my mother healthy and carefree. She looked beautiful in her two-piece bathing suit as she playfully jumped over the waves with Papa and me. And when we went for an excursion up on a hill dominating the town and the sea, she and our lady friends did silly exercises on the grass. The photos that were taken that day show Maman full of life and happiness.

A few months after the trip to Le Havre my mother fell ill and had to go to a hospital in Paris for surgery. What we thought was going to be a simple hysterectomy turned out to be much more serious. Everyday, I went with my father to visit Maman in the hospital. She never complained, waiting patiently for her health to improve. She was told nothing of her condition and neither was I. While I was sad to see my mother in the hospital, I don't remember being extremely worried, as I had no doubt she would soon get better.

In the ward next to hers was a little orphaned girl about my age, whom the hospital staff and patients had more or less adopted. Encouraged by my mother, I often went to talk to her. She had been in the hospital a long time, recuperating from burns suffered during one of the worst fights of the Allied landing on the Normandy Coast. She was from Falaise, a town near Omaha Beach, and the seat of the famous "Falaise Pocket Battle," fought between the Allied and a strong contingent of resisting Germans. In this battle, hundreds of soldiers lost their lives. The little girl's burns were on part of her face and most of her body. She showed me her scars. She was so brave, so grown-up that I didn't know what to say.

2
My Mother's Death

On March 27, 1947, when I came back from school I found my father, my grandmother, and Tante Valentine in my house. They were waiting for an ambulance. My mother was having a hemorrhage. Soon, the ambulance arrived. My mother was placed on a stretcher and taken to the hospital, my father at her side. The ambulance screeching in the villa de l'Ouest, taking my mother away, is something I will never forget.

At the hospital, they stopped the hemorrhage, but, as I realized later, my mother had cancer. The cancer, which could have been ovarian or uterine cancer, had been diagnosed when she had her hysterectomy, but at that time only my father had been told. She stayed for a time at the hospital where she had been taken, then was transferred to the *Institut du Cancer* in Villejuif (a suburb of Paris) where she stayed until the month of June.

My father visited her every day. I went with him or my grandmother on the days when I had no school. My mother was very pale; she sometimes looked yellow. At the hospital she received radium treatments, treatments that made her sick. At first, she had no strength, but after a while she recuperated a little. To reassure me, she and my father told me she would be cured and go back home. But when she finally returned home, it meant that nothing more could be done for her.

At home she tried to resume her normal life, but it was obvious that she was getting weaker. She had pains in her stomach and had to rest often. She still tried to take care of the house and do some cooking, but my grandmother had to come and help and we had to hire a housekeeper. Maman was always irritated with my grandmother. She told her that she couldn't do anything right: the food was too greasy; the kitchen was never clean enough, and so on. As for me, it was with the housekeeper that I was irritated. She was hard of hearing, and, as she could never understand what I was trying to tell her, she encouraged me to communicate by notes.

But every time I handed her a note she burst out laughing, *"Fautes d'orthographe! Fautes d'orthographe!"* ("Spelling mistakes! Spelling mistakes!") To her, it was the funniest thing on earth.

During the summer I was sent to spend two or three weeks at the home of our friends André and Jeannette in Le Havre. They were very nice to me. I had fun and went camping with their daughter Ginette, her fiancé and their friends. My father had bought me a camera; it was the first time I took photos and I enjoyed it very much. In July, the Le Havre family accompanied me back home and stayed at our house for a day or two. At that time my mother could still get up, but it was obvious that her health was deteriorating rapidly.

By the end of the summer, her pains had increased. She stayed in her upstairs bedroom most of the day, getting up with our help for only a few hours, sometimes taking the sun in a chaise longue in the backyard. I did not know the nature or the gravity of my mother's illness; nothing was said to me, the word cancer was never pronounced. I suspected she might have cancer because she had been hospitalized at the Cancer Institute in Villejuif, but when I asked, I was told that not everyone there had cancer, some people, like my mother, were treated in that hospital without having cancer.

From then on my mother's condition worsened every day; her stomach pains became almost unbearable. Now she stayed in bed all the time, and, from downstairs, we could hear her moaning. She would often moan when she thought I wasn't in the house, but sometimes when I was doing my homework in the kitchen or in the dining-room, I would hear her heart-rending wails. I would run upstairs, and she cried, and I kissed her face and hands, and I cried with her.

"I do not want to leave you," she would say. And I told her that I didn't want her to leave me. "I suffer, I suffer so much. What did I ever do to God?" she asked, even though she didn't believe in God.

I didn't know what to do. Sometimes I got in bed with her, but I had to be very careful because the slightest movement caused her pain.

"I have always been sick," she told me. "When I breast-fed your little brother, I got breast abscesses; it was extremely painful. One time, I got very ill; nobody knew what I had. It turned out to be a tropical disease that I had caught at the *Exposition Coloniale*. And another time I almost died when I had appendicitis that turned into peritonitis. Even my twentieth birthday, I spent it in the hospital!"

Sometimes Maman got angry and complained. She said that when she needed something and called from upstairs, nobody responded. She acted as if we ignored her on purpose, as if we didn't care about her. But we cared so much.

One evening when my grandmother wasn't there, I was in the kitchen by myself when my father came home. We never knew when he would arrive because of his irregular working hours and also because he always stopped at cafés for a few glasses of wine. He often arrived home, not exactly drunk, but not quite in his normal state. That night, when he came home, I could see in his eyes that he had been drinking. He went upstairs to see my mother. I didn't hear anything for a while. Then, suddenly, I heard both of them sing. They were singing the duet they sang at the Vincennes Sportif galas: *Faites ça pour moi*, and the songs they sang at our family reunions; they were singing as they always had, their voices mixing so well:

> *Excusez ma franchise*
> *Cher monsieur entre nous*
> *Il faut que je vous l'dise*
> *J'ai le béguin pour vous*

> Excuse my directness
> Dear sir, between you and me,
> I must tell you
> I have a crush on you.

> *Un souvenir, c'est l'image d'un rêve*
> *D'une heure brève*
> *Qui ne veut pas finir*

> A memory is the shadow of a dream
> Of a brief hour
> That doesn't want to end
>
> *Un amour comme le nôtre*
> *Il n'en existe pas deux*
> *Ce n'est pas celui des autres*
> *C'est quelque chose de mieux*
>
> A love such as ours
> There is not another like it.
> It is not like the love of other people
> It is something much better

They sang their repertoire, happy songs, funny songs, sentimental songs. They sang as if they would never sing again. And alone in the kitchen I cried and cried, and I knew that upstairs, they were crying as they sang. Even today, after so many years, it is hard for me to think of that evening without crying.

By October, my mother's health had deteriorated even further. She now looked older than her age. Her beautiful face had become sallow and drawn. She had almost no strength, but with the little she had, she managed to knit a cotton undershirt for my father's birthday. She asked me to write a card to attach to her present. In school I had just learned that, if one wanted to write something serious, it should be done in black ink on white paper. I used my best handwriting and created a formal black and white card that read: *Bon Anniversaire, Papa!* (Happy Birthday, Papa!), and gave it to my mother.

"Why black and white?" she said, "do you think I'm already dead?"

I could not show her how hurt I was, so I said nothing. I remade a card with all the letters in different colors. She was happy and said, "Now, that's more like it!"

All the family came to see my mother. Everyone felt helpless.

One day she told me, "After I die, I want you to have my wedding ring. You could have a stone mounted on it, or you could wear it as it is." She knew she would die soon, we all knew it. I knew it too, but I couldn't accept the idea of her death. Papa couldn't either. Since the doctors gave my mother no chance of survival, he turned to providers of so-called "miracle" remedies. He brought in bottles of water that were supposed to contain special curing chemicals, but of course, that didn't help.

Not long after that, my mother was in such great pain that she had to be given high doses of morphine. For some time now a nurse had been coming every day. Maman drifted away in another world and said nonsensical things when she talked to us. "I have seen the white wolf," she said to me one day. My grandmother told me not to pay attention. And then, my father said that it would be better for me to sleep at my friend Pierrette's for a while. I did that for a few days; then Papa came to pick me up and said that he wanted to talk to me. It was evening; the street lights were already lit. We went up the stone stairs of the villa de l'Ouest, turned left on rue Gambetta, and walked and walked while my father talked. He told me that my mother was dying, that soon she would be dead—and even though I had feared it, I had not allowed myself to believe it. Tears were running from my eyes, and my father was crying too. I do not know what else he said. We just walked in the streets of Fontenay, talking and crying, our hearts broken.

The next day, on November 30th, at the age of forty-five, my mother died. I was told I should go and see her to say my last goodbye. I went upstairs. My father, grandmother and aunts were in the room. My mother was wearing the pretty dress she had liked so much, the dark-blue one with little white dots. She looked as if she were sleeping. Someone said to me that I should give her a last kiss. I bent down and kissed her, and her skin was so cold. I cannot remember much after that, except that my aunt Valentine pressed me against her heart and said, "My poor little one, you have lost so much!" That night and the next, I went back to Pierrette's house and slept there.

Since I needed to have dark clothes to go to the funeral, I was taken to buy a dark-blue coat. Someone also said that women had to wear hats, but as I was only twelve I should wear a beret; and I had to go and buy a beret.

Soon the funeral was being prepared. In front of my house a change had taken place. Against the left part of our wooden fence there was now a mortuary that looked like a square tent with walls and ceiling made of heavy black cloth. The mortuary's open front was framed by black drapes clutched like curtains on both sides. In that little room my mother's coffin had been placed and was surrounded by a great quantity of flowers in wreaths or in bouquets, with cards from relatives, friends, neighbors, and all my playmates. To this day I cannot remember the details of the funeral. Although the procession must have started from my house in the villa de l'Ouest, I only recall it from the time we were near the cemetery. I do remember getting ready and looking at my image in the mirror with my dark coat and beret. I barely recognized myself and wondered if I would cry. And what if I didn't cry? Would people think I didn't love my mother? My memory of the procession starts on the hilly street leading to the cemetery, as I walked behind the hearse drawn by two horses. My grandmother, aunts and female cousins were by my side; the men of the family were in front, Papa walking first. Behind us were our friends and neighbors. As in a dream, I remember the cobblestones under my feet as I went up the steep street that I knew so well for having taken it so many times with my mother when we went to the cemetery. The procession passed the church of Saint-Germain-l'Auxerrois and the crumbling stone wall of the old monastery. Then we arrived at the top and entered the cemetery.

Since we were not Christian, there was no ceremony at my mother's grave. I only remember that someone gave me a flower to throw on the coffin. I threw my flower, thinking that only my mother knew how much I loved her. After that, the family gathered so people could offer their condolences. We formed a line and people shook our hands or kissed us. It was windy and cold. Everyone was terribly sad. One of my aunts said that I should not be made to stand there like an adult, and I was taken off the line. After the funeral the family went to Tante Valentine's house. That night, my cousins Miquette, Jacques, Claude, and I slept there, on the dining room floor, in improvised beds.

3
Tante Valentine, Oncle Baptiste and Roger

When I returned to school I didn't know how to act and my classmates didn't know what to do. I knew that they all thought of me as "the girl whose mother died," but I behaved normally, as if nothing had happened. And somehow it seemed to work. At least, my friends didn't dare approach the subject. The one thing I couldn't bring myself to do was to participate in choral singing; I felt it would have been disrespectful to my mother's memory. At home, my father stopped singing too. I missed my mother terribly, but I only cried in my room, where nobody could see me. I felt alone and abandoned. At night I often dreamt that Maman was not really dead, but was sick, far away, and would come back. Sometimes I dreamt that it was not my mother who had died, but my father, and when I had this dream I felt relieved, for the death of my father would have been easier to bear.

At home, it was as though my father and I had agreed not to talk about my mother. We both understood that it was our way of dealing with her death. The word "cancer" was banned from the house.

I was consulted about new living arrangements. Did I want to move next door with Tante Valentine, Oncle Baptiste and Roger, or would I rather stay at my house and live with my father? I didn't want to move out; I preferred to stay home where I had my own bedroom, my books and all my things. A compromise was worked out: I would stay at my house, but take my meals at Tante Valentine's. At noon, I would go from school to my aunt's house to eat lunch, and at 6 p.m., when school ended I would go to my house and wait there until my aunt called me for dinner. As for the nights, it was agreed that if my father came home before ten, I would sleep at home; if not, I would sleep at Tante Valentine's (this was to ensure that I didn't remain alone at night when Papa came home late, or not at all). Besides these arrangements, it was agreed that I would spend every Thursday (since there was no school on Thursdays) at Tante Yvonne's.

I soon got used to my new routine. I went home after school and waited for Tante Valentine to call me when dinner was ready. Since I couldn't always hear her calling me, she rang a bell from her open kitchen window. For many reasons, but mainly to preserve his personal freedom, my father did not consider taking his meals at Tante Valentine's. He preferred to eat at restaurants near his work, or whenever possible Chez Brusson, where the owners, in true bistro fashion, prepared a few extra meals besides theirs, keeping a *table d'hôte* for two or three paying guests. They served hearty bistro fare and announced *le plat du jour* on a slate hung under a shelf upon which stood a round aquarium, home to a small eel, forever undulating.

In theory, all this was fine, but in practice things didn't go that smoothly. My father did not adjust well to my mother's death and spent less and less time at home, leaving me almost always alone in the evenings. And when he did come home, he often had been drinking. Well aware that he drank too much, he put a stop to all criticisms by making a point of proclaiming: "My daughter never saw me drunk!" It was true. Not once did I see him incoherent or passed out, but I saw him in an altered state more times that I can count.

Every day, I wished he would come home early. If only he could be home when I come back from school at six, I thought, or at least arrive before I return from eating dinner at Tante Valentine's! For when he was home early, he was sober and we could have nice conversations. But if he arrived after nine, it meant that he had stopped at several cafés and had a few drinks too many. Then, he was not the same person. At the slightest provocation, he exploded in anger (though he never got angry at me), raised his voice, and pounded his fist on the table. For instance, the mere mention of hitchhikers made him fly into a rage,

"Can't they work and pay for train tickets like everyone else?"

He railed at people who listened to classical music,

"I don't have time for that, *moi*! I have to work to earn my beefsteak!"

Once, he even blew up when he heard on the radio a poem by Victor Hugo on the death of his child,

"How can someone who lost a child write poetry about it!"

I quickly found out what triggered his anger and learned to avoid touchy subjects. Papa could also turn "philosophical," as he put it, and sometimes talked to me at length about the meaning of life, loneliness, how he did not care about what people thought of him (he did!) . . . until I went to bed. After that, he fell asleep in the kitchen, his head resting on his folded arms on the table.

Every evening between nine and ten, I looked at the clock, wishing he would not arrive. If he wasn't home by ten o'clock, I was glad to escape and go to sleep at Tante Valentine's. But why didn't I go earlier? Why did I stick so much to the rule according to which I would only spend the night at Tante Valentine's if my father wasn't home by ten? I really don't know. I guess it didn't come to my mind to break our agreement—or perhaps I didn't want to miss the opportunity to spend some time with Papa if perchance he arrived sober.

At Tante Valentine's I was safe from my father's ravings, but I didn't really feel at ease. My aunt and uncle's home was quite different from mine. For one thing, the dinner table conversation was never very exciting. Oncle Baptiste's views of the world were rather basic. The only thing he read was the communist newspaper *L'Humanité*. He had no doubt that Stalin well deserved his nickname: *Le Petit Père des Peuples* (Little Father of the People). But politics was not my uncle's favorite subject. He preferred to talk about the weather, his garden, and the few chickens and rabbits he still kept. He also was fond of making "deep" pronouncements such as: "The onion is the king of the vegetables!" or "The stem of the artichoke is the best part!" It makes me smile now, but at that time, I just couldn't bear these kinds of statements.

Tante Valentine and I often had nice chats over coffee when Oncle Baptiste was not home. I realized how disappointed she was with her life, and how bitter she felt in finding herself in a situation she knew would never change. Engaged in her twenties to marry the brother of one of my father's best friends, she had been crushed when the young man was killed just before the end of World War I. After the war she had met Baptiste who seemed to be a very nice man. Knowing she would never love anyone as she had loved her fiancé, she had decided to marry this new suitor. Baptiste, as it turned out, was indeed very nice, but, alas, rather boring. He lived an uncomplicated life and didn't show much ambition. Truly, he and Tante Valentine had managed to save enough money to buy their house in the villa de l'Ouest, but unlike my father, who owned a car and took his family to the Côte d'Azur or other such places, Oncle Baptiste showed little interest in learning how to drive; he was content with puttering in his garage and growing his vegetables. Tante Valentine didn't dislike her husband; she even called him affectionately *"mon p'tit homme,"* but I knew she would have liked to lead a grander life, go to the opera, ride in a nice car, and go to the seaside.

Tante Valentine. (1940)

Everyone viewed her as a pudgy little lady whose greatest pleasure was to made cakes and cookies for her nephews and nieces, but I began to understand that this was far from being the complete picture: Her sister Marthe fancied herself as a Hollywood belle, and her brother (my father) was an ex-bicycle champion and a born entertainer. In reality Tante Valentine was just like her siblings: eager to be in the limelight—but it didn't show, or perhaps it did when she got angry at Oncle Baptiste for almost no reason and screamed at him in frustration.

Another cruel blow dealt to my aunt had to do with her son Roger. When Tante Valentine began to take care of me, I was twelve and Roger was twenty-seven. He was already working in Paris, at the same Swiss insurance company where he would work until his retirement, for a total of forty-five years. People had a tendency to regard Roger as simple-minded when, in fact, he was intelligent but "different." His facial expressions, his body language easily revealed that he was not completely normal. Tante Valentine was aware of the situation, but refused to acknowledge it and was obsessed with the desire to see Roger married. She tried to marry him off to every available young woman she met or even heard about. It had become a joke in the family. Even my cousin Denise in her youth had been thought of as a good prospect. At family dinners, Oncle Baptiste's second cousin from Brittany, Geneviève, was always strategically placed next to Roger, who showed absolutely no interest in her—or in any other women. He didn't show interest in men either, although it is possible he might have if society had been more open at the time. At work, Roger got along well with his colleagues. Our dinner conversation often centered on what had happened in his office that day. Among his co-workers was a beautiful blonde nicknamed *"La Pin-up,"* and a thin young man whom Roger always referred to as *"mon copain Daniel"* ("my pal Daniel"). I think Roger would have liked to socialize with his colleagues, and I remember that he got really excited when Daniel invited him a few times to some events in Paris. But outside of these rare exceptions, he had no social life of his own. He lived with his parents, participated in family festivities, and, when my aunt and uncle finally decided to follow the almost sacred French custom of taking yearly vacation trips, he faithfully tagged along. He never moved out, and, after his parents died, never changed a thing in the house.

Roger and his dog, Danny. (1950)

I had a good relationship with Roger; his tastes were quite modern and I learned a lot from him. One of his favorite pastimes was to read a movie magazine called *L'Écran Français* (*The French Screen*). He practically memorized each issue and knew all the latest gossip about movie stars. He was also aware of what was happening in Paris. For instance, since he worked near the Galeries Lafayette, he always knew when this big department store had special sales. One time, following a request made by Tante Valentine, he told us how he had to "dig and dig" into a huge pile of bras until he found one in his mother's size. He also went to museums and various exhibits, but as he hated to spend money, he mostly attended free events.

Roger got along well with his mother (except when she mentioned marriage) but his relationship with his father was tense. Oncle Baptiste, who knew how much Roger detested fixing things or working in the garden, thought of his son as a useless creature. He criticized him openly, and the fact that Tante Valentine constantly took the side of "her" son made Baptiste even more upset. Roger was quiet whenever there was an argument about him; he just grumbled under his breath, waiting for the tempest to pass. What he liked above all was to be left alone in the dining room where he kept his movie magazines and where he had his single bed. At that time the attic had not yet been transformed into livable quarters. There was only one bedroom, used by Roger's parents (whenever I spent the night, I slept on a camp bed in my aunt and uncle's bedroom). I think I understood Roger better than other people in the family. He didn't brag about his achievements, though he had many. He was quite skillful at drawing. Also, with the help of workbooks and a dictionary, he had taught himself how to read English. Later on, after I moved to America, he often added a sentence or two in English at the end of his letters and signed "Your cousin Chips," a name he had given himself, I don't know why. In popular music his tastes were more advanced than those of his parents; he disliked the radio's diet of ordinary chansons, preferring among others the wonderful songs of poet/musician Pierre MacOrlan, performed by Juliette Greco. It was through him that I was first introduced to this muse of the Left Bank's Existentialist scene. At the Tabou nightclub, one of the *"caves"* of Saint-Germain-des-Prés, with her long black hair, all-black clothes and surly tunes, she embodied the disillusioned mood of the after-war period.

And so, I was in good hands: Oncle Baptiste offered his country wisdom, Roger his sophisticated tastes and Tante Valentine her warmth and love. Even though it didn't replace my home, I felt secure with the Éoche family. Their house was very cute, made of yellow and red bricks, its front door surrounded by climbing roses. It was furnished with sturdy carved oak furniture made in his spare time by Oncle Baptiste himself (a project that had taken years to complete, to Tante Valentine's irritation). A talented furniture maker, Oncle Baptiste had left his profession (no one understood why) to work as an unskilled hand in a chemistry lab specializing in restoring taste to wine that wasn't quite right.

Tante Valentine. (1960)

Tante Valentine gave me a lot of attention. She taught me how to sew on her Singer sewing machine (the pedal kind); she made dresses for me and helped me make clothes for myself. The only thing she didn't do was to teach me how to cook. For some reason I was never taught the art of cooking, either at home or at any of my aunts' houses. Apparently, training was not judged necessary. I guess I was expected to learn "by taste." If I liked a dish, it was assumed I would be able to replicate it. Tante Valentine was a great cook, the best in the family. Now I am sorry I only asked for two of her recipes: her *bûche de Noël* and her famous chocolate truffles. I still have these recipes, handwritten on paper that has turned yellow. I was rarely brave enough to make the *bûche de Noël*, but at Christmas time my youngest daughter and I often used the *truffes au chocolat* recipe. When we were done, we kept a platter for ourselves and arranged the remaining truffles in nice boxes that we gave as presents.

I know that Tante Valentine was happy to take care of me. I was the daughter she would have liked to have. She was always understanding and approachable. The day I had my first period, it was to her that I turned, and it was obvious that she was pleased to be my "mentor."

"Don't worry, ma cocotte," she said, seeing how embarrassed I was. "It means that you are a big girl now. You'll be fine, I want you to feel comfortable, not like me when I told my mother and she said, 'Put your chemise between your legs!' Now, you stay here! I'm going to go buy everything you need." And she went to the pharmacist and bought a pink sanitary belt and two dozen cotton pads.

"Can you imagine?" she told me when she came back. "The pharmacist thought it was for me! 'No, no!' I said to him, 'it's for my little niece. It's her first time!'" (I was so glad I didn't go with her!)

The arrangements about spending the night at Tante Valentine's didn't last long. I missed the privacy of my own house, of my own bedroom; after a few months, I decided to sleep at my house, even if my father came home late, even if he didn't come home at all. I still took most of my meals at Tante Valentine's, but started to teach myself how to prepare a few dishes. It was my dream to settle in for a quiet life with my father, surrounded by the memories of my mother and all our familiar things. But it was evident that Papa wasn't yet ready for the kind of life I had in mind.

4
Things Are Starting to Change

The year was 1948. Almost thirteen, I still saw my friends of the villa, but we no longer played. We just hung around after school and talked, standing at the corner of rue Jules Ferry and villa de l'Ouest. It was obvious that our sexual awakening had begun, but we were too shy to do anything about it, except joke and hint. We still exchanged comic books and *chansons*, and sometimes went to the corner store we used to call *la petite boutique bleue* when Claude Gouge's grandparents owned it, but which had since become *la petite boutique verte* to buy magazines or tiny round metal boxes of "*coco*," a bright yellow licorice powder that we licked right out of the box. I loved to be with my friends. It was only when I was with them that I didn't think about my mother's death.

Jean Joly's First Communion. From left: Bernard, Oncle Marcel, me (so soon after my mother's death, I felt I shouldn't smile,) Tante Yvonne, Germaine Joly, Jean Joly. Others are Germaine Joly's relatives. (Spring 1948).

I had taken my mother for granted, but suddenly I had to face the fact that nothing was the same without her. What I most missed was the way she cuddled and kissed me and held me in her arms. I tried to remember her as she was before her illness, but while I could still recall the softness of her skin and the scent of her hair, when I tried to hear her voice as she called me "*ma petite caille*," it escaped me, it seemed to have vanished. I felt sad and often cried when I was by myself. Once or twice a week a housekeeper came to clean the house, but left early. When I came home from school, the house was deserted.

My father, whose loneliness was evident, turned to drinking more and more. He came home late and sometimes brought friends with him. One night, I was upstairs, sleeping—it must have been around two o'clock in the morning—when I heard a commotion downstairs. Many people were in the kitchen, talking, drinking, and laughing. I was used to these sorts of things; usually the guests didn't stay long; I just had to wait until everything was quiet again. That night, however, the chattering got louder and louder and wouldn't stop. Suddenly, someone (I later found out that it was my father) started playing the trumpet. (Where did Papa get that trumpet? I shall never know.) Aware that the noise had probably awakened the neighbors, I felt terribly embarrassed. In the middle of all this, I heard Tante Valentine's voice calling from her kitchen window out to our garden, "P'tit Louis! Stop that noise, think of '*la petite*.' She's got to go to school in the morning!" This made my father furious. He couldn't tolerate anyone telling him how to bring me up.

"I don't need your advice! Why don't you just go to bed and mind your own business!" he shouted to his sister, picking up the trumpet and blowing crazy tunes. I felt sorry for poor Tante Valentine.

A few times, my father brought women to the house. Before introducing them to me, he told me that they were "marriage prospects," and that I was to observe them and tell him what I thought. Sometimes his lady friends spent the night, which made me feel terrible, for I saw that as a profanation of my mother's memory. Three of these women I remember very well. The first one was an ex-prostitute who worked in a café near Vincennes, a café where Papa often stopped on his way home. She was young, not too pretty, and acted shy and humble. After she left, I asked my father, tears flowing and indignation rising, "How can you bring a prostitute to this house?" The poor woman (who, I recall, seemed very nice) never came back.

The second candidate was introduced to Papa and me at a Sunday lunch given by Tante Valentine and Oncle Baptiste, of whom she was an acquaintance. In her forties like my father, she was rather good-looking and laughed easily. She and Papa started dating, and in the weeks that followed I had the opportunity to see her several times. I didn't dislike her, but felt no warmth toward her—and she certainly didn't waste any warmth on me. She was from Brittany and had a funny way of pronouncing certain words; for example, she pronounced the word *"jaune"* (yellow) as *"jeune"* (which means young), and would say things like: *"Elle a une robe jeune"* ("She has a young dress," when she meant "She has a yellow dress"). It was something that I found extremely irritating. When I tried to teach her the "correct" (meaning Parisian) pronunciation, she just laughed at me. But, at least, she was respectable compared to the other prospect, and I guess I was ready to accept her (it helped that she had two cute sons, both in the Navy). There was, however, an important problem: she was totally clueless when it came to my father's "psychology." She poked fun at him and contradicted him constantly, something that we, in the family, would never have dared to do. He didn't say anything, but I knew it would never work. Finally they broke up, the difference in their personalities too great.

The third woman looked like a movie star: shapely, beautiful, with showy jewelry and expensive make-up. The day I met her, she wore a black dress close to the body, a chic flat hat with veil, and a lot of perfume. She called my father *"mon chéri, mon loulou,"* something I found utterly ridiculous, if not downright disgusting. I could tell she was a poseuse who did not know much about anything. She came to our house for dinner. We ate in the kitchen (her outfit was totally out of place—though she did take off her hat) and (I suppose) volunteered to cook. It was then that my father got a warning of things to come as she asked for a cookbook to cook plain rice! But the worst thing about this relationship was the bedroom noise. The other women had been relatively quiet, but this one couldn't help sighing and crying out, *"Ah! Oh! Chéri, chéri, c'est bon!"* and my father had to go: "Shush! Shush!" all the time. His bedroom was next to mine, and even though the walls were not thin, I heard quite a lot. The only thing I could do was sob and hold my pillow over my head. I felt miserable. I felt my mother was being betrayed. If Papa married this woman, it would be the most terrible thing that could ever happen to me. Luckily he didn't. The search was still on.

While all this was going on, I had a major preoccupation concerning my future. When my mother was ill, attention to my education had been pushed to the background. No one had registered me for the entrance test to a *lycée* (secondary school) which I should have taken at the age of eleven or twelve. As a good student I had entered the final year of the Jules Ferry primary school at the age of eleven instead of thirteen and had finished the year with good grades. When the new school year started in October 1947 (I just had turned twelve in September; my mother, very ill at the time, would die at the end of November) nobody gave much thought to my schooling. Since I was too young to graduate from elementary school (compulsory until the age of fourteen) the teachers placed me in a class that repeated the program of the final year with a few added courses designed to prepare students for the two-year business school located in the same building as the school. These courses included "mental calculation," as well as one hour of English per week with "Miss Clara," who mostly taught us how to sing: *Here We Go 'Round the Mulberry Bush* and not very much more. This program suited my father well, as he had already formed an idea of my future, picturing me as a "ground hostess" for the Compagnie Générale Transatlantique. For such a position, business school was as good a preparation as any.

At that time in France a child's entire future was decided by the age of eleven or twelve. When a child reached that age, there were only two options: take a test to transfer to a *lycée*, or remain in primary school until the age of fourteen. The second option meant that the child would have no choice but go to trade school or start working. Only *lycées* led to university education. Without taking the test to switch from primary to secondary school, the prospect for higher education was practically nil.

When I was a young girl at École Jules Ferry, only a small percentage of children took the lycée entrance test—and most of the children who did were from middle class families aware of the importance of a university education. In the villa de l'Ouest neighborhood, my gifted friend Patrick, who came from an educated family, was the only kid who took the admission test to a lycée. However, by a stroke of bad luck, he failed (his mother attributed his failure to his having played in the villa!). As a result of this early selection of lycée candidates, French higher education, while in theory open to all, remained in practice eminently elitist. (At present, things are different: at eleven or twelve, all children enter middle-schools (called *collèges*). After that they transfer to lycées, now more or less similar to American high schools.)

When I think of this period of my youth, I find it strange that Tante Yvonne and Oncle Marcel, who had done the necessary paperwork to register Bernard for the lycée entrance test, did not advise my father to do the same thing for me. This may be due to the fact that, being on my mother's side of the family, they felt they didn't have a voice. On my father's side, my cousins Miquette and her brother Jacques had not been "pushed" either toward the prospect of higher education (and the same would be true for their younger brother Claude). Obviously, the Gauthiers didn't aim for their children to go to college. Like themselves when they were young, they expected their children to work as soon as possible and contribute to the family finances.

Lycées are public schools, each with its own reputation, some being considered more prestigious than others. My cousin Bernard had been admitted to the excellent Lycée Buffon in Paris. Every Thursday, when I visited him, I was fascinated by what he was being taught, and loved to look through his books of Latin and ancient history.

When the school year was almost over I told my father that I was determined to go to a lycée at the start of the next school year, even though I hadn't taken the entrance test. This decision was entirely my own. He hesitated at first but when I told him that I wanted to be a school teacher (I was not even sure of that myself), he said, "If that's what you want to do, then you should do it!"

The two of us went to apply to two lycées for the next school year. In the intimidating admission offices we were told that I would have to take the admission test for the entry-level class: "*la sixième*" (corresponding to American 6th grade). But that wasn't at all what I had in mind! I didn't want to start at the beginning; I insisted on starting in second year: "*la cinquième*" (corresponding to 7th grade—French grades are counted downward). I felt I was on the same academic level as Bernard, and, being the same age, I didn't want to find myself one year behind him. Unfortunately, it seemed obvious that it was not possible.

"No lycée will take you in second year!" I was told firmly. "You will have to take the test for the *entrée en sixième* like everyone else!"

There remained, however, another educational channel: the *cours complémentaires*, which were middle schools going from the *sixième* to the *troisième* (sixth to ninth grade). Less prestigious than lycées and considered "proletarian," these schools offered in their last year, not only a diploma: *le brevet,* but also the possibility of taking a test to transfer to a lycée in "*seconde*" (tenth grade). My father and I made an appointment with the principal of the Cours Complémentaire de Vincennes, a very nice woman, who told us that if I passed the exam that was to be given to a group of first-year students who had flunked their finals, I could enter directly in second year. Glad to have that opportunity, I took the exam and passed without difficulty—except for a poor performance in English, competing as I was with students who had had several hours of English per week, and had chanted irregular verbs instead of the *Mulberry Bush.*

If I have perhaps given too many details on the French educational system of the time, I do apologize, but I felt I had to explain how I finally managed to transfer from primary to secondary school, something that was about to change the course of my entire life. When I reflect on these events now, I am amazed at the determination I showed at such a young age.

"I felt sorry for you," Tante Yvonne told me not long ago, "Nobody helped you with your education. You took care of it all by yourself!"

But, in all honesty, Papa never went against my wishes and was there for me when I needed him.

Before school started my father sent me on a vacation with some old friends of his who had rented a summer cottage in Les Sables d'Olonne, an Atlantic Coast resort famous for its boardwalk and its huge sand beach. The family I stayed with consisted of a couple, their nephew who was my age, and a surly overweight grandmother who had lived in Brazil and had brought back a parrot (her dear *papagaio*). I spent my days on the beach with the nephew who became my "sex mentor" in the sense that he told me all he knew about sex—at least all his big sister had told him. To my amazement, I found out what people really did in bed (no more hints like the ones I heard in the villa, but details!). I also learned about homosexuals and lesbians "who are born like that," and about ugly men, repulsive and toothless, who pay prostitutes to have sex because "men have to have sex whether they are ugly or not." (We felt terribly sorry for the poor prostitutes.) Another thing I learned about was color-blindness. My friend was color-blind; he couldn't distinguish red from green, and got mixed-up about other colors. To me, this was as fascinating as the sexual stuff. I tested him constantly. He always guessed the wrong color (but never lost his patience). I don't know if my sex life got influenced by this parallel teaching of sexual practices and color perception (albeit of the wrong colors). It is possible but not necessarily so.

It was at that time that I began to have serious crushes on men. A great love of mine was Jean Marais, the openly gay movie actor. I still slept with his picture under my pillow and dreamt that if we were ever shipwrecked on a desert island "nothing and no one could keep us apart." But my main love at the time was my uncle Albert Schuschmann. I endlessly calculated the age difference between us (thirty-two years), and hoped that when I reached eighteen, he would divorce my aunt Marthe to marry me. He was an attractive man, but it was his keen intelligence and quick wit that I found especially sexy. Apparently, a lot of women did too—it drove my aunt crazy! She, however, never suspected that I was in love with her husband. As for my uncle, he wisely chose to ignore my timid Lolita body language—if he even noticed it. Closer to reality was Patrick. But we would have to wait almost two more years before we became bold enough to hold hands in the protective darkness of the Fontenay-sous-Bois movie houses.

5
Tante Yvonne, Cousin Bernard, and a Black Elephant

When I went on my weekly visits to Tante Yvonne I walked five blocks to the bus stop, caught the bus, got off at Château de Vincennes, hopped in the métro, transferred at Châtelet, got off at Porte d'Orléans, and caught another bus to Malakoff. The trip took about an hour and a half. During the whole time, I never stopped worrying. It was not that I was afraid of taking public transportation by myself: I had done it since the age of ten. No, what filled me with apprehension was that I might be late. Tante Yvonne insisted on my being on time. Lunch was at twelve o'clock sharp! Whenever I waited longer than usual for a bus (the métro was more reliable) and realized I was going to be late, a glance at my reflection in the glass of the métro windows revealed my poor tortured face, racked with anxiety. It was unavoidable. Tante Yvonne was going to greet me with: "Late again! Can't you be on time for once?" I could already hear the tone of her voice as the dreaded sentence played over and over in my head. Every week I tried my best to leave earlier, but somehow could never manage it. I was, alas, destined to be late!

As I arrived and took off my coat, Tante Yvonne gave me her usual welcome: "Late again!" Then, taking a close look at my face, she added in the same disapproving tone, "Ma p'tite Colette, I hate to say, but your nose is dirty!"

Blushing, I immediately rushed to the bathroom and washed my entire face. But the next time I came to visit, it was: "I hate to say, but your nose is dirty!"

Before ringing the bell, I tried to give a good rubbing to the tip and sides of my nose with my glove or my handkerchief. But it was in vain. For when Tante Yvonne opened the door and gave me her "Late again!" greeting, she never failed to top it with: "Ma p'tite Colette, I hate to say, but your nose is dirty!"

Good thing that Bernard and Grand-mère Cessot were there! After our lunch, which was served on bright yellow plates in the shiny-white, germ-free kitchen, I would soon forget about Tante Yvonne, who by that time had gone to take her daily nap. Mémé Cessot did the dishes and started sewing or ironing while Bernard and I took out his Meccano erector set, read books, or went out to play.

Bernard loved to tease me. He took the greatest pleasure in irritating me, finding a thousand ways to make me angry (and I did get pretty angry sometimes), but somehow I never bore him a grudge; as a matter of fact we got along wonderfully.

I was not the only one to be teased by Bernard; he also teased other people, devising tricks that never ceased to amaze me. One of his favorites "victims" was Grand-mère Cessot. I remember the day when Tante Yvonne wanted to take a photo of Bernard and me with our grandmother (Tante Yvonne loved to take photos). We were in the Malakoff apartment, standing in front of a little Art Déco cabinet. Bernard insisted on balancing a ping-pong ball on top of Grandmother's head. Tante Yvonne protested, "Mon p'tit Bernard, please stop that!" Bernard persevered, declaring that he absolutely positively would refuse to be in the picture unless Grandmother balanced a ping-pong ball on her head. We were all exasperated. I still have the final result of this photo session. The expression on poor Grandmother's face bears a lifetime of resigned suffering (the ping-pong ball is nowhere in sight).

Bernard, Grand-mère Cessot and me.
No ping-pong ball on Grandmother's head. (c. 1948)

Bernard's tricks were often bold. Although I was sometimes quite shocked by them, I couldn't help but respect my cousin's spirit. For instance, one afternoon when Grand-mère was darning socks (at that time we economized on everything; socks were darned until their heels were practically re-woven), Bernard asked her, *"Chiche ou pas chiche?"* ("Dare or dare not?") "About what?" "Dare or dare not?" "Dare what?" "I won't tell you. Dare or dare not?" Finally Grand-mère, sick of listening to him, said, "All right! Dare!" He took a pair of scissors and, in one second, snipped in two the sock she was darning. Such actions, of course, provoked the ire of everyone, but Tante Yvonne just said, "Oh! Mon p'tit Bernard!"

After my mother's death, Tante Yvonne made a sincere effort to contribute to my upbringing. She had loved my mother, her big sister, and wanted to become a substitute mother to me, but, somehow, she missed; she had no idea how to go about it and at times could even be cruel. Puzzled by my apparent indifference after the death of my mother, she once tried to make me react. While it wasn't rare for her to hug and kiss Bernard in front of me, that particular time she went overboard, lavishing kisses and caresses on him. "Bernard, mon chéri, Mommy loves you so much! Give me another kiss, my darling. Don't you love it when I cuddle you like that? Isn't a mother nice and sweet? Look, Colette! Isn't it nice to have a mother?"

I think she believed that I would jump into her arms, tell her how much I missed my mother, and kiss and caress her, but of course she only succeeded in hurting me. The last thing in the world I wanted was to jump in her arms. Another time, pretending not to be aware I was close enough to hear what she was saying, she told my grandmother, "Colette has no feelings about her mother's death. She has a heart of stone!"

More tears in my room at night.

Besides her regular features and dark-brown eyes, everything about Tante Yvonne seemed perfect, from her raven-black hair, always fashionably cut, to her slender-fingered hands, perfectly manicured. She exercised regularly to remain thin, frequented *instituts de beauté* for facial treatments, and knew how to pick stylish clothes, often in vivid colors to highlight her exotic type. In her presence I felt awkward and had the impression that I could never live up to her standards: my clothes, my shoes, my haircuts were never right, and I did not know how to act. Tante Yvonne felt that her role was to teach me good manners and give me insights on how to dress and conduct myself in society. Her lessons were for Bernard too, but he was usually reticent and did not care about such things. She taught us table manners: the way to hold our spoon, which fork to use, how one must never drink wine when eating salad because vinaigrette spoils the taste of wine, and took us to places where we had to practice acting in the proper way. She took us to fashion shows at Le Bon Marché, the most chic of the Paris *Grands Magasins*, with its magnificent glass ceiling and its grand staircase by Gustave Eiffel. We had to sit close to the runway, write notes on our program, and check which dresses we liked best. Then, we were taken to a *salon de thé* for hot chocolate and pastries. Tante Yvonne once took me to the classy beauty parlor "Chez Claude" to have my hair cut. Monsieur Claude made me look like Joan of Arc (I kind of liked it!). Sometimes we had cultural outings at the Musée du Louvre, where we were awed by the immense statues of the Egyptian collection. Tante Yvonne also took us to the Quartier Latin, a district hitherto unknown to me. There, walking up and down the Boulevard Saint-Michel were beautiful students from all over the world. It was like being on another planet.

In the summer, we often went to the Molitor swimming pool (in the posh 16th arrondissement) where I swam peacefully, Bernard splashed everyone, and Tante Yvonne deepened her tan in her bikini. In the winter, the swimming pool was turned into an ice-skating rink. I loved to go there. Bernard did too, as it gave him the chance to practice his speed-skating among the graceful skaters. But the outing I remember best (I'm jumping ahead a little, I was fifteen then) was a visit to the movie studios of Boulogne-Billancourt.

The man who came to pick us up seemed to know Tante Yvonne well; he looked important and drove a big American car. Tante Yvonne sat next to him, Bernard and I sat in back. We took a short ride southwest of Paris. After the mysterious man dropped us at the studio, we stopped at the office and were given a pass to go see a movie being shot. The European title of the movie in the making was first called *The Tavern of New Orleans*, but was released in America under the title *The Adventures of Captain Fabian*, starring Errol Flynn and Micheline Presle, with Vincent Price and Victor Francen. Too bad Errol Flynn was not shooting that day! But we got to meet a few movie stars anyway. The set was rather simple: a section of an old-time restaurant with a bar and a few tables, the whole thing surrounded by floodlights, cameras and cameramen. The director was William Marshall, an American actor/director, who sat in a director's chair bearing his name.

Besides the three of us, there was another visitor, an American woman who was introduced to us as June Allyson. I had never heard of her at the time, but realized later that she was a famous Hollywood star. We sat with Bill Marshall and June Allyson as the scene was being filmed. A middle-aged man (I think it was Victor Francen) was being served food. He was supposed to start eating, wearing a napkin around his neck, and talk to Micheline Presle as she arrived in the room. The stage food was real, a mouth-watering pot of well-seasoned crayfish. There was one take, then "Cut!" Another take, then "Cut!" (The actor kept forgetting his lines.) In between takes, the script-girl tucked a clean napkin into the actor's collar. One time she forgot to do that, and the scene was cut again. Meanwhile, we were talking to Bill Marshall and June Allyson, both in French and in English. June Allyson was a small woman who wore on her tiny feet "real" boxing shoes which, she told us, had been made especially for her. Bill Marshall took my chin in his hands and told me I was very cute and should be in the movies. He said that, for a start, I should register as an extra; it would get me in the door. After that, we continued to watch the shooting. During breaks, when Micheline Presle spoke to her fellow actors or the movie crew, she sounded quite ordinary, not at all like a distinguished actress—which greatly disappointed me. She was very famous then, well known for her many parts, but especially for having played opposite Gérard Philippe in *Le Diable au Corps* (*Devil in the Flesh*). At that time I didn't know that Bill Marshall was Micheline Presle's husband (nor, by the way, that he had previously been married to Michèle Morgan, one of the greatest and most beautiful of all French actresses). When the scene was finally shot, the left-over pot of crayfish was given to June Allyson, who kindly shared it with us. I was flattered by what Bill Marshall had said about me; it confirmed my secret wish to be in the movies. On our way out we inquired about my working as an extra. Yes, I could be placed on the list, but I would have to register every morning and wait till the studio needed me. That was impossible. I had to go to school.

While I appreciated the fact that Tante Yvonne took me to interesting places, I always remained on my guard, for I never knew what bruising comment she would send my way, what *"pierre dans mon jardin"* she was ready to cast. It wasn't something she did to me only. In the family, she was famous for her off-the-cuff hurtful remarks. How she had acquired this pernicious trait was a bit of a mystery, but she seemed to have nurtured it for a very long time. I didn't know much then about Tante Yvonne's private life, but it was easy to see that she was not really happy with Oncle Marcel. They argued constantly, or rather, Oncle Marcel told her off and she hardly ever protested, knowing it would make things worse. When he was angry he sometimes berated her in front of other people, using rude words to embarrass her. On the one hand, he treated her as though she was completely stupid—for instance, if she ventured an opinion he would say, "Shut up, Yvonne, you are hallucinating again!"; but on the other, he made no secret to show how devoted he was to her. As we all knew, he showered her with presents. She complained to everyone about her husband, but never made any move to leave him. Their disputes put people ill at ease; consequently they had no close friends, and after my mother's death hardly any members of the family associated with them. Of Tante Yvonne's four nieces, I was the only one close to her. Denise had stopped all contacts; Simone, who did not live in Paris, had few. As for Paulette, she did remain in touch, but she complained to me that Tante Yvonne only called when she wanted to sell her (not give her) some of her clothes. In fact, except for me, Tante Yvonne never made an effort to socialize with her nieces, especially Denise and Paulette, whom she considered to be of a lower social status. As for Oncle Marcel, he never had anything good to say about Denise and Paulette, even claiming that they were "retarded." It was all very unfair, especially that his attitude toward me was completely different. He loved me, was always extremely nice, and called me his *"petite poupette"* ("little dolly"). He adored Bernard and spoiled him. But while he could be very tender, he could also be mean at times. Once, as we were having dinner, I observed my uncle pinching his son's leg under the table because Bernard had committed a minor offence; he pinched and twisted the skin, which made Bernard cry out in pain, and I suppose, resulted in a bruise.

But Bernard never complained. In fact, he didn't seem to care and continued to be as full of mischief as ever. Every time I came to visit, I heard of some new trouble he had be in. Being a rather "good girl" myself, I found that quite exciting. For instance, he had angered the other tenants of his parents' nice apartment building by riding on roller skates in the corridors and doing acrobatics on skates up and down the marble staircase, or he had had still another altercation with the building manager for playing rough games with his friends in the little kids' area of the courtyard. One day, as he and I looked downstairs from the living room window, Bernard showed me how to shine a mirror in the eyes of people who were getting their hair cut at the beauty parlor across the street. When they looked up, we quickly bent down out of sight below the window sill. Another day, the two of us went to the *Foire de Paris*, an annual exhibit of industrial products (Oncle Marcel always got free tickets through his work). To go there Bernard and I took the bus, always standing in the open-air rear deck of the bus which was called *la plate-forme*. (These wonderful old buses were retired a long time ago.) The bus employee cancelled our tickets by sticking them in a little square machine attached to his belt. Each of us had about five or six tickets, as it was a long trip. The tickets were long and narrow.

"Look!" Bernard said. "You can put a ticket on your index finger, hold your hand out of the *plate-forme* into the air, and watch the ticket turn around, just like a little windmill."

It was marvelous. I thought Bernard was so clever for knowing how to do things like that! Then a controller boarded the bus and asked for our tickets. Of course, they had all blown in the wind. To make things worse, the treacherous bus employee acted as if he had never seen us before. We had to pay our fare again, double rate. When we told our story to Tante Yvonne, she said, "Oh! Bernard!" and added, "And you, ma p'tite Colette! I thought you were more intelligent than that!"

One afternoon, Bernard and I were left alone for a while and were looking at books. A famous children's book of the time, in comic strip form, was *Les Aventures de Bécassine.* Bécassine was a young girl from Brittany who worked as a maid in Paris. She was very nice but extremely naive and didn't understand the ways of the big city. She still wore her peasant cap, wide apron and wooden shoes. Bernard had some little paper images showing Bécassine in different situations. We thought it would be a great idea to paste a few of these images on the wall above one of the day-beds of the living room. Bernard assured me that his mother would have no objection. We selected four or five of the best pictures, and used Oncle Marcel's glue to paste them on the wallpaper at the head of the bed. The effect was very cute and we loved it. We waited for Tante Yvonne to return so we could show her how good our work looked.

Needless to say, Tante Yvonne was horrified! Impossible to remove our pictures without leaving marks.

"What a disaster!" she said, although she admitted that some spare wallpaper could be used (and was) to repair the damage.

Somehow I was the one to bear the brunt of her upset. I guess it was normal for Bernard to do things like that, but for me, it was inconceivable. She didn't get angry or shout at me, she contented herself with repeating over and over, for hours, for days, even for months, every single time I saw her afterwards, "Ma p'tite Colette, I thought you were more intelligent than that!"

I am jumping a bit ahead of time, but this will fit right here: In 1949, Tante Yvonne and Oncle Marcel went on a vacation with Bernard and took me along (my father agreed to pay for my share of the expenses). During this vacation I wrote a diary, my first lengthy writing project. We went to the Île d'Oléron, off the Atlantic coast, a small island loved by tourists for its sandy beaches and delicious oysters, and stayed at the quaint "Auberge du Domaine de la Guinalière." In my diary I stated my opinion of the hotel guests, who, according to my aunt, were supposedly "high class." I was not impressed, obviously more interested in a young man named Paul, who had "very dark eyes." I did mention Monsieur le Comte and Madame la Marquise, finding the former "very reserved" and the latter impossible to identify. I also noted that I was reading *Les Misérables* when I was not otherwise busy going to the beach, riding my bicycle, playing ping-pong or tennis with Bernard, and, in the evening, Monopoly with the rest of the family. At the end of our stay I decided to show Tante Yvonne my diary, which I had illustrated with local postcards and my own sketches of the Auberge. Her only comment was: "You made spelling mistakes!" Needless to say, I was disappointed. However, except for that demoralizing remark, I had happy memories of this vacation and imagined everyone else also had a nice time. But much later, as I talked to Tante Yvonne on the telephone and mentioned our stay at La Guinalière, she said, "You were hard to please when you were a girl, nothing we did could ever satisfy you!" Now my memories are tainted with guilt.

When I visited her, Tante Yvonne often gave me clothes. She made a big ado of it, saying: "Isn't that pretty? It will look perfect on you! Isn't Tante Yvonne nice?" In fact, she usually gave me whatever she was tired of wearing. I was glad to receive her presents, but they were a blessing in disguise: when I showed the clothes to my father, he felt he didn't need to buy me any new ones since I already had all that I needed.

But very often Tante Yvonne's gifts did not really please me. For one thing, as her bust was quite bigger than mine, everything she gave me was a little baggy, or the colors, well suited to her dark complexion, were often too bright for me. She would say, "You are a brunette, you need to wear, bright, vivid colors"—not seeming to notice that although my hair was dark, my complexion was fair, a combination that, in my opinion was better enhanced by light or muted colors.

Always sure of herself, my aunt did not seem to care about other people's feelings. Actually, to put it bluntly, she had no sensitivity at all, even to the point of sometimes being a little perverse. I remember one afternoon when she, Bernard and I were in the bus, on the way back from one of our fancy Parisian outings. Bernard and I were playing "foreigners." We sat facing one another and carried a serious conversation in an invented language, adding gestures, bursts of laughter and facial expressions for the benefit of the other passengers, who, we were sure, were wondering where on earth we came from. Tante Yvonne sat apart from us. When it came time to get off the bus, she stood up and called out to me in a stern voice (giving me the formal "vous" instead of the familiar "tu"), "*Venez, Mélanie, dépêchez-vous!*" ("Come on Mélanie, hurry up!") The bad thing was that "Mélanie" was a name almost synonymous with "maid," a name everyone identified as a maid's name. I felt terribly humiliated. But she just thought it was funny; and when I told her I was upset, she said, "Bah! You have no sense of humor!"

In spite of all this, I didn't dislike Tante Yvonne. In fact, had I been asked whether I liked her or not, I would probably have answered that I liked her; but no one asked me, and I never asked myself this question. I took her the way she was. She was my aunt. Sometimes, however, after she hurt my feelings too badly, an image jumped to my mind, an image that had to do with her beautifully decorated apartment.

Close to a wall on which hung the framed drawing of a woman of "The Islands," bare-breasted, holding a large tropical fruit, her hair flowing loosely down to her waist, was a low shelf on which was placed a black porcelain elephant with its trunk raised. This six or seven inch figurine was stylish, perfectly shiny—never a speck of dust on it. Tante Yvonne had given me a photo of herself in her elegant satin robe, standing close to the shelf with the elephant.

In the evening when I was in my room in Fontenay, I often saw myself standing in front of Tante Yvonne, picking up the black elephant, and with all my strength, throwing it at her feet, smashing it into a thousand pieces.

Tante Yvonne and the black elephant.
(c. 1948)

6
Grand-mère Cessot

When Grand-père Cessot committed suicide in 1934 Mémé Cessot tried to live on her own, but soon found out that it was too difficult for her. After less than two years, she came to live at my parents' house while also spending time at the home of her daughter Yvonne's who had just married Marcel. In 1938, when my cousin Denise, following the suicide of her mother and the death of her father, moved in with my parents, it became obvious that there was no love lost between her and Grand-mère Cessot. Denise felt that Mémé had never made any effort to help her or her sisters Simone and Paulette, or even paid attention to them after the death of their parents. But aside from the friction between Denise and Mémé there was another problem, a problem that concerned the entire family: it was Mémé Cessot's drinking. My parents had to supervise her constantly in order to keep her sober. Besides the few glasses of wine she drank with each meal, she couldn't resist the temptation of pouring herself extra glasses from the unfinished bottles that were kept in the kitchen. Then, obviously tipsy, she would claim, "I didn't touch anything!"—thinking no one would notice that she had added water to the wine left in the bottles. My mother and father were often irritated with her. Mémé's drinking problem was a constant source of discord between her and my parents.

Although she was only fifty-five when my grandfather died, Mémé Cessot thought of herself as "an old woman" and became completely dependent on her daughters. Healthy, but very small and thin, she always seemed to be cold in spite of the many layers of clothing she wore. I can still see her, in her gray smock, her back touching the kitchen radiator, shaking her head and saying, *"Ah! La la la la! Mes pauvres enfants!"* (My poor children!)—which was often her way of starting a conversation.

In her youth, my grandmother had been a pretty woman. As she got older, she still looked nice, but her once large eyes were reduced to (as I told her as a child) *"des petits triangles."*

My cousin Denise recently told me that when both she and my grandmother lived at my parents' house, a friend of my father's had asked her (Denise) if she wanted to go for a ride in his new car. My cousin, who was about fifteen then, was happy to go. When Denise came back, Grand-mère Cessot, angry at not having been invited for the ride, told driver and rider that she had drunk bleach to "punish" them for not taking her along. The bleach-drinking claim turned out to be untrue, but when he heard about it, my father, who had no patience for this kind of behavior (and was weary of the constant bickering between his niece and his mother-in-law) asked Mémé Cessot to make arrangements to go live at Tante Yvonne's. It was agreed that my grandmother would come to our house on Wednesday afternoons, stay overnight, and spend the "no-school" Thursdays with my mother and me (in addition, of course, to participating in family reunions). This arrangement would work well until my mother became ill, then Mémé Cessot stayed for longer periods to help take care of Maman; but after my mother's death, she went back to live at Tante Yvonne's. In fact, the bleach incident had been the straw that broke the camel's back, for it was my grandmother's drinking that my father couldn't tolerate; he felt that it was acceptable for a man to drink, but that for a woman, it was despicable.

Living with Tante Yvonne was not easy for Mémé because Tante Yvonne (who drank mostly water) was even less tolerant than my parents of her mother's weakness for wine. After a while Mémé Cessot decided to rent a studio in an apartment building a few blocks away from Tante Yvonne and Oncle Marcel's. She paid the rent with her small pension and with the money she earned by working part-time as a companion to a young woman who had mental problems. However, Mémé never really "lived" in her studio, but used it only for sleeping. She left in the morning and spent the day at Tante Yvonne's, at our house, or at the home of the young woman she cared for.

My grandmother had another habit which was extremely irritating to Tante Yvonne: she snuffed tobacco. I was used to seeing her put a pinch of powdered tobacco on the back of her hand; sniff it with one nostril, then with the other. In her smock pocket she always kept a little wooden snuff box. For her birthday I often gave her a pack or two of snuff (little cube-shaped packs in Gauloise-blue paper) which I bought at the *Bureau de Tabac*. She always blew her nose in huge checkered white and purple handkerchiefs. Mémé's habit was repulsive to Tante Yvonne, but it didn't bother me. It was just something that my grandmother did.

Mémé Cessot adored Bernard and me. We were the lights of her life. We could do no wrong. Bernard teased her a lot, but her patience with him was endless. I was often bad-tempered, but she did not seem to mind. She never missed an opportunity to tell us how beautiful and intelligent we were. When she took us out she always gave us *"une petite pièce"* ("a little coin") so we could buy what we wanted.

From the time we were born, Grand-mère Cessot adored Bernard and me. (1936)

Bernard, Grand-mère Cessot and me at the park. (1948)

Our grandmother, understanding and discreet, had become her daughters' confidante. I am sure that my mother told her all her secrets, and I know that Tante Yvonne shared her marital problems with her. She might not have needed to do so, as Mémé knew very well that Oncle Marcel, a perfect gentleman in public, could turn horrid at home. My aunt was never reluctant to disclose her husband's "eccentric" practices. For instance, when Oncle Marcel was angry for something as mundane as the food not being to his liking, instead of arguing with his wife in private, he would fling a window wide open, and, pretending to address her, hurl gross sexual accusations to the wind for the benefit of the neighbors. If the rest of the family had not seen Oncle Marcel do anything like that, we had all witnessed his shushing Tante Yvonne at family dinners in the most humiliating way. But he was so likable to everyone else that, if we had not known that Mémé was a witness, it would have been difficult to believe everything Tante Yvonne told us about him.

Tante Yvonne and Oncle Marcel on vacation. (c. 1950)

Later on, as an adult, I became quite close to Oncle Marcel, a very intelligent man who sought to analyze his behavior more than he seemed to regret it. While I highly disapprove of his methods, I have to recognize that he did exert a certain control on Tante Yvonne, who, after he died (at a decent old age), felt free to aim her poisoned arrows in a manner that became more and more damaging.

Although Tante Yvonne appreciated her mother in her role of confidante, in other circumstances she was often ashamed of her. Not only did she criticize her constantly ("Maman, you didn't wash this glass properly!" "Maman, tuck your handkerchief inside your pocket!" "Maman, your fingernails are dirty!"), but she sometimes instructed Mémé to remain in the kitchen when distinguished guests were visiting. As for Grandmother's major problem, her drinking, it was not tolerated at all at Tante Yvonne's house, so there was little recurrence of it. However, when Mémé took Bernard and me for a walk, she often managed to stop at a café for *"un p'tit blanc"* (a glass of white wine).

Tante Yvonne's resentment for her mother dated from her childhood, a time during which she was often embarrassed by her parents' lifestyle. My cousin Paulette once told me, "Grand-père and Grand-mère Cessot spent every penny they owned, *'ils menaient la grande vie'* (they led the good life) but never bought anything nice for their house." Indeed, both my grandparents Cessot liked to eat, drink, and go out, but were not particularly interested in creating a cozy home. To make things worse, Grandmother was not a very good housekeeper; it seems that things were always somewhat chaotic around her.

Under the circumstances, it is no wonder that Grand-mère Cessot was incapable of providing any material help or even moral support to her granddaughters Simone, Paulette and Denise when they became orphaned. It is not difficult either to understand how much easier it was for Mémé to give her unconditional love to Bernard and me, not only because she had helped take care of us since we were babies, but also because she had always felt secure in the presence of her two daughters. Even if my mother and Tante Yvonne were sometimes critical of her, Mémé Cessot knew they would always love and protect her.

When Tante Yvonne was an old woman herself (almost ninety), she told me that she regretted not having shown her mother and sister more tenderness: "Mémé Cessot was so understanding. She always listened to my problems. And your mother! She was always so nice to me! She took such good care of me when I was a child. I should have told both of them how much I loved them." I had to reassure Tante Yvonne. "Don't worry, *ma tante*, there was no need, they knew how you felt." And every time we talked on the telephone, she told me, *"Je t'aime, ma petite Colette,"* and I answered, *"Moi aussi, je t'aime, ma tante."*

7
Childhood Readings

My friend Pierrette Mousset's house was different from all the other houses of the villa de l'Ouest. For one thing, it was made of wood, then, instead of facing the villa, it was perpendicular to it. When we pushed the wrought-iron gate, the dark-green house was on the right and a small concrete building was on the left, their doors facing each other. The concrete building (the Moussets called it *"le hangar"*) was used for storage and had a basement that served as a wine cellar. Connecting the house and the *hangar* and forming a "roof" over the cemented yard was a trellis covered with vines that gave shade to a big round table and a few mismatched garden chairs. In the summer, when the Moussets ate dinner under the trellis, they sometimes invited me. Wine was fetched from the cellar and food brought from the kitchen. We all were served soup at dinner and Madame Mousset always poured a little red wine in hers. (Curiously, I never heard anyone use the term *"faire chabrot."*)

"A country habit!" she would say. What she meant by "country" was her native village of Beaune-la-Rolande, the village in the Loiret where I had briefly stayed with her family at the beginning of the Evacuation.

Monsieur Mousset was a quiet man who worked as a baker at the Émorine boulangerie. He worked at night and slept during the day.

Madame Mousset called her husband *"le papa."*

"Don't make noise around *le papa*," she reminded us constantly.

She was a tall, angular woman with a pencil-line mouth and sharp bird's eyes. She looked older than the average parent. I suppose she was over forty when she gave birth to Pierrette, a long time after she had stopped working as a dressing-room attendant for Mistinguett and Maurice Chevalier, a period in her life she loved to recall. She was friendly and vivacious and used words that sounded funny to me. For example she would say, "Colette, you who are '*savante*' ('learned'), can you please help Pierrette with her homework."

The Moussets' house was so crowded with furniture that one could hardly set a foot on the floor; everything, however, was perfectly dusted and polished. Next to the dining room window, Madame Mousset kept a shrine in memory of her first-born daughter, Mireille, who died of tuberculosis at the age of twenty, about fifteen years before Pierrette was born (Mireille's dresses, neatly packed, were kept in a trunk in the "hangar"). This "shrine" was an octagonal wooden stool painted bright orange and topped with a small lace doily. It held Mireille's framed photograph and a small vase of white flowers. Pierrette and I were careful not to play too close to the orange stool for fear of toppling it.

Madame Mousset had a passion for Princesse Astrid, the beautiful Swedish-born Belgian princess who died in a car accident in 1935 at the age of thirty. She kept a photo of her beloved princess on the dining room dresser. Behind the glass doors of the same dresser were at least two dozen volumes of the *Bibliothèque Rose,* a children's books series whose main author was la comtesse de Ségur. I, too, owned books by la comtesse de Ségur, but not in such impressive quantity. Once in a while I was allowed to borrow Madame Mousset's books—after I promised to read them with clean hands. As far as I remember, there were no other books in the Mousset household.

I was not the only girl who, as a child, read Madame de Ségur's books; most women of my generation did. And although they now seem somewhat obsolete, these books—or at least some of them—are still read by French children for their charming style and colorful characters. Today, the comtesse's moral tone seems a little preachy. We also find certain chapters objectionable, as naughty children are often given "well-deserved" beatings, something that did not seem shocking at the time the books were written (around 1865). One of my favorite titles was *Les Malheurs de Sophie.* I identified with Sophie, a mishap-prone little demoiselle. Much later, I realized that the children in Madame de Ségur's books were not ordinary French kids like my villa de l'Ouest friends and myself, but were either modeled on the comtesse's grandchildren who lived with her in her castle in Normandy, or drawn from memories of her own childhood, a childhood spent in the extremely privileged milieu of the Czar's entourage. The Comtesse de Ségur, born Sophie Rostopchine was the daughter of Fyodor Rostopchine, adviser to Czar Paul I. During Napoleon's siege, in 1812, it was Fyodor who had issued the order to burn Moscow. Fyodor Rostopchine went into exile in Paris where his daughter Sophie married the Comte de Ségur and gave birth to eight children. When her husband seemed to have lost interest in her, she retired to her Château des Nouettes, and, at fifty-seven, began writing books for children, books that would be enjoyed by millions of readers. While I want to believe that la comtesse's influence on me was to foster my passion for reading, I also have to admit that she left me with a vague longing for a golden age, when little girls with festooned dresses and ribbons in their hair roamed freely in their private parks under the watchful eyes of their devoted maids.

I read a lot when I was a child. Like most children, I knew by heart the fairy tales of Charles Perrault, from Cinderella and Sleeping Beauty, to terrible Bluebeard. I also read Grimm's tales, and adored Andersen's. I often went to sleep with princes and princesses in my thoughts. But when I was afraid that a wolf or a witch were coming to get me, or that the Ice Maiden was ready to give me her kiss of death, I had the perfect remedy: I conjured up a stageful of ballerinas!

I collected books of folk tales from the French provinces where ghosts and devils reigned. I also owned a book of Slavic stories full of noble *boyars* and double-crossing *Tziganes*. My collection included a whole series of the illustrated lives of famous French historical figures: the saintly Joan of Arc who heard voices while keeping her sheep, the good Louis IX (Saint Louis) who administered justice under an oak tree in the Bois de Vincennes, the cruel Louis XI who put prisoners in small iron cages, and the magnificent Louis XIV, *Le Roi Soleil*, who held court at Versailles.

At school, in the early grades, we memorized La Fontaine's fables with their wonderfully sketched animals whose faults and foibles taught us useful lessons; later on, we learned poems, mostly by Victor Hugo and Lamartine, and had to recite them in front of the class. Later still, we studied and discussed passages from many literary works. On our weekly "library day," the teacher opened a glass-fronted bookcase in the classroom, took out a book and called out its title. Students were encouraged to express their opinion: "It's good, I read it three times!" or "It's boring! Too many descriptions!" After these critiques, we did or didn't raise our hands to borrow the book. I remember that we read popular French authors: George Sand, Jules Verne, Alphonse Daudet, Victor Malot (whose grave, by the way, is in the Fontenay-sous-Bois cemetery), but it also strikes me that some of our favorite titles were translations from the English language: *Jane Eyre, Wuthering Heights, The Mill on the Floss, David Copperfield, Little Women, White Fang, The Last of the Mohicans*, etc.

Unlike the Moussets, who only treasured the *Bibliothèque Rose*, my parents kept a variety of books around the house, but these books did not interest me: Alexandre Dumas was too hard to read, Pierre Louÿs' novels (I could tell by the covers) were about half-naked women in fancy versions of ancient Rome, detective stories had no pictures, and the books on Jean Jaurès and Socialism, as well as the many trade-union pamphlets did not appeal to me. My father loved Jack London, but I don't remember seeing any books by him at home. Actually, more than book readers, my father and mother were passionate newspaper readers, a habit that I caught from them at very young age. I subscribed to *La Semaine de Suzette* (*Suzette's Week*) and *Fillette* (*Little Girl*), two magazines that Maman also loved to read (in spite of Papa's teasing).

Grand-mère Cessot was the only person in the family who used the Fontenay-sous-Bois library. This "library" was a small office with a counter enclosed in a sort of cage. A woman behind the counter communicated with the public through a square opening in the bars; behind her we could see shelves filled with books. I assume that my grandmother just told the woman what kind of reading she wanted and took whatever was given to her. She always brought home three or four books: popular novels by Eugène Sue or Émile Zola, or romances of the kind that made my parents shrug their shoulders—which didn't prevent my grandmother from devouring her books with unbounded pleasure.

In the villa de l'Ouest, we exchanged comic books. Some of the most popular were *Les Pieds Nikelés* (the adventures of three scoundrels) or Alain St. Ogan's *Zig et Puce* (a little boy and his penguin). But my favorite was *Bicot*, which was about a little boy with a red coat and a round cap. Bicot, who had a pretty older sister, lived in a strangely neat street with lawns in front of houses, and played a game with a ball, a glove and a stick. I had no idea he was American. I discovered later that this comic book was the translation of *Winnie Winkle*, and that Bicot was none other than Winnie's little brother, Perry Winkle. Bicot had many friends who always met in a special place they called their clubhouse, which made me think that it would be a great idea if all the friends of the villa de l'Ouest also had a clubhouse (or, as we say in French *un club*).

At the end of my garden, by the henhouse that stood empty since the war was over, was a small shed where my father stored odds and ends. The plaster walls inside the shed were covered with cobwebs and the floor strewn with dead leaves. I showed it to my friends who agreed it would make a wonderful *club*. After my father emptied the shed, we all worked at cleaning it up. When we were finished we brought in some chairs and decorated the walls with pictures. It turned out that the preparations were more fun than the results. When our *club* was finished, we sat around not knowing what to do. One thing I remember is that Dédé Anciaux, pretending to hold a movie camera, did not leave Patrick alone: he constantly pretented to "film" him, going "bzzz, bzzz, bzzz." It was mildly funny for a minute, but Dédé would not stop. Every time we met in the clubhouse, he would bring his "equipment" and go: "bzzz, bzzz, bzzz." It drove Patrick crazy—and the rest of us too. We soon abandoned our clubhouse and went back to playing in the villa de l'Ouest.

Other readings of my childhood made a strong impression on me. One was a pirate story: *Le Fils de Gaspard Le Rouge* (*The Son of Gaspard the Red*), which left me with a love for tall ships; another was a children's book, forgotten now, given to me on my birthday by my cousin Roger. Titled *Simone et les Blanc-Blanc*, it was the story of a little girl who went with her parents to Martinique. When, for some reason, Simone's parents had to return to Paris, they left their daughter for a time in the care of the large Blanc-Blanc family. Simone was very happy and had fun playing with all the children (it was obvious that the author was using the story to describe Martinique and its customs). Until then, I knew nothing of black people. There were no black kids in my school since no black families lived in the area. An African face was rare, seen occasionally in the métro. I became fascinated by the Blanc-Blanc family, especially by the mother, Madame Blanc-Blanc, a large woman with a round face, who was an expert at twisting a colorful scarf into a headdress and who possessed a comfortable chest where Simone could rest her head. It is now a rather embarrassing image, but at that time I had never heard of stereotypes and viewed Madame Blanc-Blanc strictly as an individual. Craving for caresses, I longed for Madame Blanc-Blanc. When I was sad at night, I imagined her by my side. I pressed my head on her soft breasts while she patted my hair with her soothing hand. Today, as I reminisce about this, I find it befitting to offer my gratitude to Madame Blanc-Blanc, who was there for me when I most needed her.

By contrast, there was a children's book I didn't like at all. It was called *Les Aventures de Frère Lapin* and was my first purchase in a used book store. I had passed this store many times, but had never dared to enter. Finally, heart pounding, I went in by myself, picked a book and paid for it, acting as if it were something that I had done a million times. From the picture on the cover I thought the book would tell the adventures of a cute little rabbit, but soon discovered that the rabbit wasn't cute at all. He was cunning and sly, always ready to trick some other animal. Successful most of the time, he himself was tricked one day when, through the ruse of a fox, he got stuck to what was described as a scarecrow made of tar. I thought this was the strangest thing I had ever read. What author could think of a thing like that? Of course, I found out much later that my little French rabbit was not French at all. He was in fact "Brer Rabbit," the trickster from Uncle Remus' stories, the one who got stuck to the tar-baby. These stories, perhaps a mixture of African tales and slave defiance, were something that, at the time, I had no way of understanding.

EIGHT

1948 - 1950

1

New School, Colette and More

In October 1948, a month after my thirteenth birthday, I started school at the *Cours Complémentaire de Vincennes*. I took the bus to school and was happy to discover that I had the same schedule as a handsome red-haired young man. I thought about him a lot and wrote him love notes, undelivered, of course. I gave him a name: Martial. In my notes, his hair wasn't red but "auburn." Though I shamelessly looked at him, I cannot say for sure that he ever noticed me.

When I did not take the bus, I rode my bicycle. As I was often late, I had to pedal at top speed. I was lucky sometimes when a pickup truck passed close by; I grabbed on to the side of the truck, held onto it and rode effortlessly through traffic (I didn't tell my father).

My school was in an old gray stone building surrounded by high walls. It looked like a stylish (but somewhat decrepit) mansion. We entered through an iron gate and crossed a little garden. On the right was the residence of the concierge, on the left, the office of *Madame la Directrice*. Straight ahead was the school itself. Like my elementary school, the *Cours Complémentaire de Vincennes* was an all-girls school. (The school does not exist any more; it has been razed and replaced with apartment buildings.)

If *cours complémentaires* were considered proletarian compared to lycées, this was not the case for the Vincennes establishment, which was an ex-private school recently converted into a public school..

The *Cours complémentaires* were created in 1880 to allow working class children to extend their education beyond primary school. While children of the bourgeoisie received an excellent education in the lycées, the *cours complémentaires* tended to offer an education of lesser quality, with teachers not always qualified. This went on for some years until the government, recognizing it was unfair, ordered a series of reforms between 1945 and 1959 which resulted in making *cours complémentaires* comparable to lycées. By 1975, when new institutions called *collèges* (junior high schools) were created, the *cours complémentaires* ceased to exist.

The *Cours Complémentaire de Vincennes* did not follow this pattern. The private girls' school which occupied the building would have had to close (for financial reasons, I assume) had not the government taken it over. Its old name *Cours Lamartine*, still appeared on the façade. The good thing about this takeover was that the former teachers (all women) were retained. And what teachers they were! Most of them held the *agrégation* (a prestigious higher education diploma). I was very lucky indeed to find myself surrounded, almost by accident, by a group of remarkable women, who, each in her own way, would contribute to changing my life.

Every three months, students were ranked according to test results. In the classrooms, the best students sat in front, the less successful in back. As a new student, I found myself sitting in the back rows (which turned out to be fun). I was moved at the end of the first trimester, and from then on, stayed in the front rows, regularly ranking in the first ten, and often the first five in the class. My initial months at the new school were uneventful until I met Colette Brun, who was to become my lifelong friend.

Colette was very popular. Before the teacher arrived and the class began (we didn't go from class to class, teachers came to our home room), she told funny anecdotes to the girls sitting close to her, while other girls gathered in the nearby aisle to listen and laugh. Since I didn't know anybody, I didn't dare to approach this little group. When, encouraged by Colette, I got closer, I found her delightfully funny; she was like a stand-up comic, telling jokes about members of her family to make us laugh, while at the same time leaving no doubt about her affection for them. Our friendship started slowly. I soon realized that there was much more to her than being the class entertainer. In fact, when I got to know her better, I found her to be serious and reflective, though with a good sense of humor. As months went by, we continued to become closer. I found it easy to share confidences with her. She was always receptive and understanding. Besides what I could call "an attraction of the soul," we had things in common: we shared the same first name, we were both born in September (she was one year older than me), both our fathers were printers, and we both lived in Fontenay-sous-Bois. This last common point meant that we generally met in the morning bus. She lived a few stops beyond mine and was already in the bus when I boarded it. After school, we took the bus home together.

My friend Colette Brun in the Tuileries Gardens. (1950)

Going to a new school didn't prevent me from seeing my villa de l'Ouest friends. We no longer spent time in the villa, but whenever we had a chance we went out together to explore different districts of Paris. We often went to *les Grands Boulevards*, walking from Porte Saint-Denis to Place de l'Opéra. No longer the place where strolling *boulevardiers*, swinging their canes and whistling a tune, flirted with *midinettes* (haute couture seamstresses), the boulevards had nevertheless kept their festive character. There were many improvised booths from which salesmen demonstrated their merchandise, surrounded less by buyers than by gawkers fascinated by the salesmen's colorful pitch. There were also animated cafés, theaters, movie houses, and many stores that we got to know well. I particularly remember the *boutique de farces et attrapes* (jokes and gags store), with its little laughing-man automaton in the window. We also went to the Eiffel Tower, going up by elevator and down by the stairs (a memorable descent). We explored Montmartre. From métro Place Blanche, near the Moulin Rouge, we climbed the steep rue Lepic, went to Place du Tertre and on to the Sacré-Coeur. Once in a while we visited the Musée du Louvre. There, our friend Lili had a surprise. Apparently new to the museum, when she turned her attention to Greek statues of nude heroes and athletes, she could not believe her eyes—and even less lower them.

With my villa de l'Ouest friends on the *Grands Boulevards*. From left: Robert Chourlay, me, Patrick, Pierrette, Lili, Jean Grosso, Jacqui. (c. 1950)

In the summer, we went to Nogent and walked along the river Marne, looking at the boaters and listening to music coming out of the *"dancings."* And, of course, we never missed the big yearly fair, *la Foire du Trône*, on Place de la Nation. All my friends loved to go on rides, but I didn't go, the rides made me motion-sick. What I enjoyed most at the fair were the small blown-glass animals that a booth keeper created before our eyes. I always bought some, holding them so very delicately in the métro. But most of them broke before I got home (or shortly after, if they survived the trip).

It was around that time that Patrick and I fell in love. We didn't say a thing; it was all in our eyes. At night, sitting up in bed, I wrote him love letters on a minuscule notebook of lined green paper. These "letters," all starting with *"My dearest Pat"* (in "real life," nobody, including me, ever called him Pat) were, as far as I remember, full of clichés and childish romanticism. After writing seventy-two of them (for some reason, I remember that number), I realized how silly they were and threw them all away. Good thing Patrick never even knew they existed!

If my love was mostly an illusion, Patrick, poor dear, truly gave me his heart, a heart that I would later negligently break. But at that time I was sincere, and I became deeply touched when he gave me a present, the first I had ever received from a boy: a Toblerone chocolate bar. (He had style.) Sweet love in every sweet bite.

Patrick and I even had "our" song. Nowadays every kid learning the piano plays Beethoven's *Für Elise*, but when I was young, it was not particularly common. After several years of taking piano lesson with the piano teacher who lived across the street from my parents' house, I asked my father if I could go to another teacher. I had not learned to play a single melody, and since I hardly ever practiced my scales, my knowledge of music had remained elementary. My new teacher was an older lady, about sixty-five, always dressed in elegant clothes, velvety and black, as if she was ready for the opera. She always held a white handkerchief in her hand. I addressed her as *Mademoiselle*, as I had my previous teacher, who was a spinster. But the new teacher insisted on *Madame*. Right away she started me on *Für Elise*, and I soon learned it to the great pride of my father. When I made a mistake, she shook her handkerchief over the keyboard, and I apologized, *"Excusez-moi, Mademoiselle!"*

My friend Patrick. (c. 1950)

"Madame!" she corrected me sternly.

She loved to gossip and asked me a lot of questions about my previous teacher,

"I have heard that she always keeps a glass of wine on the piano, and that she teaches *chansons* to her students. Is that true?"

"No! Not at all! That is not true at all, *Mademoiselle*."

"*Madame!*"

She also told me how awful men were, not during the day, but in bed, at night.

"You will see, ma petite, they won't leave you alone, they will keep begging you and begging you to do that awful thing!"

Once, she asked me to follow her to the kitchen where she wanted to show me something. I had never seen a kitchen like that in my whole life! It was like a scene from *Great Expectations*: all the cupboards, counter tops and shelves were crowded with empty glass bottle and jars, everything completely covered with dust and cobwebs. I was so taken by the sight, that I have now forgotten what it was she showed me that day.

To come back to "our" song; it was none other, of course, than *Für Elise*. When I heard Patrick whistling the melody in front of my house, I came out to talk to him, or if I started playing it on the piano, he miraculously appeared. Sometimes, he sang words to it: *"Aux derniers rayons du soleil d'or"* ("By the last rays of the golden sun"). Beethoven's piece had been turned into a chanson, popularized by the *chanteur* Armand Mestral.

About a year passed between the time we fell in love and the time we held hands at the movies. And after that, almost two years would pass before we shared our first and only kiss.

2
Sainte-Aubierge

Tante Marthe, Oncle Albert and Miquette lived on rue Saint Sébastien in the Popincourt district, not far from the *Quartier du Marais*, which at that time was still Paris' main Jewish neighborhood, not the picturesque art district it has become. From the St. Ambroise métro station, it was a short walk on Boulevard Voltaire to their apartment. The Boulevard, sometimes crowded, always animated, was lined with shops and sidewalk stands which sold *souvenirs de Paris*, scarves, umbrellas, presents of all kinds. I especially liked to visit at Christmas time when it was dark early and the asphalt was shiny with rain or melting snow. Glittering clothing boutiques and toy store windows were crisscrossed with strings of tinsel. Restaurants tempted passers-by with their displays of oysters, mussels, dark-pink sea urchins and tiny *chapeaux de gendarmes* (black hat-shaped shellfish) laid on beds of crushed ice and seaweed. *Charcuteries* exhibited rows of little pigs sculpted out of *pâté*, with eyes of truffles. The brightly-lit windows of *boulangeries/pâtisseries* overflowed with *éclairs, babas au rhum, mille-feuilles*, (napoleons), *choux à la crème*, and *tartes aux fruits* whose sparkling glaze reflected the surrounding lights. The sweet smell of *pralines* (roasted almonds dipped in pink sugar) filled the air. Pralines were as much a part of the Parisian winter holidays as were roasted chestnuts.

Whenever I visited my aunt and uncle I was always warmly welcomed. Tante Marthe, unlike Tante Yvonne, never criticized my appearance or anything I did (actually, she was not really interested in me, absorbed as she was by her own preoccupations), but she was nice and that suited me fine. Oncle Albert was nice also. He teased me sometimes, but always gently. I was no longer "in love" with him by then, but still had much admiration for his dead-pan jokes and easy repartees, wondering how he could think so fast. He had a special "style" that would later be imitated by some members of the family—with limited success. But in the

Schuschmann household, it was my cousin Miquette who was my favorite. She was still like a big sister to me and I always felt comfortable and happy in her presence. We shared our love secrets, and if I didn't have many yet, she had plenty. My cousin had become a beautiful young woman with a face impossible to forget and a remarkable body. She was already, as she put it later, "cursed with big breasts" (now we might say "blessed.") Curvy and narrow-waisted, she was, in my opinion, a world-class beauty. Her complexion was milky-white with pink highlights, her high cheekbones accentuated the slant of her deep-blue eyes, and her temptress' lips revealed the brightness of her teeth. Influenced by her mother who acted like a movie star, Miquette had adopted expressions and postures that would have been fine in a Hollywood movie of the time, but were rather overdone and perhaps too dramatic for a sixteen-year old in Paris. Her blue eye shadow and bright-red lipstick made men think that she was mature and available, when in reality, mature she was not yet, and available she was not at all. What she was looking for was love, pure, true love, perhaps with kisses, but certainly not with anything else. And these men, these *cochons*, always wanted the same thing! She had many amours, hopelessly fell in love again and again, but in the end had to break up in disgust. I didn't tell anyone about Miquette's stories, that is, not anyone except Colette. Soon *Les Amours de Miquette* became one of our favorite subjects of conversation; together we commiserated on the fate of my poor cousin.

My cousin Miquette. Later photo. (c. 1960)

Most of the buildings on rue Saint Sébastien and in the neighborhood were old, their gray facades darkened by city soot. My aunt and uncle lived in such a building. Upon entering it, we followed a narrow corridor and climbed wooden steps, not always well swept. From the dingy stairwell windows we looked down onto an industrial and commercial courtyard. Not far away, on rue des Gravilliers, in the *Quartier du Temple*, Oncle Albert's parents lived in a similar, but even older building where the rent was cheap and where it was easy to set up a workshop. There, as they had for many years, they worked at their power sewing machines, manufacturing workers' cloth caps. Tante Marthe now also spent time at their apartment, working at a sewing machine. It was still by selling such cloth caps (as well as women's purses) at outdoor markets that Tante Marthe and Oncle Albert made their living. Miquette helped with packing, unpacking, and selling the merchandise. At the age of fourteen she had been put to work and had worked ever since. After she finished school at fourteen, no one ever asked her if she wanted to continue studying or learn a trade. Willing or not, she had been expected to help the family.

It was at about that time that Lydie, Oncle Albert's daughter by his first wife, renewed contact with her father. From the time her parents had separated, at the beginning of the war, Lydie had been brought up by relatives. She was about my age. I can say I was a little in awe of her, intimidated by her exotic beauty. Her skin was light copper; her black hair tightly pulled back outlined the perfect oval of a face smooth as stone and pierced by the most beautiful green-yellow eyes. Now it appeared that she was going to be Miquette's sister and my cousin; she had decided to come and live with my aunt and uncle. But somehow, it never happened. She disappeared for long periods. All in all, I only saw her two or three times.

In spite of the fact that Tante Marthe and Oncle Albert didn't make a lot of money, they loved to go out. They often ate at restaurants in Paris or took trips to the country to drink champagne with their friends.

"And so what if our friends are pimps and prostitutes? They know how to relax, to enjoy themselves." they said.

On a more restrained note, they also liked to go to radio shows, to which they took my cousins and me when I happened to be around. At that time we had no television; many variety and talk shows took place in radio studios. We were the "live audience" and got to see many celebrities, among them the popular band leader Raymond Legrand (his son, Michel Legrand, would also become a famous composer) and the legendary opera singer Lili Pons. I particularly remember one guest, the beautiful ballet dancer, Ludmilla Tchérina, one of the stars of the movies *The Tales of Hoffmann* and *The Red Shoes*. She was accompanied by her husband, who, after being asked if there was something that irritated him about his wife, casually answered that when she shaved her legs, she borrowed his razor and returned it blunt. I couldn't believe that these almost mythological people would do and say such mundane and shameful things! At that point I had just started to shave my legs (with my father's razor), something I would not have dreamt of mentioning to anyone.

My aunt and uncle also took us to the cinema, not to ordinary movie theaters like the Palais-des-Fêtes, but to the biggest and fanciest Parisian movie houses: the immense Gaumont Palace or the Rex, which had a ceiling like a planetarium, full of twinkling stars. They were also music lovers, especially enthusiastic about Gershwin. Their influence on the family was such that their admiration for *Rhapsody in Blue* prompted my cousin Roger, who hardly ever attended paying events, to take me to a Gershwin concert. Besides listening to music, Oncle Albert read a lot. It was through him that I discovered several classics of science fiction, as well as popular novels such as Cronin's *The Citadel*.

Even though Tante Marthe and Oncle Albert had the reputation of being more carefree than the rest of the family, I never heard anyone criticize them, not even on the day, when, almost out of money, they told us that they had used their last few francs to go to the movies. They were just considered free spirits. However, when my aunt bought ready-made food at the *charcuterie* (or worse, served sandwiches for dinner), it was something that was frowned upon. It was too radical a concept. For a woman, to do such a thing was considered mad, shameful, almost a mutiny.

I do not know what made my aunt and uncle, these genuine Parisians, decide to move to the country, but suddenly, they declared that they had had enough of the city; they couldn't breathe; they wanted to live in the open air, far away from the noise and the agitation of Paris. And when they moved, they did not do things half-way. They didn't pick a quiet provincial town, or even a small village. They picked Sainte-Aubierge, a spot completely isolated, which consisted of a single house, a chapel, a natural spring, and a wash-house no longer in use.

Talking to my cousin Miquette some time ago, she made me realize something I hadn't considered at the time: that this move was unfair to her. And I do understand. There was nothing in Sainte-Aubierge, no cinemas, no stores, no friends, no men. She was of dating age then, and in spite of the enthusiasm she showed at first, she must have soon realized that country life was not such fun after all. She complained that her mother never had her interest in mind, but "used" her, first by making her work at selling merchandise (and later at manufacturing it), second, by expecting her to provide more than her fair share of help around the house. I think it is true, although I am quite sure that Tante Marthe didn't plan it that way. Focused on her married life as she was, she probably didn't put much thought into how her actions would affect her daughter, neither at that time, nor in the future.

I stayed in Sainte-Aubierge quite often, especially during Easter or summer vacations. Sainte-Aubierge is in the Brie Province, about fifty miles east of Paris, outside the village of Mauperthuis. The train deposited me in the small town of Faremoutiers where Oncle Albert, accompanied by all my cousins, picked me up in his car. I always looked forward to spending time, not only with Miquette, but also with her brothers Jacques and Claude. Since my aunt had lost the custody of her sons after the war, I didn't get to see my two cousins as often as I saw Miquette. I mostly saw them when they visited their mother, or sometimes when they came to Tante Valentine's. As children we had played together in Oncle Baptiste's garden and had gone with Tata Valentine to see the animated Christmas windows; now that we were teenagers we were happy to find ourselves together again. Jacques was full of gallant attentions toward me, and Claude, still childish, was always up to mischief. Both were handsome and smart, and I loved their company.

The locality of Sainte-Aubierge came alive once a year. Originally a place where pilgrims worshiped a saint of the Middle Ages (an abbess who died in the seventh century), it became around Easter time the site of a large

The chapel in Sainte-Aubierge. Old Postcard.

fair that spread itself out on the meadows in front of the house. The small chapel, closed the rest of the year, was open for a few days to the fair-goers who came by the hundreds. They prayed if they felt like it, but mostly went on rides, shot guns in booths, or danced under a big tent stretched not far from the house. In the tent, a live band played on an elevated platform while people danced on the specially installed hardwood floor or relaxed at the café-bar. The fair was great fun and lasted three or four days. People lined up to go inside the ancient stone structure that protected the fountain; they tasted the water, cool and pure, said to grant eternal bliss to lovers; and visited the wash-house. The partially roofed wash-house looked like a small swimming-pool surrounded by an enclosure, also built of ancient stones. (My cousins and I felt sorry for the washer-women of the past whose hands must have been numbed by the freezing spring water.) We ran into crowds wherever we went. The merry-go-round music played until late in the evenings. The smell of sugar candy was in the air.

My cousin Miquette in front of the chapel. (1949)

Except for these yearly festivities, Sainte-Aubierge was extremely quiet. Its only house, the one where my aunt and uncle lived, was an old farmhouse which must have belonged to a rich farmer, perhaps a relative of the present owners. The farmer's house had been remodeled and divided into two residences: a small one, which my aunt and uncle rented, and a large one which the owners kept as their summer home. Of the farm, there only remained a barn still stacked with hay, and, at the back of the house, a stable in disrepair, a couple of empty sheds, and a few pieces of rusting equipment.

Outside, grass grew on gently rolling slopes, and a short distance away a forest began. My cousins and I often went to the forest, enjoying our walks on soft moss or crackling leaves. In the spring, we picked violets and wild strawberries, and pointed out to one another the brightly colored mushrooms we spied under the trees. I still long for the smells and sounds of this friendly forest, and always wanted to go back. But not long ago my cousin Jacques told me that, in fact, he did go back.

"What a disappointment!" he said, "There is no more forest. It has been decimated." It made us very sad.

Looking through my photo album I find only a few pictures of our time in Sainte-Aubierge, but two of these, which I took of my cousin Claude, seem to capture our spirit: on the first, perched high in a tree, Claude strikes a pose that evokes a bow and arrow, feet wide apart, one hand holding onto a higher branch; on the other, sitting on one heel, he straddles the spout-shaped stone from which the flow of water coming from the spring cascades into the wash-house. In both photos, he looks like a mischievous young Pan, with sunshine playing in his hair.

My cousin Claude in Sainte-Aubierge. (1949)

In their enthusiasm for country life, my aunt and uncle acquired some pets, a few of these traditional, the others friendly farm creatures. I remember their three dogs: Pernod, Pastis, and Anisette. The dogs got along very well; one could see them sleeping under the kitchen table. Anisette, the small fluffy terrier, leaning either on Pastis, the golden retriever, or on nice old Pernod, a mixed hound, black and brown, with a strong body, short legs and long silky ears. Pernod's favorite place

293

was an old Louis XVI chair whose legs had been cut off. When my cousins and I went for a walk, Pernod always followed. He loved to go in the water (there was a river nearby), but could not stand to see us swim; he was convinced we were drowning and frantically came to our rescue by pouncing on us (and making us almost drown in the process). We just loved him. One day, as we were crossing a bridge over the river, we decided to sit on the stone parapet. Suddenly, Pernod put it in his mind to join us. He jumped from the street but, miscalculating the width of the parapet, he flew over the ridge, diving straight into the river (nothing bad happened to him: he just swam to shore). I will never forget the sight of old Pernod taking an Olympic dive to our great astonishment. After that, the simple mention of Pernod's dive was enough to get us giggling.

When my cousin Jacques came to visit me in Sonoma in 2003, he reminded me of some Sainte-Aubierge animal stories that I had forgotten.

Besides the dogs, my aunt and uncle also kept as pets two goats, a couple of hens, a rooster, a duck, and a rabbit. They also fed three or four abandoned cats that had the reputation of killing vipers. The goats, tied to long ropes on the hilly meadow in front of the house, were very naughty. They forever tried to eat whatever they could, but were particularly fond of our magazines, the clothes we dropped by mistake, and, of course, our straw hats. After milking the goats, my aunt poured some milk in a big dish that she set on the ground. The dogs and cats made a circle around the dish to drink the milk, while the duck—a baby still yellow—splashed happily in the middle.

Jacques also told me that Pernod was a thief, but a thief who had the good sense of bringing his booty to his masters. Once, he stole an egg and carried it in his mouth without breaking it. Another time he picked up a wrapped package of sliced ham, the lunch of some people who were camping nearby. My aunt apologized to them, went to the village *charcuterie* to buy a replacement for the campers, and served Pernod's ham for our own lunch.

Sainte-Aubierge has passed in the family lore as a sort of idyllic land of our childhood. Two images, both from Jacques' memory, have almost the color of myth: Jacques, playing toreador with a cow in a meadow, in front of his mother, who is laughing, laughing; our cousin Roger, in the middle of the river where we are all bathing, his dripping hair in his face, waving a stick and shouting, "I am Neptune! I am Neptune!"

There was something else about Sainte-Aubierge that fascinated me. It had to do with the owners' part of the house. My aunt had a key to it. Entrusted to go inside to air out the rooms she once in a while let us go there, provided we didn't touch anything. When we were allowed to go, we made sure not to displace any objects—sometimes with exaggerated precautions—and always left the place exactly as we found it. One evening when my aunt had guests we even got to spend the night in the forbidden wing of the house. Lying on a big bed, the four of us tried to convince one another that the house was haunted. The shriek of the owl that lived in the chapel made us almost believe it.

Up to that time I had never been in what is called *"une maison bourgeoise."* My house and Tante Valentine's were decorated simply, their furniture already a little old-fashioned. As for Tante Yvonne and Tante Marthe's interiors, they were both tasteful, but modern. By contrast, the owners' residence was in true "bourgeois style" with antique furniture, oriental carpets, oil paintings, and a library whose glass cases were filled with leather-bound books. The bedrooms were rich with country armoires and fluffy beds with carved headboards, the *salon* replete with stylish sofas and slim-footed armchairs. A small and rather mysterious dressing room was one of our favorite spots; it held a mirrored table overflowing with perfume bottles, lipsticks, makeup jars and powder puffs, all thrown about, as if waiting to be used. I fell in love with this house and explored it as if it were a fairytale castle. I wanted a house just like that when I grew up. Of all the rooms, I especially liked the library. My cousins and I would sit on the floor and look at the books. There was a marvelous volume with the picture of a frog on transparent plates. When we lifted one transparency we could see the frog's circulation system with red arteries and blue veins; another transparency showed the nervous system; and there were more layers still. It was always a treat to go to this house, but my aunt rarely gave us permission to do so.

For a long time, the owners did not come. But one day, not long before my aunt and uncle left Sainte-Aubierge for good, they arrived. It was at the time of the Easter festival and I happened to be there.

The lady of the house was friendly. She had a husband, Monsieur Silvagni, a renowned painter and gallery owner—whom I didn't meet, and a step-son, Philippe Silvagni—whom I did meet. Philippe was tall and distinguished. He had a thin mustache and large brown Italian eyes with long lashes. He was sixteen, in *seconde de lycée* (10th grade); I was thirteen, in *cinquième de cours complémentaire* (7th grade). He immediately began flirting with me, and spent much time with me at the fair. He even helped with my aunt and uncle's improvised business: a "bicycle garage" in their yard, for the duration of the fair. Philippe asked me for my address in Fontenay-sous-Bois and promised he would be in touch (a promise that he kept, to my great surprise).

Eventually, after less than two years of country life, my aunt and uncle got to dislike living in Sainte-Aubierge: the nearest grocery store was almost a mile away, the neighbors were standoffish, winters in the country were no fun at all (they hated the mud), springs were no better (they couldn't stand the carnival). In other words, they were bored. Moreover, they were broke. They couldn't pay their bills and even less their taxes. The fact is, when they left Sainte-Aubierge, it wasn't on a nice note: their possessions were taken out of their house, stacked in their front yard, and auctioned to the highest bidder. Of course, all the villagers were there for the show. Pernod and Pastis were given to people in the country, while little Anisette was lucky to find a very nice home in the villa de l'Ouest, almost next door to my house.

3
A Lot about Printing and a Little about Kissing

"And what does a kiss feel like?" I asked Pierrette.

"Oh! I don't know, kinda like a snail crawling on your lips."

This certainly wasn't what I expected. At that time, my notion of kisses had more to do with Hollywood romance than with mollusk locomotion. Pierrette was sixteen, but I, at fourteen, would have to wait to do my own experimenting. At least now, when Patrick and I went to the movies, we held hands. It was exciting at the beginning of the film, but after a while when our hands became clammy it became embarrassing. We kept our fingers locked because we didn't know what else to do, but it distracted us from what was happening on the screen.

As for Papa, he still came home late at night or didn't come at all. Most of the time I had dinner at Tante Valentine's, but, now that I had more homework, I returned home right away and spent my evenings working at my desk, in my bedroom.

When I got up in the morning, my greatest pleasure was to talk to my father. Then, his mind was sharp and he was always in a good mood. Our morning conversations centered most of the time on his work as a newspaper printer.

I knew quite a bit about printing already since so many members of my family were printers. Before the turn of century my grandfather Cessot was already a newspaper printer. Later, my grandmother, my uncle Félix, my mother, my father, Tante Yvonne, my cousins Paulette and Denise's husbands, all worked *dans la presse*.

The general term for newspaper printers was *imprimeurs* (printers), but the initiate referred to them by their specialty: *linotypistes* (linotype operators), *typographes* (typographers), *rotativistes* (rotary press operators), or in abbreviated form: *linos, typos, rotos*. My father was a *clicheur* (stereotype plate-maker). This profession which bore the official name of *stéréotypeur-galvanoplaste*, has now ceased to exist. It was eliminated with the transition to offset printing in the fifties and sixties and the arrival of computers in the eighties.

The newspaper printing district in Paris, *le Quartier de la Presse*, located in the 2nd arrondissement, was centered around the métro station Sentier, where rue Montmartre (which is not in Montmartre) crosses rue Réaumur. It included many surrounding streets such as rue du Sentier, rue du Croissant, Faubourg Poissonnière, etc. Close to *la Bourse* (the Stock Exchange), this district was not far from where *le Musée Pompidou* is now. It was there that most newspapers had their printing plants, in older buildings with enormous underground spaces where huge rotary presses sometimes ran all night. My father worked rue du Croissant for *l'Imprimerie Centrale du Croissant*, a mid-sized printing shop which did not print dailies, but a variety of weeklies or monthlies: *l'Argus* (the official automobile publication), *l'Éducation Nationale* (the Education Ministry newspaper), *le Libertaire* (the anarchist mouthpiece), *Juvénal* (a conservative satirical review), etc. In nearby streets were printed *Le Figaro*, *L'Équipe*, *L'Humanité*, *France-Soir*, and other titles.

My father often brought home several newspapers, as these were freely exchanged among printers (though he did buy his own favorite daily, *Le Parisien Libéré*). Avid newspaper readers, both my father and I spent much time in the kitchen, our papers balanced on the sugar bowl at breakfast or the bottles of wine or Eau de Vichy at lunch, reading and discussing the news. Not the most polite way of doing things, but so wonderfully pleasurable.

Having been brought up among printers, I was familiar with the various steps of newspaper production. Now that the old way of printing exists only in the past, I think it will be useful to describe these steps, if only to give a better idea of my relatives' daily lives.

After the journalists had written their copy and delivered it to their editors for review and approval, the copy was passed on to the linotype operators. Sitting at their seven-foot-tall black machines lined in a row, the linotype operators typed the copy on their machines' keyboards. My mother was one of these operators. The typed text was not produced on paper, but could be seen in relief on the thin edges of small metal plates called *lignes* (lines, or "slugs"). The characters on these column-wide lines were cast in molten lead from reusable molds inside the machine. The metal lines gathered automatically in the upper part of the linotype machine, forming text that read backward, very much like the words on a rubber stamp. To check their work, the linotype operators read the lines backward without difficulty. I remember that my mother never ceased to amaze me with her backward-reading talent. I also remember the few times when, as a child, I was taken to her printing house. Maman typed a metal line with my name on it and gave it to me, still a little hot.

From the columns of metal lines, proofs or galleys were printed and sent to the composing room (located on the printing house upper floor) where they were checked by *correcteurs* (proofreaders) who sat in small glassed-in offices. After the corrections were made, and lines were retyped, new proofs were taken. The proofread copy was then handed to the *metteurs en page* (compositors) who worked on high tables referred to as *"le marbre"* (in the old time, these tables were actually made of marble). The *metteurs en page* designed the newspaper and prepared a *maquette* (a dummy), working with proofs of text, titles, and photos.

The blocks of metal lines, duly corrected, were then picked up by the typographers who set them in a rectangular iron case (*une forme*) and secured them with "keys." Together with the metal lines arranged in columns according to the compositors' design, were titles, photos and illustrations that had been produced on metal through a photogravure process.

My grandfather, a typographer, had begun his career before the introduction of linotype machines, when the text was still composed by hand with movable type. In his youth, he had learned the traditional printing trade, selecting metal characters one at a time from a double box called *une casse* (a case), where capital letters were stored in the upper case and small letters in the lower case. As for my grandmother, at the beginning of her career, she had been trained in lithography, a process later replaced by photogravure.

Once the newspaper was composed in metal inside the *forme*, a proof was taken by rubbing ink on the metal, applying a piece of paper on the characters, and carefully tapping the back of the paper with a brush. Typographers and proofreaders re-checked this almost final proof for errors or typos, called *coquilles* ("shells"). As this process was going on, it was said that the newspaper was still *"sur le marbre"* ("on the marble"), upstairs, and that it had not yet "fallen." It meant that the compositors were still busy, and that the *clicheurs*, who were downstairs, couldn't start working yet. Finally when everything was duly reviewed, *le bon à tirer* (the printing authorization) was issued.

The streets in the *Quartier de la Presse* were amazingly narrow. It was hard to imagine they hid such enormous establishments. Besides printing houses, they also harbored a great number of small cafés, typical Parisian bistros. There was a reason for this multiplicity of cafés: printers didn't have regular work hours; they reported in shifts, some at approximately the time the newspaper was supposed "to fall." However, this was not very precise due to the fact that sometimes the copy was not delivered on time, late news needed to be included, or some problems arose with the composition. When that happened—and it was most days—the printers had to wait in cafés, until someone from the printing house came to announce: *"Le journal est tombé!"* (The newspaper "has fallen!") My father and his team of about five or six *clicheurs* always waited at a special café in the rue du Croissant, where they were well-known and considered "family" by the establishment. There, my father, who in the past had jokingly called all his friends *"P'tit Jules,"* saw the name stick to himself and was called by *la patronne* and some of the customers: *"Monsieur Jules."* I often went with Papa to "his" café, where I was known as *"la fille de Monsieur Jules."*

The frames containing the pages set in metal characters by the typographers were handed to the *clicheurs* who verified one more time that the size of margins, the spaces around the illustrations, etc., were correct (and—even at this late stage—also pointed out corrections whenever they discovered some *"coquilles"*). After final approval by the *clicheurs*' team manager, a cardboard imprint or matrix, *le flan* (the flong), was produced by using a press to take an imprint of the metal composition. This cardboard (or rather papier-mâché) flong, which now bore hollow imprints, was placed in a machine that gave it a semi-cylindrical shape.

The manager of my father's team was Louis Vélard, a very funny man with a crooked mouth, a broken voice, and a gift for Parisian slang. My father and I sometimes went to the restaurant with him and his wife, a woman older than he was, very witty, who had been the madam of a "high-class" *maison de plaisir*, and looked like an aging movie star with her furs, jewels and frizzy dyed hair. All the *clicheurs* at *l'Imprimerie Centrale du Croissant* had worked together most of their lives. They were good friends, and often ate out or went fishing together on weekends.

Now the curved cardboard imprint was given to my father, whose specialty within the *clicheur* team was to operate the stereotype machine. From this cardboard matrix, the machine produced a cast—in an alloy composed mostly of lead—through a process of galvanoplasty. The machine was extremely precise and melted the alloy at high temperature. After checking the gauges my father pressed a lever to make the molten metal drop in a special compartment. (I have a photo of him at work, a leather apron around his waist, his hand on the machine locking device, a gauloise stuck to his lip.) When the metal had cooled, my father extracted the *cliché* (stéréotype), a thick semi-cylindrical piece of shiny metal whose outer surface bore characters in relief. After a final inspection, the *cliché*, now ready to make an imprint on paper, was sent out to the rotary press.

Although my father's specialty was to run the stereotype machine and his co-workers also had their own areas of specialization, the *clicheurs* were familiar with all stages of printing, and often participated in a great variety of tasks. The fact that these tasks—all done under time pressure—required a great deal of precision and concentration did not prevent the team members from joking and teasing one another in a battle of wit and a marvelously creative way of using the language (the slang of printers is well-known and has even found its place in a special dictionary).

One may wonder about the dangers of working with lead, especially in over-heated, windowless spaces. The printers, well aware of the health risks, took some precautions (knowing that these were not always fool-proof). My father, who went to work wearing city clothes, changed into work clothes as soon as he arrived at work. At the end of the day, before putting his city clothes back on, he took a shower. It was something that was part of the safety regulations, which also included regular medical checkups.

The heavy *clichés* were picked up by helpers who put them on carts and took them to the underground floor. There, they were secured to the big rotary presses which had already been fitted with *bobines*, huge reels of blank paper. (Everyone is familiar with these presses, often pictured in movies, with newspapers coming out at top speed from rolling cylinders.) My father took me downstairs a few times to show me the big presses; and what I remember best about them is how incredibly noisy they were. The rotary presses were operated by *rotativistes*, who, according to typographers and *clicheurs*, did not possess as many skills as other printers (at least that's what I always heard). Finally, the newspapers, printed, cut, and folded, were ready to go. They were bundled and taken to distribution firms, such as the Messageries Hachette, also located in the *Quartier de la Presse*. The parked trucks and loading activities created monstrous traffic jams in the extremely narrow streets.

I hope that these notes will give a better idea of a profession which played such an important role in my family's life. I also hope they will help convey the spirit of the morning conversations when my father and I discussed the printing world. These conversations brought us very close together, something that neither he nor I needed to acknowledge.

If an important aspect of working *dans la presse* was the printing milieu itself with its jokes, language, camaraderie, even its cafés, there was also another side: it was the workers' demands, the trade unions, the strikes. My father was the trade union representative for the *clicheurs* (and sometimes for all the printers) of *l'Imprimerie Centrale du Croissant*. Year after year he was reelected to this position by his co-workers.

Printers were not part of the bourgeois class. They were blue-collar workers, but with a difference. Not only were they the highest paid among workers, but, thanks to their familiarity with the written word, their proximity to journalists (at work and in the bistros), and their reputation as a group which historically created and printed the militant brochures that would often contribute to changing the social order, they were considered special, quasi-intellectual as it were.

As part of his trade union duties my father attended meetings, both with workers and with management, and it is evident that he was respected by all. He presented the workers' demands, bargained with the print-shop owners, coordinated with other union delegates, and, when it was unavoidable, carried and followed the order to strike. Trade unions in France were not all based on specific trades as they usually are in the United States; instead there were three or four major unions open to all workers regardless of trade. Papa was a delegate to the GCT (*Compagnie Générale du Travail*) which was affiliated with the left and had close ties to the Communist party. A more moderate union, the FO (*Force Ouvrière*) had been created in 1946 from a dissident faction of the CGT, and a Christian workers' union existed as well. While a number of printers were members of the other unions, most of those in my father's shop belonged to the CGT—even though some of them disagreed with the CGT's communist affiliation. As for my father, he was a leftist, voted communist, but never wanted to become a member of the Communist Party. He didn't read the communist newspaper, *L'Humanité*, which he found doctrinaire and boring. He also detested the cult of personality lavished on Stalin. While he (and he wasn't the only one) was not yet aware of the atrocities committed by the Stalinist regime, he felt that a man who wielded such immense power could only be a dictator—and he detested all dictators.

After the difficult years that followed the war, French workers demanding better conditions went on prolonged general strikes in 1947 and 1948. The CGT remained the trade union that best represented the printers' interests and was at the forefront of their struggle.

Through negotiations or strikes, printers made gains unique in the French industry. They obtained three weeks paid vacation—and later four—plus extra paid days at Christmas. They gained medical and retirement benefits that supplemented the already improved French Social Security system. Most of all, they secured an excellent salary. Newspaper printers were considered a model: whatever they obtained, other industries requested. They were often closely followed in their gains by the automobile industry.

My father was very conscientious about his work with the union, and I loved listening to him talk about it. In the kitchen, in the morning, when he gave me the latest news, I followed the negotiations and cheered at the gains. He also kept me up with events in the life of his co-workers, and shared with me some of the jokes and anecdotes he heard at the printing shop or in the cafés.

It was at the time of our morning conversations that I started reading the weekly anarchist newspaper, *Le Libertaire*, one of the papers that found its way home. I liked to argue that "intelligent people" have no need for government and should be free to live their lives as they saw fit, as long as they respected other people's rights. I felt sympathy for the underprivileged and anger toward "the ruling class," knowing, in fact, very little about either.

But my political awareness, effervescent as it was, wasn't to become the dominant element in my life. Other interests (especially love) were soon to take a more important place.

I was at Tante Valentine's house one afternoon after school, when someone rang the bell by the outside gate. Tante Valentine went to look,

"It's a young man," she told me, "he says he wants to see you."

"A young man?" I couldn't think who it might be. I went out to the gate. It was Philippe Silvagni, the son of the Sainte-Aubierge house owners! I couldn't believe it.

"How did you find me?" I asked.

"I went to the address you gave me at 10 Villa de l'Ouest, and since no one answered the bell, I tried next door at number 12 to see if the neighbors might know where you were." (I had not told Philippe that I sometimes was at number 12, my aunt's house. It was just a coincidence that he found me there.)

Tante Valentine asked me to let *"le jeune homme"* in, and offered him coffee and cookies. I explained to her how we had met. Philippe told us that he happened to pass through the neighborhood where he had just delivered one of his father's paintings.

"Where did you deliver it?" asked Tante Valentine. She was curious. She knew almost everyone in the district.

"At 46 rue Roublot," Philippe said.

Later on, when I walked him to the bus stop, he told me that it wasn't true. He hadn't delivered a painting. He had seen the street sign for rue Roublot in passing, and had just made up a number. (But Tante Valentine did uncover his fib. The next day, she went to number 46 and found out that there was nothing there, just an empty lot.)

"I had to see you," Philippe told me, "I kept thinking about you."

He was very convincing, but I was a little afraid. He was so mature (close to seventeen), so sophisticated, so gallant. He tried to kiss me when we parted but I pulled away, perhaps influenced by Pierrette's description of a kiss. I was not ready yet. And, of course, there was Patrick (although my feelings for him were beginning to change). Philippe and I promised to write or call. We wrote a few times, but never pursued this fledgling liaison. This brief episode did something to me, though. It made me think that boys were interested in me, even older boys, even fancy boys whose fathers owned art galleries. I didn't quite know what to make of it, but I vaguely felt that the world was wide, the choice was great, and love would most likely be found outside of my neighborhood.

4
Corsica

In the summer of 1950 my father and I took a vacation in Corsica. One of my father's friends at work knew someone on the island, Madame Jaspart, who lived in the little coastal town of Erbalunga.

"She will help you find a place to stay," the friend had said. "And by the way, she is married to a gendarme, hope you don't mind!"

"Well! Here goes my reputation!"

We took the train and first stopped in Marseilles, where, as good tourists, we had bouillabaisse at the port, strolled on the Canebière, and climbed the many steps to Notre-Dame de la Garde, the cathedral that dominates the city. It was very windy that day. The photos in my album show me laughing and trying to hold on to my skirt. From Marseilles, we took the train to Nice. The train between Marseilles and Nice follows the coast closely. Papa and I enjoyed catching sight of the blue of the sea and the white of a sail every time we emerged from one of the numerous tunnels that cut across the hills. In Nice, we had to wait for the ferry to Corsica; it left in the evening for a crossing that would last all night.

Marseilles. (1950)

We stayed on deck to enjoy the starry sky, I suppose. But we hadn't planned on a change in the weather. When a storm hits the Mediterranean, it is usually bad, and the storm that developed that night was a particularly nasty one. No rain, just a very choppy sea. I got terribly seasick. The only way I could maintain my countenance was by pretending I was a prisoner who was being tortured. I knew that my agony wouldn't stop unless I betrayed my friends. I kept repeating to myself, *"Je ne trahirai pas mes copains!"* ("I will not betray my friends!") And I did not. I held on till the end—though I was quite green when I got off the deck. Later, I told that little story to my father, who, to my embarrassment, repeated it to everyone.

We rested a while when we arrived in Bastia in order for me to feel better; but soon, I was dismayed to find out that to go to Erbalunga we had to take a bus for a trip of almost an hour on a coast-hugging road—which meant a turn every few seconds. Needless to say, my arrival in Erbalunga was not the most glorious. At the time, I could not have guessed that, of all the places I ever visited, this area of the Cap Corse would forever remain dear to me, leaving me attached to it as if it were my native land.

The beach and village of Erbalunga, viewed from my window. (1950)

We were welcomed by the friendly Jaspart couple. After Monsieur Jaspart and Papa had exchanged a few glasses of wine, Madame Jaspart took us to the lodgings she had reserved for us. We left the town and walked for a while along the shore. Then, what a surprise! Nothing will ever compare to the new quarters we were shown! We had two rooms in a house built on rocks at the very end of the beach, the only house there.

At the opposite end of the beach, we could see the old village of Erbalunga, one of the most picturesque in Corsica, with its red-roofed houses huddled behind the ruins of an ancient Genoese tower built on a narrow promontory. Spread inland between the old village and "our" house was the newer part of town where the Jasparts lived. The pebble beach, which began at the foot of the tower, stretched its soft curve and ended into a cliff of ragged brown rocks beaten by the sea, the rocks where our house stood.

We met the landlady, a distinguished single woman in her forties, who lived with her mother in the main part of the house. She explained to us that she and her mother occasionally rented rooms, but "only upon recommendation." One of these rooms faced the beach; it had a view of the tower and the old village in the distance; the other faced the outer edge of the rocks with a view on the open sea. Papa took the seaside room and I took the beach side one. The landlady warned me that I would have to get used to the noise of the pebbles moving rhythmically back and forth with the motion of the waves. At first, I was just too happy to finally lie on a bed, then, as I began to feel better, I followed the noise of the pebbles, first with all my attention, then in a vague somnolence, and soon, in my dreams.

It was our good luck that we knew local people because we were able to immediately take part in the life of the town. Madame Jaspart had a daughter, Paulette, who was my age. Paulette, tall, skinny, and wearing glasses, was warm and welcoming. She introduced me to all her friends, and, from then on, I shared the activities of the local teenagers. We lounged on the beach, swam, talked, played with the younger children, discussed the village gossip, and always had a lot of fun. My new friends, proud of their native Corsica, were eager to tell me about its language (they taught me a few words), its not-to-be-missed sights, and its legends, including ghosts in grottoes and miracle-working saints.

The proximity of the sea was invigorating. I loved to swim in the warm Mediterranean. I dove from the rocks below our house, and swam as far as I could, until the shore became a line dotted with tiny houses and trees. At one point, my father, realizing that he had lost sight of me, became frightened and quickly swam to my rescue. He found me totally surprised to have worried him so much. Good thing he didn't watch me when I went rock climbing! My friend and I walked to another beach where craggy cliffs rose between two and three stories high. In my bikini and barefoot, I climbed the rocks, intuitively finding places to grab onto, feeling more and more exhilarated as I got closer to the top. Climbing rocks is like climbing trees. It comes naturally and makes one feel like an animal.

Besides that, of course, there was love, love all around, but, unfortunately, love not shared. I fancied a sailing Adonis, but the object of his attention was a pouty Parisian girl who came to Erbalunga every summer, a girl who wanted nothing to do with him. A well-built, tanned young man whose eyes burnt for me (and who had taken to calling me the Mermaid, *la Sirène*) only met with my indifference. And I had no interest whatsoever in a younger fellow, who complained in his Corsican accent: *"Tu me tranches le coeur en rondelles de saucisson"* ("You are cutting my heart in slices of salami"). As for poor Paulette, she had no romance at all. She was at an age when tall girls are more like thin-legged cranes than slithery mermaids.

From left: Madame Lamour, Papa, Paulette Jaspart, me, the Parisian girl, children. (1950)

Meanwhile, Papa was not wasting his time either. One could sometimes find him on the beach in company of his tireless admirer, a woman named, quite appropriately, Madame Lamour. But she was not his ladylove, it was obvious. A little too old for him and rather plain, she was something of a bore. As a matter of fact, he was forever trying to dodge her. He'd much rather stay in town with his new pals, the gendarme and his buddies, playing cards and drinking wine.

Monsieur Jaspart took my father on some of his rounds in the *maquis*, the vegetation of shrubs and bushes that grows on the Corsican hills. The hills of Corsica are famous for sheltering fugitives from the police (and during the war, partisans). Now, the Corsican Nationalist Movement, whose goal it is to sever Corsica from mainland France, is very active, but, at that time, the bandits in the *maquis* were not political revolutionaries, but smugglers of various kinds of goods. The gendarmes knew their way around the hills and seemed to be familiar with the bad guys' hiding places. My father told me that his gendarme friends collected ham and wine offered by the smugglers as a gesture of goodwill to make sure the law would not give them too much of a hard time.

Every evening my father and I ate dinner at a hotel-restaurant located on the promontory, in the old village. We took our meals sometimes inside, sometimes in a patio brightened by big pots of geraniums. There, we were close to the ruins of the Genoese tower, standing tall, as if still defending the village that it protected in the 16th century against the raids of the Barbary Coast pirates, one of them the dreaded Barbarossa from Algeria (who was perhaps the model for the *Gaspard le Rouge* of my childhood readings).

The establishment was quite elegant. I liked to sit in the restaurant with my father, proud to be part of *les gens chics* (the chic crowd). I put into practice the good manners Tante Yvonne had taught me. Alas, Papa slurped his soup! At first I said nothing, but, as days went by, I gathered my courage and said, "Papa, do you think you could make less noise when you eat your soup?"

I should have known better. That was not the sort of thing one could say to my father, especially when he was already excited by the wine drunk during the day with Monsieur Jaspart, plus the bottle he had already half-emptied while waiting for the food.

"I have worked all my life to earn my beefsteak! I have earned the right to eat my soup the way I want. Nobody is going to tell me what to do. I don't give a damn what people think!"

Now that he was raising his voice, I was even more embarrassed. I blamed myself for bringing up the subject. For a while, we said nothing. But luckily, these little altercations didn't last. My father and I couldn't stand any bad feelings between us. The smallest discord made us feel terribly upset. Taking little steps, we started to chat about this and that, hurrying to make the situation right again. And I'm pretty sure that, in the days that followed, Papa made a big effort to eat his soup silently. As for me, I learned not to correct Papa's manners.

One day, my father and I took the train from Bastia to Ajaccio, capital of Corsica and birthplace of Napoleon, for an excursion that was to last a few days. There, we lodged and took our meals with a family that someone in Erbalunga had recommended to us. The family consisted of the mother (a widow), her teenage daughter, and a little boy. Although the rooms were bright, the food was good, and the family nice, my father and I couldn't help feeling uncomfortable as we were treated, not only with respect, but even with a bit of obsequiousness, as if we were "the masters," and our hosts "the servants." Of course, the family couldn't have guessed that their reverence didn't sit well with my proletarian father and his libertarian daughter. The young girl, beautiful and soft spoken, was about my age. She showed us the town and accompanied us to the beach. I liked her very much but could never get her to say *tu* to me, as she insisted on giving me the respectful *vous*. I thought about her a lot after we left, and wrote her postcards from Paris.

Back to our house on the beach, my father, *sportif* as ever, decided that we ought to rent bicycles and go from Erbalunga to Saint-Florent, a trip of about twenty miles that involved crossing the whole width of the

Cap Corse, the thin arm that forms the northern part of the Island of Corsica. We started early and pedaled with energy. But between one shore and the other there is a steep hill, and soon we had to walk our bikes. It was a long and tiresome walk in the heat, but, after reaching the summit, the lengthy descent was thrilling. We did the same thing on the way back, stopping once to pick big bunches of beautiful pink flowers that we hung all over our bikes; we wanted to give them to our nice landladies. As we rode, many people shouted to us, "No, no! Don't keep these flowers! Throw them away! Poison!" We had picked belladonna, a plant used for medicinal purpose, but poisonous, and certainly, best not given as a present!

The most romantic event (how I wish I could live it again—differently!) of our month in Corsica took place shortly before our departure. One night, the boys of the village decided to give a serenade to "the Mermaid" who was soon to leave their shore. They brought their guitars, and when night had fallen, came under my window to sing for me some marvelous Corsican songs. But my window was right on the beach and the pebbles that were pushed up and down by the waves were both awfully noisy and gently lulling. And so, I heard absolutely nothing of this charming serenade. I slept all the way through. My father didn't hear it either, but, at least, he had the excuse of being on the sea side of the house. Only the landlady and her mother heard and enjoyed the music, but they didn't appear at their window, knowing the serenade was not given for them. The next day, informed by the landladies of the events of the night, I knew that I had to thank my friends. I couldn't bear telling them that I hadn't heard anything at all, so I said that I had heard a "little bit toward the end." In fact, when I think of it now, I can hear it, that serenade on the beach, I can hear the waves breaking, the pebbles rolling, the sound of voices and guitars rising, fading, and disappearing in the wind.

Then it was time to leave. I will come back, I promised my friends (and myself), I will come back. Papa and I took the bus to Bastia and then the ferry for Nice. The crossing was in the evening and the boat would briefly sail south along the coast of the Cap Corse before going onto the open sea. This meant I was going to see my dear Erbalunga once more! It was night now, the sea was calm, the boat rode slowly on the waves, and the Genoese tower appeared, with the old village behind it. Then we could see the beach with our house at the very end. And on the beach my friends had lit bonfires to say good-bye, to say how happy we all had been. Four, five, six, maybe more bonfires on the pebbles of the beach, burning and making me cry. Thank you, thank you, my dears, I will love you always.

5
Papa Finds a Wife

According to the songs my father sang I was able to guess the state of his love life.

"*Qui j'aime? Problème! Je ne sais moi même*" ("Whom do I love? Problem! I don't know myself"): he had fallen for a woman, but was not sure how the affair would turn out.

"*Parlez-moi d'amour, redites-moi des choses tendres*" (Talk to me of love. Tell me again those tender things): he was doing quite well.

"*Reviens, veux-tu, ton départ a brisé ma vie*" ("Come back, please do; your departure shattered my life"): he had been dumped.

"*Je n'appartiens à personne, mon coeur n'est pas un captif*" ("I don't belong to anyone; my heart is not a captive"): he was looking again.

I knew he had his own life, but I felt a little abandoned. The worst example of this came on New Year's Eve. He had promised to come home early. We were going to eat the dinner of lamb stew and white beans that I had lovingly cooked. I waited and waited. In my vision of happiness I could see myself sitting in the kitchen after dinner with my father, both of us poring over a volume of the World Encyclopedia borrowed from Oncle Albert. Reality was different. No volumes of the Encyclopedia were ever borrowed. Papa didn't come home that night. My tears fell in the white beans. I sadly recorded the event on a loose leaf of my notebook.

My father sat down with me one day.

"I want to talk to you," he said, "I am alone and still young. I have to rebuild my situation."

He never used the words "remarry" but always talked in terms of "rebuilding his situation." I knew what he meant.

"I understand, Papa," I said bravely. "I hope you find someone nice."

It made me sad to think of a new woman in the house, but I realized that my father's crazy life could not go on forever.

"I noticed two neighbors of ours," he continued, "a blonde and a brunette. I believe they are sisters. They often walk in the villa de l'Ouest with two small children. I think the children belong to the blonde. Anyway, it's the brunette I am interested in."

I had only vaguely noticed these two ladies who had recently moved in the neighborhood; their house was not exactly in the villa de l'Ouest, but at the end of a little path that ended in the villa.

"How would you feel if I tried to meet the dark-haired woman?"

Somehow, I felt that this time my father was serious: he had never needed my approval before taking out one of his "fallen women." I had been faced with the *fait accompli*.

"It's all right with me," I said.

A few days later I heard him sing: *"Qui j'aime? Problème! Je ne sais moi-même"* (the news was good, if still uncertain).

Papa had initiated a conversation with the dark-haired lady. He had found that she was not married and lived in the downstairs rooms in her sister's house. Her sister, the blond lady, had a husband and two little boys.

"There is one thing that bothers me about her," Papa told me, "it's her first name: Fréda. Who ever heard of a French woman named Fréda? Why can't she have an ordinary name like Alice or Marguerite?"

It's not so bad," I said.

Fréda, soon after meeting my father. (1950)

"I really think I will have to change her name. She told me that before she was born her parents had picked the name Alfred for a boy, but when they had a girl, they called her Alfréda. She had been "Fréda" ever since. Let me see—I could call her Fernande, no—Alberte, no. I just can't think of anything close."

In the end, he did not change her name. We all got used to calling her Fréda.

I could see that my father really liked this lady, and I knew he was desperate to settle down, but, right away, I decided that, even if Fréda and I got along well, she was to understand that she would never replace my mother.

Fréda had been married but never had any children. Several years before meeting my father, she had divorced her husband, an alcoholic who had since died. Completely free, about forty-two (my father was fifty), rather good looking (short, busty, girdled, dyed black hair), she was a responsible woman who loved her family and was especially devoted to her two little nephews. Papa's choice was good. Fréda proved to be the best wife he ever could have found.

Papa and Fréda in the backyard. (1950)

A few months after meeting my father, Fréda moved in with us. Some time after that, she and Papa were married in a private ceremony at City Hall. I was not present at this ceremony which took place—perhaps to spare my feelings—when I was away on vacation.

All this may sound fine, but in reality things were not easy for me. Fréda did not seem to have any understanding of who I was. She often criticized me and hurt my feelings. It was obvious that it was difficult for her to accept my father's unconditional love for me. For my part, while I was obedient, worked well at school, and was never deliberately obnoxious toward Fréda, I made sure to keep a certain distance, something that was probably extremely irritating to her.

However, although we were very different, we did make an effort to get along. I respected Fréda's intelligence and the good home she created for my father and me, but I just couldn't warm up to her. For one thing, I didn't like her voice, low and a bit raspy (a smoker's voice—she was now trying to limit herself to one cigarette after lunch). I didn't like either the fact that she wore a little too much makeup and had pencil lines instead of eyebrows. But these were just details. The worst thing about her was that she was critical and sarcastic (as many French people are) and sometimes couldn't help being downright mean. She made unkind remarks about everybody, especially my relatives (when Papa was not there) —but spared hers. She didn't outwardly argue with me; her modus operandi was through insinuations. I could tell that she had nothing but contempt for my love of art and literature, often implying that I was wasting my time.

"Some day," she told me, "you will realize what life is really about."

Feeling that she associated reading with idleness, I was embarrassed to read in front of her, even my school books. If I heard her coming near my room when I was reading, I quickly closed my books and started writing something, for at least, writing proved that I was "doing" something. Although later in life she became an avid reader herself, at that time, she had a disdain for books, and didn't seem to understand why I wanted to keep on studying beyond secondary school. She had a niece my age who worked as a *"petite main"* (apprentice seamstress) in the haute couture house of Jacques Fath. She would probably have liked for me to do something equally "real."

It is no wonder that Fréda was bitter: she had had a very hard life, first in her youth, then during her first marriage. Raised in a suburb northeast of Paris, she had spent her childhood in a rundown neighborhood, not far from the fortifications. To live on the fortifications carried a stigma: it meant you were the poorest of the poor. To live close-by, as Fréda did, was only slightly better.

The first three lines of fortifications, areas of defense around Paris, had long ago disappeared having been built over as Paris kept growing, but the fourth (and last line), dating from 1840, still remained (it is now covered by the *Boulevard périphérique*). These last fortifications were no longer used for defense, but consisted of large grassy areas which were at first used for promenades and picnics, but had later become the sites of shanty towns.

Although Fréda didn't frequent the shanty-towns, she told me that she and her friends had once befriended a group of Gypsies who lived in a camp right on the fortifications. They had visited the Gypsies and had even been invited to a wedding at their camp. She also told me that, at that time, she had only one dress that she wore every day to go to the factory where she worked. She washed her dress on Friday night and wore it with a white collar to go dancing on Saturday. Since her father, a heavy drinker, had died young, her mother worked very hard, cleaning people's houses, to bring up her children: five girls and one boy (the boy, to everyone's sadness, had become an alcoholic and left the family).

Fréda's mother now lived in the villa de l'Ouest with her daughter Renée ("the blond lady"). Her four other daughters visited her regularly. They all adored their mother and tried to grant all her wishes; I had never in my life witnessed such devotion. She was an extremely nice old lady, very frail, who most of the time sat in an armchair with a blanket on her lap.

While I recognized that Fréda's family was closer and more easy-going than my own, it was obvious that her relatives were not as interesting as mine. Two sisters, Renée and Adrienne, had married two brothers, Frédo and Lulu, who ran a body-and-fender shop. Nice but loud, both men drank a lot and loved merrymaking. The family always laughed heartily at their jokes, even when they were not funny. Everyone always seemed to have a good time. I got along best with Fréda's oldest sister, Titine, who was the most reserved of all. The youngest daughter of the family, Ginette, who had received some education thanks to the help of her sisters, was an office worker. Her husband, André, a plumbing contractor, was deservedly recognized as the cleverest and wittiest of the bunch. Suddenly my father, now surrounded by his new sisters and brothers-in-law, became deeply involved with his new family. He started spending most weekends in their company, especially appreciating the fact that they loved to take fishing trips, and that card-playing was their distraction of choice.

My own family found this new involvement a bit disconcerting. Tante Yvonne told me that my father had married "below his class." Oncle

Marcel, who had been my father's fishing partner, became sour at having been dethroned by the brothers-in-law, *les beaux-frères* (he uttered this word with contempt). My cousin Denise claimed that Fréda's male relatives were vulgar (which was not true), and drank too much (which was true). Tante Marthe and Oncle Albert, and Tante Valentine and Oncle Baptiste, who all appreciated Fréda's qualities, didn't dislike her relatives but didn't associate with them, for in truth they were too different from them.

For me it was also a bit hard. Whenever possible, my father and Fréda wanted me to accompany them on their weekend fishing trips (Papa had bought a new car and a little camper). My presence was also more or less required at Sunday lunches and holidays with all of Fréda's relatives. I participated as much as I could, but never had very much fun. It is not that I was a snob like Tante Yvonne, it is just that, after a while, I found the trips boring and the family lunches (which always ended in card-playing) even less entertaining—although I had to admit to myself that Ginette's husband, André, was pretty witty. I usually spent my time with Fréda's cute little nephews (and not, as was probably expected, with her teenage niece, Nicole, who loved to be with the adults and who played cards with them). I tried to escape these family affairs as much as I could, as I much preferred going out with my friends of the villa de l'Ouest, my cousins, or Colette, my new friend from school.

With Fréda's nephews, Robert and Michel. (1950)

In 1951, when vacation time arrived, my father decided to return to Corsica, so we could show Fréda our wonderful Erbalunga. We were able to rent rooms in "our" house, but this time there was no serenade. While my father and Fréda kept company with the gendarme and his wife, Madame Jaspart, I met with my friends of the year before, or went to the beach with

Paulette Jaspart (who had become even taller). We talked a lot, sharing gossip about the local boys. That year, sitting on the warm pebbles of the beach, I read *Gone with the Wind*, and, as all girls my age, empathized with Scarlett and her wrong choice of men. I most admired Scarlett's philosophy: "I'll think about it tomorrow," which I would use for years to come when things became too hard for me to bear. I also read *My Son, My Son!* by the Welsh writer Howard Spring, a tragic story of disappointment about two men, each with a son who grew up to be exactly the opposite of what their fathers had expected. I thought of this novel as "the best book I ever read." Once again I left Corsica with sadness, promising to return. But that time, my promise was not kept. I never did return.

French cancan in the backyard: an infrequent blending of two families and friends. From right: Nicole (Fréda's niece), me, my friend Pierrette, my cousin Miquette; my cousin Claude dressed as a girl, a friend of Fréda's family. (1949)

NINE

1950 - 1951

1
Friends and Teachers

My friend Colette remembers everything about our school: the classrooms, the green-haired concierge, the closet where we hid at recess to read our books on rainy days, the names of the girls in our class, every school trip we ever took. I'm afraid I have forgotten quite a bit. Most of the details have become blurry, when they haven't completely disappeared. For this story, though, I am not going to add what my friend has pulled out of the dark, except perhaps for the concierge's green hair, which, I am sure, was the object of much schoolgirl merriment.

How can I describe my friendship with Colette? To celebrate it, many more pages would be needed, perhaps even a whole book if we were to include all the letters we exchanged (and which both of us saved). Our friendship, which started when I was thirteen and she fourteen, sustained us all our life, and, to this day, remains unchanged.

When, new in school, I approached Colette carefully, she readily welcomed me into her circle of friends. And all at once, in her group of lively girls who laughed and made fun of everything, I felt comfortable and wanted. There was something different about Colette; one could see it right away. Under long straight lashes, her large brown eyes, luminous and soft, displayed her soul right there, at the surface. When she looked at me, I knew she understood my quest and my sadness. I fell in love with Colette, but it was not a sensual love; it was what could be described as a passionate friendship. I thought about her night and day. Sometimes, at home, I made childish drawings of the two of us, two figures viewed from the back walking hand in hand on a long road that disappeared into the horizon. That was the life I wanted: to be with her forever. This intensity of feeling was, of course, due to my age and my immense need for love, but I didn't think of it that way, I just knew that I had found Colette and I needed her, and that she had found me and she needed me. We became friends, inseparable friends.

My best friend, Colette Brun. (1951)

The professors in our school (in France, secondary school teachers have the title of professors) were, as I mentioned earlier, all distinguished women with high educational background. They formally addressed us by our last name *Mademoiselle Gauthier, Mademoiselle Brun*, and sought to make each student learn everything within the curriculum and beyond. Devoted to their profession, they paid attention to each one of their students. For the first two years, our professor of French literature was Mademoiselle Rauly.

Mademoiselle Rauly cast a heroic figure. Her straight jet-black hair, cut just below the ears, would have squarely framed her face if some untamed strands had not forever insisted on flying out of place. She wore either knee-length tight skirts or mid-calf pleated skirts, always with black leather boots. Outside, she favored a black cape about the length of her short skirts. Her face was square, her eyes brown and fiery, her features chiseled. When she became angry, her olive complexion turned to red, sometimes even purple. She projected strength and determination. She didn't walk, she paced. With big gestures, she seemed to emulate her heroes: Napoleon and Victor Hugo. When we were rowdy, she silenced us in one second with her imperious look and efficient *"Mesdemoiselles!"* Standing up and crossing her arms when she expected an answer from a student or from the class, she gave us her famous *"J'attends!"* (I'm waiting!), almost as classic as Zola's *"J'accuse!"* She was an excellent teacher who introduced us to the 17th century classic plays of Corneille,

Racine, Molière, the Romantic poets of the 19th century, and even the more contemporary works of Gide, Valéry, Aragon, etc.. We respected her, although sometimes it was hard not to poke fun at her exaggerated poses and the habit she had of sitting on the radiator. Not only did she excel inside the classroom but she strongly believed in the educational power of field trips. The destination of these trips reflected her original mind. Once, she made us stand under a bridge in Paris, our assignment being to note sights, sounds and smells. Another time, she took us to an exhibit of pines and fir trees, and another time still, to Victor Hugo's house, Place des Vosges, where, with her customary enthusiasm, she introduced us to the poet's superb pen-and-ink drawings. On a visit to Clemenceau's house (another one of her heroes), I remember mustachioed portraits and a bar of soap the great man used.

Mademoiselle Rauly, who was both our literature and history teacher, made us appreciate—I could even say love—the quaint Place Dauphine and its Louis XIII buildings with their rounded portals and ornamental white and red bricks. She pointed out that, on the place Dauphine side, the back rooms of the Palais de Justice housed the *Imprimerie Royale* (Royal Printing House) where, until the Revolution of 1789, books and pamphlets were printed with permission of the King. From the Place Dauphine, she had us cross the Pont Neuf, stop to look at the statue of King Henri IV, and, going down some steps behind the statue, she led us to the small Vert Galant Garden which forms the very end of the Île de la Cité. There, she had us stand as if at the prow of a ship with the Seine in front and on both sides. Mademoiselle Rauly explained the meaning of the word Vert Galant (Green Gallant), the nickname of King Henri IV himself, this old lecher, still green, still chasing women. But he was a good king and how sad we were that in 1610 (a date all French students memorize and remember for ever) he was assassinated by Ravaillac. As we sat in an outdoor café, drinking hot chocolate at Mademoiselle Rauly's expense, we discussed with some relish the quartering of Ravaillac and imagined how his limbs, tied to four pulling horses, were torn away from his body. Trips with Mademoiselle Rauly were always fascinating.

Although Colette was my best friend, I had several other friends in the class. One of them was Lyliane Giraud. Lyliane was somewhat of a celebrity for something that had happened in the first year of school, the year before I started my studies in Vincennes. In 1947, the great hero of the French Resistance, Général Leclerc, had died. On the day of his death, the sad news was announced in each class. When Lyliane heard the announcement, she had a nervous attack; she started sobbing loudly, her head on her folded arms at her desk, to the students' astonishment and the teachers' perplexity. This event had been reported to me in hush-hush tones. There was something else we all knew about Lyliane: she had weak ankles and was prone to accidents. As we went down the steps of the Vert Galant garden, she twisted her foot and, once again, sprained her ankle. She could barely walk, but did not complain. Lyliane was a pretty girl with a round face, dark round eyes, a peachy complexion and a fleshy mouth. At that time, she was a little plump, which was not good for her fragile legs. I am still friends with Lyliane who, as an adult, became a beautiful (and complex) woman.

From left: Lyliane Giraud, Jacqueline Heurtault, Colette Brun. In back, a friend and me. (1951)

I had another friend, Jacqueline Heurtault, a girl with paper-pale skin, who was neither plain nor pretty, and whose inquiring eyes behind serious-looking glasses seemed to try to find the hidden meaning of everything we said. She talked in a high-pitched voice, was a little affected, and developed an almost obsessive attachment to me. Later on, at the end of our studies at the Cours Complémentaire de Vincennes, when everyone scattered in different directions to find their way in life, Jacqueline, Lyliane and I would be the only three students to transfer to the Lycée Sophie Germain (at that time called Collège Sophie Germain) in the Quartier du Marais.

But at the moment our main preoccupation was with day-to-day life at school, which consisted of classes, tests, and, once in a while, a special event. At the occasion of Mother's Day, all the girls were called to meet in the assembly room. One after the other, the teachers made moving speeches in praise of mothers. Some of the girls also stood in front of the assembly to talk about their mothers, either in their own words or in the words of famous authors. This event was hard for me to bear and I started crying. Colette gently consoled me.

When I first attended the school, our mathematics teacher was Madame Chrétien, a jolly woman, pink and round who was liked by everyone. With piles of books under both arms, some falling to the floor, she would ask, "Am I supposed to be here?" Almost invariably, she was not. "Oh! Sorry! Wrong classroom!" And she would leave with a happy giggle.

By contrast, in the upper grades, the mathematics teacher, Madame Vaudène, had a dour personality. Her head looked like a skull on which a layer of leathery skin had been stretched. On the top of that head grew sparse yellowish hair in frizzy little tufts. Her skeletal body was hung with drab gray clothes. When she went outside, Madame Vaudène wore a cape, not an elegant cape like Mademoiselle Rauly's, but a long black one, with a wide hood. On her heavy black bicycle, Madame Vaudène enveloped in her cape looked like a figure of death straight out of a Jean Cocteau movie.

Of the four personal encounters I had with Madame Vaudène, three were bad, and one was nice (I think).

I was not very good at math; I did my homework and studied the lessons, but the results were never brilliant. If I did manage to end up with an average grade it was because half of the final test was an essay question on "mathematical theory," for which I studied hard. When it came to the other half, which consisted in solving algebra or geometry problems, I was not good at all. Madame Vaudène called me to the blackboard one day and asked me to solve an equation in front of the class. I didn't know how to do it; I just I stood there with chalk in hand. She let me stand for a long, long time. The class was completely silent. Then Madame Vaudène said, "Well, Mademoiselle Gauthier, if you think your pretty face and your curly hair will help you in life, you are wrong! Go back to your seat!"

Another time, following the day of the school assembly for Mother's Day, she caught me by surprise and said to me in front of my school friends, "You are using your mother's death to make people feel sorry for you!" It was too much; that remark literally made me sick. I couldn't stop crying, and when I went home I developed a fever and couldn't go to school for a few days. I don't know why she said that, especially since I tried not to mention my mother's death and acted as if nothing bad had ever happened to me. But after that, I began wondering if Madame Vaudène was right, if indeed I had not been "using" my mother's death. I resolved to hide my feelings even more, and never to talk about my mother at school for fear that what I said would be misinterpreted. In such moments, I was happy to have Colette as my friend. She was the only one who understood me.

The third and worst personal encounter with Madame Vaudène gave me nightmares for years to come. There was a rule: when we left school, we were not supposed to linger in front of the gate, not even to wait for friends whose classes ended at the same time as ours. We did anyway, because our friends usually appeared after a few minutes. One day, after school, I was waiting outside for Colette. I was not planning to stay long since I knew she was bound to come out right away. But Madame Vaudène saw me.

"Circulate, Mademoiselle Gauthier, you know you are not supposed to stand here!"

I left, went to the next street and stood at the corner. I assumed Madame Vaudène would go back inside the school, but she suddenly reappeared.

"Mademoiselle Gauthier, move, go home!"

I went away again. But Colette and I had planned to take the bus home together as we usually did, and besides, I had her bus tickets in my school bag. Madame Vaudène was gone now. I stayed in the same small street but went a little further back and hid behind a car where I still had a view of the students as they came out. All of a sudden, Madame Vaudène arrived on her bicycle, her black cape draped around her.

"You are still here, Mademoiselle. I order you to go!"

This time I left for good, but instead of going toward the front of the school, I went down the small street where I had stood, and which ended in a narrow passage. By then I was running. My plan was to follow the passage, turn left, go back toward the front of the school and try to find Colette. I ran and ran. I wanted to turn around the block but the streets were not at right angle; I took one street, then another. I was far now, saved, I thought, when suddenly, I raised my head, and, right in front of me, blocking my way with her huge black bicycle was Madame Vaudène, the horrible skull face showing its teeth, the eyes reduced to slits, the cape of death floating around her.

"Ha, ha! Mademoiselle Gauthier, you are trying to defy me! Follow me to school! This matter will be brought to Madame la Directrice and you shall be severely punished!"

I had to follow her. By that time I was trembling and crying. She took me inside the school and left me in a classroom where Mademoiselle Rauly (who was my homeroom teacher) was sitting by herself, correcting papers.

"This student must be disciplined!" Madame Vaudène told her. Then she left—no doubt she had to go home; she had wasted too much time. Mademoiselle Rauly could not understand what all the commotion was about. I was still crying, trying to explain the whole thing; I showed her the bus tickets, but, to her, the matter was not important, and although Madame Vaudène had asked her to pursue it further, it was obvious she had no intention of doing so. But this event had been traumatic for me. I will always remember the grinning face in front of me and the nightmarish sensation of fear and helplessness.

On the last day of the school year we had a celebration with lemonade and cookies; the entertainment was provided by the students. The star student was *"La Déesse de L'École"* ("The School Goddess"). It was Mademoiselle Rauly who had called her that because of her good grades and piano-playing ability. The nickname had stuck. We didn't like "The Goddess" because she was "too perfect," as well as pretentious, but we had to admit that she did know how to play the piano. After the Goddess' classical piece, several students did comical skits, and I recited a poem by Jacques Prévert: *Page d'écriture,* about a little boy who began to chant his multiplication tables along with the rest of his class while looking out of the window. Seeing a beautiful bird, he became completely distracted, and his mind flew away with the bird. I recited it like a little play, with gestures and a lot of feeling. After that, I went to talk to my friends and eat cookies. Then, Madame Vaudène came to me, a smile revealing her yellow teeth.

"I love the poem you just recited," she said, "Would you do me the favor of reciting it once more, just for me."

Of course, I was terribly nervous, but I recited the poem for her. She seemed happy and looked at me kindly.

"Thank you very much!" she said.

That was my fourth personal encounter with Madame Vaudène.

During my first year at school, there was another terrorizing teacher, our sewing instructor, but nobody took her seriously because sewing did not count in our grade point average. Her name was Madame Dupont, but we all called her "Ramses II" for her uncanny resemblance to the mummified Egyptian legend. She taught us sewing, starting with common stitches, following with embroidery stitches, then pattern-making, how to sew sleeves onto a dress, how to affix a collar to a blouse, and, finally, how to make a perfect buttonhole with buttonhole stitches. We worked and worked at that last project, which consisted of producing three buttonholes on a little piece of fabric. When Ramses II, carrying a big pair of scissors, walked up and down the aisles between our rows of desks, we had to hand her our work in progress. And when she felt that our sewing wasn't up to her expectations, she brandished her scissors, introduced their point into the openings of our piece of fabric, and sadistically cut up our wonderful, cherished, almost finished buttonholes.

I don't want to give the impression that I was terrorized by my teachers; in fact, it was quite the opposite. Most of our teachers were easy to like, and one of them, even, was easy to love. It was Mademoiselle Villa, Professor of Spanish. Not that she was nice; she was the most demanding and, for sure, the most feared of all teachers, especially when we hadn't learned our lessons. She called on us at random and we'd better know how to conjugate irregular verbs; her drills were fast and merciless. But Mademoiselle Villa was absolutely beautiful and I (and I was not the only one) was in love with her. I dreamt about her. I wanted to be close to her. I studied my Spanish very hard. She walked like a queen, her gorgeous body molded in clothes so refined that the likes of them had never been seen at our school. Her face, of Mediterranean type, was perfectly shaped, her skin smooth and tanned, her thick black hair severely combed in an elegant chignon. She had an aquiline nose, very Spanish, which everyone knew was too big, too pronounced for her beautiful face. But what attracted us like bees to nectar were her eyes, large, sea blue, lined with long dark curly eyelashes. What was she thinking, this Mademoiselle Villa? What indeed was she thinking when I approached her desk and gave her my assignments? She looked into my eyes, very deeply, sexily, possessing me as it were, and letting me possess her. I was confused, upset, excited. I didn't want to tell my friends that she did that to me—and wondered if she did that to them too. After the Easter holiday when she came back to teach, we were all shocked to see that she had had plastic surgery. Her nose had the same shape as before, but it was smaller, in proportion. After that, her beauty had no limit. One of the girls bragged that she had seen her in her underwear, but we all knew it was not true. What did I want? What did I hope? I don't remember longing to kiss her, to touch her. I had no clear idea. The only thing I wanted was to love her. Shortly after her nose repair, she announced that she was getting married and would not return to teaching in the fall.

Madame la Directrice, our school principal, who had been the former private Cours Lamartine's headmistress, was a refined woman of the French bourgeoisie, with authority and connections. At her invitation, one of her friends, a high official of UNESCO, the educational unit of the United Nations (UNESCO's headquarters are in Paris), came to our school as a guest speaker. Impeccably dressed and a little pompous, he explained to us how we could do something good for other children in the world. He told us about a school in the desert in the newly founded country of Israel. The families were dispersed far and wide, and when it was time for school to start, it was difficult to call in all the children. What was needed was a bell, a bell that the teachers could ring to signal the beginning of classes. Mademoiselle Rauly felt it would be a good project for our class, and we all set out to collect money to buy *la cloche* (the bell). Finally, when we had enough, a bronze bell was purchased: it was six or seven inches high and darkish gray. As Mademoiselle Rauly thought it didn't look cheerful enough, we painted it gold. When the UNESCO official was told that we had the bell, he invited the whole class to Headquarters to deliver it. The event was staged and called *"Une Cloche dans le Désert"* ("A Bell in the Desert"). I must mention that, in French slang, the word "cloche" means a person a little stupid, someone not quite right in the head. And so, needless to say, one of the consequences of the project was that Mademoiselle Rauly acquired the endearing nickname of *"La Cloche."* At the event, we were made to stand for a professional photograph in front of a large map of Israel while the UNESCO official held a wooden stick pointing to the destination of our cloche. I remember being picked as one of the students who had to stand next to him. We were all told to look at the map. I have always wondered if this picture got published in a newspaper or a brochure, or if it still languishes deep in the cellars of the UNESCO archives.

One day, at school, the teachers told us that the City of Vincennes was sponsoring a contest for best essay on the occasion of *"la Semaine de l'Amabilité"* (Courtesy Week). We were used to writing essays, which were assigned to us as weekly homework and end-of-quarter tests. I wrote mine. It was declared best in class, then best in school. Sent to the City of Vincennes, it won best in the city. The prize was a modest sum to be deposited in a savings account opened for the occasion. The following year, the City of Vincennes again sponsored an essay contest, this time in honor of Mother's Day. Somehow, either the teachers forgot to give the students the assignment on time, or they didn't feel like giving it at all, but, knowing that they had to turn in an essay to the City of Vincennes, they decided to ask me to write one. They would pretend it had been found best in school. Mademoiselle Rauly and Mademoiselle Salex, the school's other French literature teacher, came to see me and explained the situation, asking me to be discreet about it. Then, they made me sit in a classroom all by myself, and gave me about an hour to write my essay. It was sad for me to write about my mother, but I tried my best. I was almost finished when both teachers came in to apologize: They were very sorry; they had forgotten that my mother was dead.

Mademoiselle Salex, who became my French literature teacher in the third year, was one of my favorites. The other girls didn't like her very much; they found her boring and obsessed with Latin. She did love Latin, having been a Latin teacher when the *Cours Complémentaire* was the *Cours Lamartine*. A "classic" program had been offered then, but in our present school we didn't have the choice between "classic" and "modern." Our program was entirely "modern," with two foreign languages: English and Spanish. We had no Greek and Latin, which meant that if we eventually transferred to a lycée, it would have to be in a "modern" program. This was very sad for Mademoiselle Salex. But to compensate for the loss of a formal Latin course she didn't miss a single opportunity to point out to us the Latin root of French words. This taught me a lot, to the point that sometimes I think I know more Latin than some students who actually took it.

Mademoiselle Salex was tall and thin; she had very white skin and dark hair; her demeanor was modest and her severe clothes made her look like an old maid. She had a scar from reconstructive surgery for a harelip, something that probably made her self-conscious and shy. However, I personally thought she was very pretty because of her extraordinarily beautiful eyes. Her eyes were wide open like flowers, light brown, shiny and soft. She always looked at me deeply, not sexily like Mademoiselle Villa, but with sweetness and affection. Once, she whispered to me as I was close to her desk, "You are my favorite student." It made me blush, and I didn't tell anybody.

It did not strike me as shocking that some of our teachers may have been lesbians—not that I am implying anything about Mademoiselle Salex. I was actually thinking of Mademoiselle Rauly. It was suspected that her "partner" was Mademoiselle Gédalge, our music teacher. But I didn't speculate on this possibility, assuming they were just close friends—and I don't believe my school friends spent too much time speculating on it either. We just didn't talk about things like that.

Mademoiselle Gédalge was, I think, the daughter of the composer André Gédalge, who counted among his disciples Ravel, Milhaud and Honnegger. She was a wonderful music teacher. She taught us music appreciation by bringing records ranging from Bach to Gershwin and encouraged us to go to concerts. Colette and I went on Sunday mornings to the Concerts Colonne at the Théâtre du Châtelet, where we heard classical music under the direction of the greatest conductors of the time. These concerts, organized especially for high-school students, covered various epochs and genres of music; they were not a requirement but many of our friends attended them also. Colette and I never missed any. Mademoiselle Gédalge, a strong woman with an imposing face and wild black hair, directed us in choral singing and taught us various classical musical pieces that she made us practice under tight discipline. For one of these pieces, a baroque song based on the sixteenth-century Ronsard's poem, *Mignonne allons voir si la rose*, our choral group was selected to sing at the Théâtre du Palais de Chaillot, near the Eiffel Tower, for a national competition.

Afraid I would ruin our chorale' chances, I just mouthed the words. Perhaps because of that, we won and even had the honor to be heard on the radio station *France-Inter*.

The only times we left our homeroom to go to other classes were for our music lessons, the gym (where, among other things, we practiced "rhythmic dance" in little white tunics), or the chemistry laboratory located on the upper floor of the school. If I have only a vague recollection of our scientific experiments, I remember distinctly the large lab room which was also used for our annual physical exam, consisting mostly of radiography of the lungs. We had to strip to the waist. As we were modest, we were embarrassed to see one another half-naked. The room was crowded with nervous girls, and since at that time people didn't use deodorant, the odor of perspiration was definitely noticeable. In the confusion, I couldn't help stealing a few looks around, and, wouldn't you know! Besides all her other achievements, it was "The School Goddess" who turned out to have the best-looking breasts of us all: firm, well-formed, and pointing straight out like pistols!

This brings to mind a quiet day when, sitting at my desk in the second row, I was listening to the teacher. From her seat in front of me, one of my friends, Françoise Magnaval, suddenly turned around toward me and announced:

"The History of Breasts through the Ages!"

Then, she turned back to face the teacher, but as soon as the teacher began to write something on the blackboard, Françoise turned toward me again:

"The Middle Ages!"

She had stuck her metal ruler under her sweater. On her flat chest, the ruler made a form looking as if her breasts were squeezed inside a suit of armor.

She turned back, pretending to be interested in the lesson. Then, suddenly, when the teacher wasn't looking, she turned around toward me again:

"The Renaissance!"

Stretching her sweater to the maximum with the ruler, she now had an enormous chest. She quickly turned back, waited for the right moment. In a flash, she turned around again:

"Modern Times!" Her breasts were now lopsided, Picasso style.

"What's so funny, Mademoiselle Gauthier?"

"Nothing, Madame!"

We did have a pretty good time at that school! There was also our obsession with MEN. In a girls' school, the mere sight of a man provokes the greatest excitement. When a repairman happened to come to our class, even if he was old and ugly—even more so if he was old and ugly, we opened our eyes wide, and said with fake rapture: "A MAN! A MAN!"

Then one day, I fell in love with a guest lecturer—maybe we all did. With his deep tan, his curly reddish hair, his eyes of the purest blue, and his well-cropped short beard, he looked like masculine beauty personified. He was a South African anthropologist studying the Zulus. His voice and his accent were irresistible, and he could speak the Zulu language including the "clicks." I became convinced that he had kept his eyes on me the whole time of his lecture. I dreamt about him, longing to be held in his arms. And from that day onward, I nourished an undying love for anthropology.

2
14th of July

Whenever I heard Yves Montand's song *"C'était le soir d'un Quatorze Juillet"* (It happened one evening on Bastille Day), I was reminded of my own evening on Bastille Day, although mine had nothing to do with the romantic song.

I was fifteen then. Papa and Fréda were at home with Fréda's family, celebrating, playing cards, and drinking. When I asked permission to go out with my friends after dinner, Papa wanted to know where we planned to go.

"Close to the Mairie de Fontenay," I told him. "We are going to listen to music, dance in the streets, and watch fireworks."

It was what people did on Bastille Day. Papa said I could go, providing I was back by midnight. It wasn't so bad since my regular curfew was 8 p.m. I knew I was expected to be on time; if I was late, I was sure to get a reprimand accompanied by a "Don't you know I sacrifice myself for you" speech. My father, who felt the weight of being solely responsible for my upbringing, made a point of knowing my whereabouts. As most fathers, he was particularly concerned with the preservation of my virginity. Even at this early stage he had warned me several times that if I ever got pregnant before getting married he would commit suicide. He had said it so convincingly (I'm sure he believed it himself) that I never doubted he would make good his threat. Besides his warnings and admonitions, he always added something about the neighbors, concluding with: "What would the neighbors think?" He seemed to be haunted by the neighbors' opinion, to the point that I was convinced the neighbors were the true rulers of his life. As a result, when I went out with my friends, I was always careful to be home on time (or at least almost on time). I was very much afraid to displease my father.

Jacqui, Patrick, Pierrette, Robert Chourlay, and Jean Grosso came to pick me up. It took about twenty minutes to walk to the Mairie. Bastille Day's festivities were already in full swing. Paper lanterns hung on strings surrounding each dancing area, and between the lanterns dozens of little *bleu, blanc, rouge* (blue, white and red) paper flags flapped gently in the wind. We could choose among different styles of dances, each with its own music: accordion for old-fashioned people, a full band for ballroom dancing, or modern rhythms for boogie-woogies. Some of the dancers held a glass of wine in their hands; children ran through the crowd; lovers hugged and kissed. There was laughter all around. Everyone was having fun.

My friends and I looked at the dancers, but since the boys in our group were shy about inviting us, Pierrette and I danced with each other or with a few young men brave enough to ask us. Time passed quickly. My friends wanted to sit at a café terrace but I knew that if we did I would be late since it was already almost midnight. I told them I had to go home, but they laughed at me, called me Cinderella, and said that on the *Quatorze Juillet* people stay up all night. I sat with them, but didn't feel good about it. They talked and laughed and did not hurry. Several times I reminded them I had to go (it was after midnight by then), but they told me to relax; there was nothing to worry about. Then I said I would walk by myself.

"No, no, wait for us. We'll be ready in a few minutes!"

At last, we left the café; I wanted to walk fast but my friends were dragging on. I knew my father would be angry with me, and I was terribly worried.

Finally we were two blocks away from the villa de l'Ouest. We were all in a group when I saw my father approaching. I detached myself from the rest of my friends and walked toward him, ready to apologize for being late. But when he saw me, he stopped and stood still. As soon as I was close enough, without waiting for me to talk, he took a step and slapped me across the face, very hard. He had never struck me before. I was shocked. I didn't know what to do. Why did he have to slap me? And why in front of all my friends? Wouldn't a speech have been enough? I started sobbing and ran home. When I arrived I went straight to my room and closed the door. I couldn't stop sobbing. I looked at my mother's picture on my shelf. Fréda found out what had happened and tried to console me. There was only one explanation: my father was drunk. I had guessed that much, but it didn't undo the hurt. There and then, I made a promise to myself: when I grew up I would leave my house and go away. Away, as far away as possible.

The next day, my father apologized, which made me cry some more. He said it was because he was terribly worried that he acted so fast. It was obvious that he didn't know what to do to make things better. He didn't tell me he loved me more than anything in the world (we never said things like that), but he knew that I knew.

It did take some time for me to forgive him, but, of course, I did. However, the fact that throughout my youth I lived in fear of displeasing my father shaped my attitude toward men, making me fearful of displeasing them. It was something that would burden me for the rest of my life.

3
Life at Home

When my father married Fréda, she was working in a bindery in one of Paris' industrial districts. Her job was to bind small address books and pocket diaries. Since my father would have considered it a personal dishonor to have a wife who worked in a factory-like situation, he asked Fréda to quit her job. Fréda did not mind, she had enough to keep her busy at home. Besides, she was now able to spend more time with her mother, sister, and little nephews who all lived practically next door. However, she would have liked to keep her friends. One of them, Caitlin, was a nice lady with bright clothing and a lot of makeup who was married to an American and lived in California most of the time but spent several months in France every year. My father was introduced to her, but did not like her very much, so Fréda dropped the friendship. Another friend, Roberte, was a younger woman Fréda had met at work. She had two sons by a married man (or was it a priest?) who had set her up in an apartment. He paid the rent, took care of his sons' expenses and visited regularly. My father, although he was not known to be strict about morality (except when it came to his family) objected to Roberte's lifestyle. Again, Fréda broke up the friendship. This may appear dictatorial on the part of my father, but it was not surprising. In his time and milieu, while it was perfectly all right for men to have friends, it wasn't the custom for their wives to go "gallivanting" with friends of their own. Women were supposed to associate only with the family. My mother, Tante Yvonne, and Tante Marthe didn't have personal friends who visited them or who invited them to their houses. Tante Valentine was the exception: she had two good friends, Madame Abalin, her colleague at the creamery, with whom she went to the opera, and Madame Bousquet whom she visited or who came over for tea. (Poor Madame Bousquet was forever accompanied by her execrable mother-in-law.) But, as I mentioned before, it seems that Tante Valentine was looking outside the family for something more cultured, more elegant. Seen by most as a good cook, a little lady in apron and slippers, she longed for a fancier life.

Almost as soon as Fréda moved in with us she wanted to make changes in the house. Understandably, my father agreed to the remodeling plans. The main bedroom was cleared of its goatskin rugs and satin bedspread; the knickknacks on the night table disappeared; the large oval portrait of my brother was taken down (Fréda found a small picture of him as a baby, framed it, and placed it on the night table—a sensitive gesture which must have touched my father). The wallpaper was changed. The vanity, replaced by a convenient chest of drawers, was moved to my room. Except for this addition, nothing was done to my own bedroom. Not long after my mother's death, the pink wallpaper had already been replaced by a light yellow one, of a more modern design (my father hung wallpaper himself with impeccable workmanship). At that time to surprise me Tante Valentine had dyed the white muslin curtains of my glass-fronted bookcase and the white lace throw on my desk bright canary yellow. I hadn't been particularly enamored with the results, but hadn't complained for fear of hurting Tante Valentine's feelings.

The most important change was in the kitchen. Fréda did not like the big cupboard with sliding doors, the one that had hid our radio during the war; she wanted a modern kitchen with "elements." The cupboard was dismantled and cabinets were built on the walls. A refrigerator was introduced, and the whole room was repainted bright white. I didn't mind, but there was one change I didn't like at all: the wonderful pulley lamp with its light pink porcelain shade, the lamp that my mother pulled up or down to produce just the right amount of light for reading or sewing, was taken down and replaced by a ceiling neon tube. This fluorescent light made us look ugly, and, worst of all, it had a continuous hum. I could hear this hum all the way upstairs in my bedroom when I was studying or reading and I hated it.

There was something else that Fréda changed: from the time she had met Papa, she had never called him "P'tit Louis." He was now "Louis."

My aunts Valentine, Marthe and Yvonne somewhat resisted his new name, but for his nieces and nephews Tonton P'tit Louis had become Tonton Louis.

More and more, I took to gazing out of the window and daydream with "languid indolence," as Jane Austen would put it. In fact, it was obvious that I was becoming different from my parents, and that, soon, I would be looking for a life outside the family.

Although I had new friends at school, I still went out with my old friends of the villa de l'Ouest. Most had begun their adult life, as several of them were a few years older than me. Pierrette was now working in a factory for the pharmaceutical company Roche which had a facility in Fontenay-sous-Bois.

"What do you do exactly?" I asked her.

"I work on a machine that sticks labels on medicine bottles."

"Do you find it boring?"

"You get used to it!"

She did not seem unhappy. When I went to pick her up, she enjoyed talking about the people who worked with her. My villa friends and I still went to the movies on weekends. We also still took walks in Paris, particularly on the Champs-Elysées or the Grands boulevards.

Patrick remained the friend with whom I communicated best. Now attending a private business school, he also had other activities. With some friends, he had formed a band in which he played keyboard.

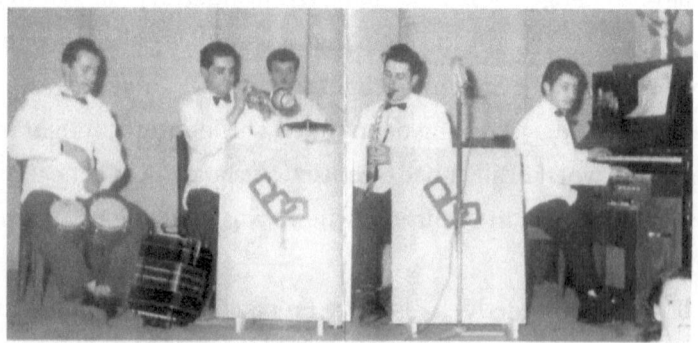

Patrick (at the keyboard) with his band, the BP. (c. 1951)

Raymond, one of the band members, was rather cute. Pierrette, Colette (who by then had met my villa friends), and I declared we were "in love" with him. At that time, Patrick had taken to dressing differently. He now wore striped shirts, very tight pants and black shoes. His hair was slicked on the sides, and he wore on his finger a large ring with a flat stone. My feelings for him fluctuated. The truth was that I was not physically attracted to him. One thing, though, that I did appreciate was his musical taste. I had never liked the sentimental songs sung by Edith Piaf, Lynne Renault, etc., that my family listened to on the radio. Among the singers I did like was Yves Montand. I had gone to see him in an unforgettable performance at the Théâtre de l'Olympia. Now, Patrick introduced me to George Brassens and made me aware that this guitar-playing singer was in fact one of France's major composers and poets. Patrick also introduced me to some others of his favorites: the Canadian singer Félix Leclerc, also a poet, and Les Frères Jacques, an avant-garde singing group.

Jacqui was now preparing to go to the military service. He had grown sarcastic and did not understand Patrick's new ways. After his military service, he lost contact with the rest of us. Later on, during one of my visits to France, I asked Pierrette if she ever saw Jacqui.

"I see him sometimes on the street," she said, "but when he sees me he looks the other way and never says hello."

I didn't keep in touch with Lili and her sister Michou, or with Robert, Dédé, or Claude Gouge. I wrote to Jean Grosso when he was in the military service in Algeria, but I enclosed anti-government articles cut out from my anarchist newspaper *Le Libertaire*. Jean very discreetly asked me if I could send him only letters—without enclosures. In my naivety, I had not realized I could have put him in trouble. When Jean came back, he moved away from the villa de l'Ouest and we no longer heard from him.

For several years I wrote or visited Pierrette. She had left the Roche factory, married and had a son. Later, I heard that she and her husband had bought a house in Brittany. My cousin Denise recently told me that Pierrette is a widow now. Like me, she must be a grandmother. Patrick was the only member of the villa "gang" I had kept in contact with.

We had lost touch for a long time but eventually found one another. He had a successful career in business, got married, and had children and grandchildren. He and his wife, Noëlle, retired in Nîmes, where I twice visited them. Sadly, Patrick, the nicest of men, died on October 14, 2008.

Back to the years 1951/52: although Fréda went along with my father's whims, she was more outspoken than my mother had ever been. To my surprise, Papa seemed to accept Fréda's slightly rebellious attitude. I guess he was happy to have a nice home life, without much to complain

My father and Fréda with my cousin Denise's daughter, Martine, dressed as Bécassine. (1956)

about. He had regained his habits. He still kept his *cahiers* at the end of the kitchen table; some contained his home accounting records, others (the ones full of mysterious calculations) were, I discovered, statistics based on horse race predictions made by specialists in various newspapers. Papa methodically scored all their tips, noting how many times they had been right or wrong. When he felt he had accumulated enough information, he played the leads given by the most successful predictors. He bought racing tickets at the corner *bureau de tabac* every Sunday, investing a small amount, sometimes winning, sometimes losing, but never very much.

My life at home was not altogether unpleasant. I did not dislike Fréda in spite of the fact that she still "threw stones in my garden." I realized that she was not really trying to be hurtful; she just couldn't help being critical. The only thing I couldn't get used to was her almost Victorian Puritanism. In my family, we had always spoken quite freely about almost everything, but, suddenly, the slightest allusion to anything sexual was frowned upon. Fréda had a way of finding impropriety when there was none, sullying the most innocent actions.

I remember a remark that was quite shocking to me. Colette and I were still inseparable; sometimes Colette would walk me home from her house, then I would walk her back home, then she would walk me home again. (We lived about six blocks apart. To go to her place we had to climb two flights of outdoor steps connecting one street to another. Her house, in the upper part of Fontenay, was in a small street, also called a "villa.") Fréda told me one day, "You shouldn't spend so much time with Colette."

"Why?" I asked.

"People will start wondering about the two of you. They might think you have a 'special friendship.' You know what I mean!"

I didn't know what to say. It was so unfair.

I also was offended by the fact that Fréda often hinted that I was promiscuous when in reality I was completely innocent. Once, I asked my father if I could go out with my friends to pick lilies of the valley on May Day instead of going with the family. My father said I could, providing my friends and I would go to the same spot in the woods as the family. I objected, saying, "I don't want my friends to think that I'm always in my parents' shadow like a good little girl." Upon which Fréda interjected with a smirk, "Do you really believe your friends think of you as a good little girl?"

When Fréda hurt my feelings too much, I went to Colette's house. Sometimes I spent the night there. Colette's parents were very nice, and I was always welcome. At bedtime, Colette's mother would warm up the sheets with a flat iron, and in the morning she prepared nice bowls of café au lait and buttered bread. When I went back home, I often found that Fréda had placed a bag of candies on my pillow. I thanked her, but we never discussed the reasons for her gift.

If I criticize Fréda, it is not to say that I was blameless myself. Like all adolescents, I had different faces. At home, I tried to act unfeeling and *blasée*. Whenever I remembered to play that part, it worked: I exasperated everyone. However, in private, I was overflowing with emotion: love, ecstasy, despair poured out of me like water. My father and I understood one another. He realized that there was more to me than what I showed. We never talked about my mother, but he knew she still had a big place in my life, and, in the same way, I knew she still had a big place in his life. I thought of her a lot and still cried when I was alone my room, but now, with my face full of tears, I looked at myself in the mirror, and cried some more.

Colette and I having fun in her parents' garden. (c. 1952)

It was my mother's spontaneous caresses that I missed most. French people are a little wary of impromptu gestures. In the morning, they get up and kiss everyone on the cheeks. When they meet relatives or friends during the day, it's still more kisses; and when they go to bed, it's the same thing: kiss, kiss. But it's perfunctory and often done without warmth. Now, when my cousins or friends do something nice and I respond by giving them a hug (I have lived in the U.S. a long time), I feel them tense up, as if I had done something abnormal.

Even between Colette and me there was a certain distance—and that in spite of the bubbling volcano of our friendship. We kissed when we met and when we parted, and sometimes held hands when we walked, as girls used to do at that time, but all that was done without emotional or sensual exuberance. I could not turn to Fréda for a warmer kind of love as there certainly was nothing gentle about her. Tante Valentine was nice, but a little gruff. As for Tante Yvonne, she had been successful in driving away any tender feelings I might have had for her. So, at home, my only recourse was to act as if I didn't need anybody. My father was the only one who knew better. Somehow we formed a sacred, silent pact, which was never discussed, and which would never be broken.

When I was about fifteen, I started writing down my thoughts, my dreams, whatever was important to me. I didn't keep a formal diary but wrote on little pieces of paper or on pages torn from my notebooks. On a shelf of my bookcase I kept a box in which I dropped what I called *"mes petits papiers"* ("my little papers"). The never-sent letters to Patrick were there, so were writings about my mother, about Colette, and about a friend of my father's I had a crush on. Good thing I gave my father's friend a made-up name: "Dominique" (I didn't like his real name). He must have been in his forties, an exceptionally handsome man with steely blue eyes and prematurely silver hair. I was very jealous of *La Danseuse* because it was said that she had received his favors (which I highly doubt). He was married but separated, and the rumor was that his mistress was Madame Naudé, the wife of the new café owner at 36, rue Jules Ferry—the Brussons had retired; "Chez Brusson" had become "Chez Naudé." I raved about "Dominique" (who knew nothing about it) and wrote him passionate letters, which of course I didn't send, but put away with my *petits papiers*. Then, one day, I realized that someone had touched my box and read my papers. Was it Fréda? Did she believe everything I wrote? Did her cutting remarks about my so-called "loose life" originate from what she had read? Did she believe in a real "Dominique?" I was quite upset, and, from then on, decided to hide my writings. I took an empty copybook, pasted envelopes on the pages and stuck my folded "little papers" in the envelopes. I also pasted some drawings I made, and sometimes added cut-out pictures or dried flowers. In the end, after a few years, I had about five notebooks, which I always put away among my school things, so no one would find them. I later dismantled these notebooks, keeping only a few of the little papers, most of them having turned yellow with time. Some were silly, some were touching or amusing. And some were useful for the writing of these memoirs. Here is one, about Patrick:

> "Again, as every time she saw him, she felt a deep emotion invading her. I do not know a face more complicated than his, she thought. And while they exchanged a few words, she hesitated as to where she would rest her eyes. On his eyes? They always surprised her, for she never expected to find them so pale. On his lips? She did not recognize them, surrounded as they now were by an irregular mustache, about which one could not tell if it was blond or red. She thought about his hair; it was greased and straight. She remembered that morning not long ago when she had seen him happy, his hair flying in the wind. But she had to keep up with the conversation, and, while observing him, she kept thinking, both about what she was going to say, and about what he would think of her. She abruptly became afraid he would realize that she had powdered her nose to hide her pimples, and she suddenly blushed. He looked at her, stirred also, a little surprised at her blushing."

4
The Hairdresser and the Stocking Mender

Louison Bobet is a legend: winner of many races including the World Road Race Championship, winner of the Tour de France three years in a row, he remains to this day one of the greatest bicycle champions that France has ever known. In 1952, already a great champion, he lived (to our honor and pleasure) in Fontenay-sous-Bois, about a block and a half from the villa de l'Ouest. The only problem was that we never saw him. He was always in training somewhere else. Once in a while we were lucky enough to catch a glimpse of his wife in the garden of their house. Some people bragged that they knew her, but personally I only saw her once—and that from a distance. I did, however, have my hair done by the same hairdresser.

At the corner of rue Jules Ferry and rue Roublot was a small beauty parlor with only one hairdresser, the owner herself. She was a good-looking woman, very nice. After a shampoo, she rubbed my head with cologne water for what was called *"une friction."* It felt very good. Every time I went to her salon, she told me that she did Louison Bobet's wife's hair. She also said I should model for coiffure magazines because my hair was beautiful and manageable. I did have nice hair, jet black, coarse and shiny, with just enough curls to hold any kind of styling.

"I like the hairdresser," I once told Fréda.

"Well, you should be careful!" she said.

"Why?"

"She is *une femme à femmes* (a women's woman)."

I had never heard the expression, but Fréda's remark piqued my curiosity. It sounded intriguing, and I continued going to the salon. However, nothing out of the ordinary ever happened. The hairdresser still gave me a *friction* with eau de Cologne, still told me I had beautiful hair, and still mentioned that Madame Bobet was one of her clients.

* * *

During World War II and for many years afterward, silk or nylon stockings were so expensive that women tried to make them last as long as possible. This gave birth to small businesses specializing in stocking mending. Runs in stockings were re-woven in such a way that repairs were invisible. The stocking menders worked sometimes out of dry-cleaning shops, sometimes from their own little booths. Sitting behind a window, a stocking stretched on a sort of embroidery ring, they re-wove the runs using a metal instrument that looked like a fat crochet needle with a tiny hook at the end. A stocking mender had opened her shop, a pre-fabricated booth, in a parking lot on rue Gambetta, a short distance from the villa de l'Ouest steps. I had not yet taken my stockings to that booth for re-weaving.

On the last day of school there was a children's show at the kindergarten located at the corner of the villa de l'Ouest and the rue Jules Ferry. Since one of Fréda's little nephews was going to be in the show, I went with the family to the school event. It was very cute; the children were adorable as they acted in their little plays; the parents sat on chairs lined up under the horse chestnut trees of the yard, patches of sun falling over their summer clothing.

There was a woman there. I had already seen her in Fontenay, a black woman, very beautiful. Since she was the only black person in the whole neighborhood, gossip had circulated about her. It was said that she was the daughter of a French woman and an African army officer, but no one was sure. She had recently moved to Fontenay with her children. When the school show was over, I happened to leave at the same time as she did. She was walking right in front of me, holding her little child by the hand. Her body moved sexily as she walked in her high-heeled shoes. The back of her bare legs especially attracted my attention. Her calves were firm and perfectly shaped. Not overly muscular, but well-defined nonetheless, they formed an almost square shape with every step she took. To me, this young woman's beauty, her allure, the perfect form of her legs, and the honey color of her skin were fascinating. She represented self-confidence and perfection such as I would never be able to attain.

I took my stockings to be mended, and, as one might have guessed, the pretty woman was the stocking mender. After that, every time I went to her little booth, she looked at me, joked, and smiled—which made me blush. Once, I had to ask her for a favor: I needed my stockings fixed right away. After she had done them for me, I told her, *"Merci, vous êtes très gentille!"* ("Thank you, you are very nice!") It doesn't seem like much, but it was something an adult would say. It made me feel as if I had said something daring and personal.

Whenever I returned to her booth, she welcomed me with a smile and a bright light in her beautiful dark eyes.

"Here comes my favorite customer!" she would say.

Once, her boyfriend was sitting with her in the booth.

"Here is the girl I told you about. Isn't she pretty?" she told him.

"Yes," he said, and, looking straight into my eyes, he asked me, "Why don't you visit us sometime?"

I became a little frightened. The boyfriend was not the kind of man I was familiar with. He rode a motorcycle and wore black leather clothes. He was very tall, blond, with a handsome face and very wild hair. His eyes were strange, much too shiny for ordinary eyes, very green, light green, and they looked at me deeply, in an alarming way. There, in front of me was a whole world I knew nothing about. I retreated. I still took my stockings to be mended, but, from then on, acted like a schoolgirl. After a while the business closed. Women no longer needed to have their stockings mended; they just bought new ones. The little booth was dismantled, and my beautiful stocking mender disappeared, I don't know where.

5
Sixteen

At sixteen, I was pretty and (except for my nose) I rather liked myself. I liked my green eyes, my dark hair, my well-aligned teeth. My body, I liked too (though I hated my feet). I spent hours in front of the mirror and danced alone in my room like Leslie Caron in *An American in Paris*. When I took the bus, I stood on the open-air rear deck to exercise my "Power," which consisted in singling out a man on the street and looking directly into his eyes as the bus rolled along. Invariably, the man looked back at me and kept staring until the bus disappeared. I could feel "Desire" in his eyes. Once on firm ground, I assumed a more modest expression.

I hated my nose. It was too big and too straight. To try to make it at least look aquiline, I slept with my pajama belt tied around my face. The flat pajama belt, by pressing against my nose (though frequently disturbed during the night) would, I thought, help me achieve an elegant Jewish look, but it didn't work.

I was in my last year at the Cours Complémentaire de Vincennes. My studies were going well and my friendship with Colette was secure. Other

girls wanted to be my friends; one especially, Monique Bernard, wrote me letters asking for my attention. I liked her; she was funny, told wonderful tales from her native Brittany, and knew how to make fun of me without hurting my feelings (few people could do that—I was very touchy). But I couldn't be friends both with Colette and Monique, at least not with the same depth of commitment. It was the same for Jacqueline Heurtault, who still sought my attention. I did go out with her sometimes, but remained devoted to Colette. But, while Colette was equally devoted to me (we spent practically all our free time together), she had another friend with whom she shared something quite foreign to me, something that wasn't part of my life: leftist politics. Yes, I still read

Le Libertaire and professed to be against the government. Yes, I felt compassion for the underprivileged and unfree of the world, but I was not really committed. On the other hand, Colette and her friend Jeannette were absolutely serious. They kept up with workers' demands, joined protest marches, and went to political meetings. I didn't dislike Jeannette and wasn't upset about her spending time with Colette; no, as a matter of fact, I liked her. She was what one could call "jolly," always in a good mood, always cheerful and fun to be with, but I didn't feel closely connected to her.

At school with (from left) Françoise Berthet and Monique Bernard. (1951)

In retrospect, I realize she probably felt the same way about me. The three of us sometimes went out together. I also had a chance to meet Jeannette's parents, who were very warm people. They were Jewish, originally from Poland. I particularly liked her father, a tailor, whom I got to know rather well, as he made clothes for Papa and me at his shop in Paris.

It was under the influence of Colette and Jeannette that I joined a communist youth group, which I ended up quitting after two meetings because of a quid pro quo involving no less than my "Power." I don't remember why I chose that particular group, perhaps because its members were involved in putting together a show, and I was interested in the stage. The group leader was named Serge. He was in the process of training six or seven young people to do theatrical skits based on the lives of heroes and heroines of the Soviet Union. At the first meeting, he asked me to pick a heroine. Totally unfamiliar with the subject, I just sat around. At the second meeting, Serge suggested I should mime a Soviet heroine who died as she stood in front of a train during a war protest. It was all a little strange to me. I didn't really see the point of these skits.

In Vincennes with Jeanette. (c. 1951)

Serge was very handsome, and I thought he responded to the looks I gave him (I'm sure he did). I said to Colette and Jeannette that I found him really cute, and that it appeared that he "liked" me. Well! My secret was repeated. I was "denounced" to Serge. While it was reported to me that he had generously declared "Let's forget the whole thing," I was too embarrassed to ever go back to the group.

I was much more in my element playing the coquette with poor Patrick and driving him crazy with an "I like you, I don't like you" attitude. Whenever he was on vacation, he sent me tender postcards: "I think of you," "I remember *The Last Rays of the Golden Sun* (Für Elise), the song we used to play on the piano." He also quoted another song, one that better pictured our situation: *Si toi aussi tu m'abandonnes*, the French translation of the High Noon theme song: *Do Not Forsake Me, Oh My Darling*. But it was *Autumn Leaves* that would forever describe our relationship:

> *Les feuilles mortes se ramassent à la pelle*
> *Les souvenirs et les regrets aussi*
> *Tu vois, je n'ai pas oublié.*
>
> Autumn leaves are gathered in shovelfuls
> So are memories and regrets
> You see, I did not forget.

(Music by Joseph Kosma and words by Jacques Prévert, a poet we all loved.)

Somehow, Patrick's sadness did not seem to touch me very much. On Sunday mornings I put on nice clothes to meet my friends at the Roublot market place. The food market was held in a big hall with a turn-of-the-century roof of metal beams and opaque glass. There, housewives compared the quality and prices of the merchandise displayed: cheese, charcuterie, meat, fish, vegetable, fruit, pastries, and flowers, or they chatted while standing in line, their senses assailed both by the wonderful scents and the loud voices of merchants calling out the freshness and low price of their goods.

Next to the covered market, temporary stalls or booths were aligned on both sides of the street, offering new clothing, purses, household goods, toys, etc. Young people met in front of the covered market and walked back and forth by the street vendors, talking and laughing, and sometimes purchasing one or two things their mothers had forgotten to buy.

Occasionally, in the evenings, the indoor space of the Marché Roublot was used to hold sporting events. I attended the boxing matches with my father or my friends. The boxers were local young men, in the categories of welterweight, lightweight, or featherweight. We had fun going to these matches. We shouted at our favorites, "Hit him! Don't be a baby! Destroy him! Knock him out!"

My father was proud of me for getting so involved with the matches. He probably hoped that my enthusiasm would lead me to become passionate about other sports. At school, I was one of the fastest runners and highest jumpers, and I could climb rope like a sailor, but I wasn't interested. My father often said with regret, "My daughter is good at sports, but she is not competitive."

If I had a laissez-faire attitude about sports, I worked hard at remaining among the best students. I was now in the last year offered by my school (9th grade), and it was time to think about the future. Most of the students would take an exam called *le Brevet*, and either go to secretarial school or work, but a few would go to *lycées* which led to university. There was a test to transfer from a *cours complémentaire* to a *lycée*. Luckily, because of my grade point average, I didn't have to take this test and was automatically admitted to Collège Sophie Germain, a high school in Paris. (Here, I want to briefly point out that, when I was a student, the terms *"lycée"* and *"collège"* were more or less interchangeable. Later on, after a series of educational reforms, the term: *"collège"* came to designate junior high schools, while the term *"lycée"* became reserved for high schools. To avoid confusion, the Collège Sophie Germain was then renamed Lycée Sophie Germain, as it is known now.)

There was a crisis of sorts during my last year at my school in Vincennes: at the beginning of the school year, Colette and I, who had always been in the same class, were separated. Because of the number of students, there had always been two divisions: A and B for each grade. If a student was placed in a specific division, she could request to transfer to the other one "to be with her friends." Now, it seemed obvious that the school was applying a tracking system (although the teachers denied it). There was an "advanced" class and a class for less gifted students. I got very upset and wrote a letter to Mademoiselle Rauly, asking her to please put Colette and me back together. In my letter, I not only emphasized my friend's scholarly abilities, but I described (how relevant was it? I have no idea) Colette's admirable character, writing something like: "Colette is a very generous person. She gives money to beggars in the street, and after she finishes school she will go take care of lepers in Africa." My letter had no effect; there was nothing I could do; we spent the last year in different classes. But while Colette never made it to Africa, there were already signs that she wanted to devote her life to helping people in need.

I was not that altruistic, although I did volunteer to read books to blind people along with other girls of my class (Colette included). My passion at the time seemed to have been to record everything I did or saw. I still have a little text written as a birthday present for Grand-mère Cessot—it was the second "literary" present I gave my grandmother; the first one was titled (already!): *Remembrance of the Villa de l'Ouest*. This new text, in all its naive complacency, described a show followed by a luncheon organized by my school for senior citizens of the City of Vincennes. I was one of the chosen "waitresses." I explained to my grandmother without a trace of false modesty how each class had picked three of the most "gracious and amiable" girls to act as waitresses. In spite of my present embarrassment at quoting this silly composition, I think it paints a typical scene of the time:

> "Madame la Directrice tells us that our role will be to greet the old people at the door and take them to their seats. . . . Soon, a girl with a lovely smile comes to announce that the spectacle will start with a piano piece played by Jacqueline (the School Goddess). . . . Then comes a scene from a Molière comedy, to the joy of our dear old people. . . . After that, two girls dressed in long red dresses and black lace shawls do a Spanish dance. . . . We are lucky to have among us a girl who is in the corps de ballet of the Châtelet. Wearing her tutu, she turns and flies on pointes. The old people demand an encore. . . . Madame la Directrice announces that we are honored to welcome a special guest: Mademoiselle Suzanne Flon, of the Théâtre des Variétés, who will recite a few poems. The spectacle is over; the old people go out to the yard while we prepare the tables. Soon they are back inside, chatting gaily. We first bring them a good ham sandwich, then a piece of cake with cream. Wine is poured in their glasses, which makes them very happy. The next dish is a gorgeous piece of flan. After that, there is a fruit salad, and finally: coffee and cookies. . . . At the end, there is a raffle with

presents donated by students. An old lady who won a packet of rice is not pleased. I exchange her prize for a bar of chocolate and a box of cookies. Everyone is happy. The old people ask if they can kiss the waitresses. Of course they can! Now it's time to clear the tables. We are allowed to eat and drink whatever we want. We almost have indigestion from chocolate and cookies, but we drink wine and coffee to give ourselves the energy to do the dishes. We are exhausted; our white aprons are all soiled; our feet hurt; but we keep on smiling because we feel that, at least, we have given a little dose of happiness to the old people."

And an overdose of sugar, I would say!

In the summer of 1951 I took a vacation in London with Bernard, to visit his pen pal, Kenneth Farrington. Ken had already been to France and had stayed at Tante Yvonne's house where I had met him. Ken, Bernard, and I had gone out together to various sites in Paris, Ken practicing his French, Bernard and I our English. Once, during Ken's visit, Tante

At Tante Yvonne's: Colette, Bernard, Ken and me. (1951)

Yvonne prepared a special luncheon and asked me to invite a school friend. I invited Colette, of course. Tante Yvonne, who had made a special French meal, decorated the table with little British and French flags; she loved to do things like that. Back in London, Kenneth wrote to me and the two of us also became pen pals. To this day, Bernard and I are still friends with Ken, who later became an actor and is well-known in England.

It is during this trip to London that I started loving all things English. Bernard and I were very well received by the Farringtons. I was given Ken's little sister's room decorated with pretty chintz curtains and Humpty Dumpty wallpaper. In the morning Mrs. Farrington brought each of us a cup of tea in bed. In the evenings we lounged in the cozy living room, sinking in the sofas and soft chairs—nothing like my rigid dining room in Fontenay. Ken walked around the house reciting Shakespeare. We visited London: the Tower, Westminster Abbey, Saint Paul's Cathedral. Mr. and Mrs. Farrington drove us to the countryside, stopping at pubs where people sang popular songs, standing around a piano player. I loved every bit of it. I also felt happy with Ken and Bernard, who, being sixteen-year-old boys, were both quite fond of me simply because I was a girl.

At Ken's house. London. (1951)

Bernard and I returned to Paris after a couple of weeks, taking the train from Victoria Station to New Haven, the boat to Dieppe, and then the train to Gare Saint-Lazare. This would be the first of numerous trips to England where I tasted a way of life I found so much more pleasing than my everyday French life.

Bernard and me in London. (1951)

Hôtel de Sens, around the corner from my school.

A vacation before school starts.

TEN

1951 - 1953

1
Sophie Germain

In October 1951 I started in *classe de seconde* (10th grade) at Collège Sophie Germain, an all-girl secondary school named after a famous female French mathematician and physicist. I still have a booklet with the rules of the Collège; here are some of these rules:

> 1/ Students' conduct: Conduct must be absolutely correct. Makeup is prohibited. Students must arrive and leave according to the itinerary established by their parents. Students must not linger either in the street, in front of the school gate, or at the métro station; they must never draw attention to themselves in any way.
> 2/ Students' conduct inside the establishment: Students must wear a long-sleeved smock of unbleached linen (smocks of color—and needless to say, black smocks—are no longer tolerated), on which the student's last name, the first initial of her first name, and her class number must be embroidered in red cotton thread (chest: left side). For physical education, it is required that the student bring navy blue shorts and white gymnastic shoes, to be carried back and forth in a special bag. These objects and this bag will also bear the student's name and her class number. It is firmly recommended that the student wear long pants for outside sessions of physical education in winter, which will prevent colds and bronchitis.
> It is prohibited to leave any article of clothing or any books in the collège, or bring jewelry or sums of money non-indispensable to school life. The school declines all

responsibility in this matter. The use of a *poche* (pocket), always with the student, is particularly recommended for holding billfolds and coin purses. No books or objects can be brought to the collège without authorization. A teacher's signature is indispensable if a non-school book or publication is to be brought. Any political or religious propaganda is prohibited, as well as the wearing of badges.

It is prohibited to throw pieces of paper, orange peels, etc. in the garden, the yards or hallways, as well as in the classrooms. Any student infringing upon this rule will be punished by one bad mark. It is similarly prohibited to trample the school's little flower bed (*une mauvaise note*).

Who would have thought of trampling the school's tiny flower bed anyway? The rules go on like this for four pages. Another passage will surprise:

Madame la Directrice holds office hours for parents on Saturdays from 1 to 3 p.m. and (exceptionally) on other days by appointment.

(We had school on Saturday morning).

The school was headed by three figures of authority: *la Directrice* (the Principal), *le Censeur* (Vice-principal) and *la Surveillante Générale* (Head of Discipline). All the school personnel were female. The *Surveillante Générale*, an ugly shapeless woman, whom the students had nicknamed "Titine," was an absolute terror. We had to line-up in front of her when we left the school grounds for lunch as she verified our passes and looked at us one by one, scrutinizing our faces for any trace of makeup. If she found the slightest hint of mascara or detected half-erased lipstick, she would send us to the restrooms with a disdainful: "Mademoiselle! Go wash your face!"

For disobeying the school rules we were given *mauvaises notes* (demerits). Each demerit diminished our monthly grade in *conduite* (behavior) by one point. Throughout the year, we were supposed to maintain a *conduite* grade point average of ten out of twenty. If a student's final grade in behavior was nine, she had to repeat the year; if the grade was under nine, the student was dismissed. Punishment for various offenses also brought hours of detention to be "served" in a study room on Saturday afternoons under the supervision of *pions*, or *pionnes* (university student proctors), who promptly reported us to the authorities whenever we misbehaved. In my first months, intimidated by the Collège rules, I was afraid to get in trouble in any way.

Besides me, the only two students from the Cours Complémentaire de Vincennes who had transferred to Sophie Germain (others had stopped their studies or gone to other lycées) were Lyliane Giraud, the very sensitive girl with weak ankles, and Jacqueline Heurtault, the "intellectual" who persistently sought my friendship. There was no escaping Jacqueline now; we often rode the métro together and shared free time between classes. This, however, allowed me to appreciate her intelligence and wit, and her special gift for "analyzing" everyone and everything. I also became closer to Lyliane and often visited her at her home. Since Lyliane came from a bourgeois milieu (her father owned a local enterprise), the atmosphere at her house was much different from what I was used to at home. Her parents' apartment in Vincennes was richly furnished and decorated. Whenever I came to visit, her mother served us tea in grand style. She brought out fancy tea things on a tray and gave us cookies, cake, or little open sandwiches. After arranging everything on the table, she left us alone to do our homework or share school gossip. I could hardly have imagined Fréda doing anything like that.

To project a bit in the future: I remained friends with Lyliane, who will continue to appear in my story. As for Jacqueline, I am sorry to say that my move to the United States interrupted our friendship. Jacqueline would continue her studies to earn a PhD in Natural Science. She became a noted specialist in the study of arachnids, wrote scientific books and articles, and taught classes at the Paris Museum of Natural History. She even had a pseudoscorpion named after her: "I. jacquelinae." Jacqueline died in 2000.

Studies at Sophie Germain were not easy. Emphasis was on math and science. Since these were my worst subjects, I thoroughly applied myself. After three months we had our first end-of-quarter tests in all disciplines. For some reason I did very well, and when all grades were averaged, I ended up ranking first in my class. I could hardly believe it! My father was honored. However, I relaxed a bit afterwards and never duplicated this feat. While I did continue to be a good student in literature, English, Spanish, geography, history, and even biology, I never became good in algebra, geometry, trigonometry, physics, and chemistry. Nevertheless, I always managed to keep a decent grade point average. I never worried too much about my results except at the time of *"compositions"* (quarterly tests), when students were put under great pressure. (Education reforms have now done away with the dreaded *compositions*, as well as with the ranking of students.) For several weeks before the tests, we had to cram mercilessly. I studied every day past midnight, falling asleep book in hand, and got up at 5 or 6 a.m. to review my subjects.

It was during one of these early morning study sessions that I decided to try smoking. Some of my friends already smoked cigarettes, so I wanted to keep up with them. Luckily, my father always left a pack of Gauloises around. At 5 or 6 a.m. Papa and Fréda were still asleep. The kitchen, bright white and neon-lit, was quiet and deserted. It was the perfect moment to take out a Gauloise, strike a match and light the cigarette. It was absolutely disgusting! The taste made me sick. Little pieces of tobacco stuck to my lips. I wondered how people could enjoy something like that! Maybe this is why I don't smoke. A Gauloise at dawn, you should try it!

The Lycée (ex-Collège) Sophie Germain is on rue de Jouy, in the Marais district. The Quartier du Marais, now fashionable, wasn't yet so chic in the fifties, as major restoration didn't start until the sixties. On the right bank of the Seine, between Place de la Bastille and rue des Archives, the Marais was, in the seventeenth and eighteenth centuries, the district of the nobility, who lived in grand houses built in classical style. In these houses, or rather mansions, called *hôtels particuliers*, receptions were given for people of the court, and literary salons held for famous writers and philosophers. But little by little people of the nobility moved away, and, by the time of the 1789 Revolution, most of the mansions had been abandoned. The Marais became the Jewish district of Paris. Often used as warehouses, the classical buildings, blackened by time, were barely noticeable. In the narrow rue de Jouy and neighboring rue de Fourcy a few quaint food shops sold Jewish and Polish specialties. However, at the time I went to school, most of these small businesses were already boarded up.

The Collège Sophie Germain was located in an old building whose wings stood around an inside court. During my time at the school, this building was rather decrepit and no one seemed to pay any attention to its architecture. Later on, I would learn that it was none other than the 15th Century "Maison de l'Hermitage," which in the 17th century became the Hôtel de Fourcy and was occupied at a time by a *Conseiller du Roi*. In 1882, the classic old mansion was chosen to house Paris first secondary school for girls, a school which eventually became the Collège, then the Lycée Sophie Germain. A vast restoration plan begun in 1991 contributed to returning the building to its past glory.

Next door to the collège was a large black building (I assumed it was some sort of government office) which was also later restored to its seventeenth century magnificence. This building was the Hôtel d'Aumont, a duke's palace built by the most famous architects of the time. A short distance behind my school stood the beautiful castle-like Hôtel de Sens, with its corner turrets and huge portals, one of the few remaining Parisian medieval residences. It was already being restored when I went to Sophie Germain, but the crumbling apartment buildings at its sides (which were later razed and replaced by new buildings in the "old style"), had remained standing and were still inhabited, their window ledges brightened by pots of geraniums. During one of our drawing classes, which were sometimes held in the backyard of our school, we were given the assignment to draw the Hôtel de Sens. I have kept my drawing; it hangs on my wall, a reminder of my school days in Paris.

To go to school I took the bus, then the métro, and got off at Saint-Paul-Le Marais (at that time just called St. Paul). With my habit of not leaving until the last minute, I was often late. The rule was that, if we were less than five minutes late, we were allowed in class but would get one bad mark. More than five minutes late, we got one bad mark and had to wait out the first period in the office of Madame La Directrice. More than once, I found myself in that office, but it was by no means an unpleasant experience. The office, softly carpeted, was all wood and sunlight. While Madame la Directrice was busy writing at her desk, I sat in a comfortable chair and was allowed to take one of the leather-bound books out of the small glass-fronted bookcase. I had a favorite book, a few chapters of which I would read every time I was late. It was titled *Les Aborigines d'Australie*.

My drawing of the Hôtel de Sens

Until then, I didn't know anything about the Aborigines, but I became fascinated by them. Again, as after the lecture given at my former school by the smashingly handsome South African Zulu specialist, I thought of becoming an anthropologist.

Once I got used to the rules of discipline, life at Sophie Germain was not all that bad. First of all, the classes were interesting; I especially enjoyed the literature program which consisted, in the first year of our studies, of Greek and Latin classics in their French translations. I also liked the English class which was taught by a wonderful teacher, Mademoiselle Marcelle Sibon, translator of the works of Graham Greene. In Spanish class, we read passages of Don Quixote in the original text, going over every sentence—if not every word—according to the French method of *lecture expliquée* (explained reading), a method which, if sometimes tedious, is sure to deliver wonderful rewards in the end.

Besides our regular physical education periods, we could choose a sport as an elective. I picked crew. It was not the competitive sport that is usually associated with "real" crew. Actually, one could have called it "paddling on the Seine." However, as is usual with crew training, our sessions started at six o'clock in the morning. We were divided into two teams, each team in a canoe holding six girls, three paddling on one side, three on the other. Once we managed to get coordinated, which was no small matter, we just went gliding along. Speed was not of the essence. Can one imagine anything more delightful than boating on the Seine in the morning, slowly cruising along the sides of Île de la Cité with the new sun shining on Notre Dame, turning around Île Saint Louis, whose historical gray houses were barely visible through the trees? We started at Pont Marie which was close to our school and went as far as Pont de la Tournelle with its statue of Sainte Geneviève, the patron-saint of Paris, the water of the Seine, a mirror of green and silver.

Notre Dame and Île de la Cité. Postcard

If I appreciated Sophie Germain in general, its main appeal for me was the students. I never had any trouble getting along with other girls, and had many friends in the school, some of them I admired for being "math geniuses." One girl who was different (I think she was a bit crazy), managed to "draw attention to herself" and was expelled after a few months. At noon, in good weather, my small group of close friends and I went to eat our sandwiches in the Notre Dame gardens, a short walk away, where we enjoyed looking at boys, flowers, tourists, mothers with their little children, and the flying buttresses of the old cathedral.

There was a girl who wasn't part of our group but whom I liked very much. She had one close friend but otherwise didn't socialize much. Her name was Gisèle Bélard. Her essays in literature were well-written, clever, and to the point. Her math tests were always done quickly and correctly. Without a doubt she was the smartest girl in the class, superior in all subjects. In my opinion, she was also the most beautiful. She looked just like a Renoir painting: round face, golden hair, skin with almost invisible down, soft as a peach. I was intrigued by her, but she was reluctant to communicate. I once invited her to go with Colette and me to the École du Louvre where we attended evening classes in art history (always eager

In the Notre Dame garden. From right: Jacqueline Heurtault, me, Lyliane Giraud (in front) and other friends. (1953)

to learn everything possible, we took these free classes offered by the Musée du Louvre). She came once, but that didn't help me to know her better. At the very end of our studies at Sophie Germain, I was sad to learn that the brilliant Gisèle didn't plan to attend the university. She was going to get married and work in an office.

One of my favorite friends was Fanny Panderia. Her family was from Spain, but Fanny had been brought up in Paris. She was very cute, with big shiny dark-brown eyes and curly black hair. She sat next to me in Spanish class. If we appeared to listen intently to the chivalrous adventures of Don Quixote, our attention was not always on the text. Way down on the floor, under the desk, something was happening. Fanny would take off one of her shoes and I would take off one of mine, then she would gently kick her empty shoe on my side and I would slip my stockinged foot in it. It was most exciting. Her shoe was warm. Throughout my body, I could feel the charming glow of dear Fanny Panderia.

With all my work at Sophie Germain I had no time for love. I did, however, manage to get my first kiss, although, after waiting so long, I was no longer in love with the kiss-giver. Patrick and I had walked Colette to her house one evening and we were on our way home. I had taken Patrick's arm, perhaps to get closer to him, perhaps to protect myself against the cold, as he was wearing his warm (and fashionable) duffel coat. After going down the steps of the villa de l'Ouest, we lingered a while. It was foggy; there was a bit of snow on the ground. We ended up kissing, but it was without passion, at least on my part, since I felt nothing but friendship for Patrick. I had not meant to mislead him. I just had followed "my instinct." At my age (eighteen) I was more than ready for concrete experience. Besides, it was rather exciting to kiss a boy right in front of my house, knowing that my father would have a fit of dishonor if he caught me. But the whole thing did not make me happy, mostly because I knew I was causing more pain than pleasure to Patrick, who, of course, would not fail to entertain renewed hopes about me since I continued to show him love one day, friendship another, indifference when I felt like it—enough to keep him wondering.

But I couldn't spend too much time thinking about love—or whatever that was. What I had to do was to concentrate on my studies. In July 1953, I was to take the *Baccalauréat*, a difficult national test, the crowning of the secondary school program. Without passing the first part of that test, as well as the second part, given the following year, there would be practically no chance of entering the university. At that time, more than a third of the students failed the exam. We were going to be tested in all subjects—both in writing and orally—by teachers whom we did not know, in unfamiliar lycées in Paris assigned to us at the time of the test. We were under immense pressure, taking mock-exams all year around, and cramming as much as we could. Nothing much else but studying was on my mind during that school year. I woke up early, went to bed late and studied during weekends. Fréda cooked fish for me—it was good for the brain. Finally June arrived. I took the written exam and passed. What a relief!

Between the written and oral exams I had a dental appointment; I went to it but, unfortunately, I had an accident: the point of the drill detached itself from its socket, flew in the air and landed on my lip, cutting it deeply. I had to have stitches; the wound was covered with gauze and tape, making it difficult for me to talk. I was very upset, wondering if I was going to be able to take the oral test—and also worrying about "my beauty." Fréda was supportive. She made soup for me since I couldn't chew well, and didn't make any comment when I drank my soup from one side of my mouth while looking at myself in a mirror! After a few days, my lip started to heal, just in time for me to take the oral exams. The final result of the *Baccalauréat* showed that I had passed with honor, but at that point I didn't care, I was just happy to be through. Papa and Fréda were thrilled, the sisters and brothers-in law raised their glass to my success, Tante Valentine, Oncle Baptiste and Roger congratulated me warmly. I gave the news to Tante Yvonne and Grand-mère Cessot, who in turn gave me the news that Bernard had passed too. What joy! Colette, who had anxiously waited for the results, was much relieved. It felt so good to be loved!

2
Barcelona

After all these efforts, it was agreed that I needed a vacation. Papa offered me a trip as a reward for my success. When I told him that I dreamed of going to Spain, he contacted a journalist friend whose family lived in Barcelona. The friend sent his younger brother to give us more details. I immediately "fell in love" with the brother, a painter (artist) who was not only charming and handsome, but also noticed my picture of the Hôtel de Sens and found it *"très artistique."* This young man (who, alas, I never saw again!) and his brother were the sons of a Spaniard, Pablo Montez, from an earlier marriage. Their father was now remarried to a younger woman (he was in his mid-sixties, she in her early forties) with whom he had two children. We were told that Pablo and his wife, Maria, would be happy to earn a little income by hosting me. Papa accepted the conditions, and it was decided that I would spend a month's vacation in Barcelona. It would be a good opportunity to practice my Spanish. Only Pablo spoke some French, the rest of his household did not speak any foreign languages.

At that time Spain was still under the dictatorial regime of Franco. The first thing I noticed upon arriving in Barcelona was the great number of *guardias* (militarized policemen from the *Guardia civil*). These policemen could ask people for their identification papers at any time. It did happen to me one day as I was resting on a bench; a policeman approached me and asked me to show him my passport. It also soon became evident to me that people couldn't freely express their disapproval of the regime; they avoided talking about politics.

However, except for the *guardias*, the atmosphere in Barcelona didn't appear repressive; hundreds of people, Spaniards and tourists alike, walked up and down the Ramblas at all hours of the day and evening, since life in Spain goes on way past nightfall. Often, there was Catalan music and dancing on the streets; the friendly dancers encouraged spectators to join in the dance circles, and I soon learned to dance the *sardana*. As I walked in busy streets lined with shops full of goods for tourists, I admired the beautiful Spanish people, women in elegant white dresses and high-heeled shoes, men in light summer suits that enhanced their tanned complexion and dark mustaches.

Walking on Las Ramblas. (1953)

Life at my hosts' was not on a grand scale. For a long time, I didn't know what Pablo did for a living until I found out that he polished shoes at a little stand next to a café in a busy area of town. Besides polishing shoes, he sold black market cigarettes and a few packages of candies and chewing gum (he had a special arrangement with the café). Maria did not work; legally blind, she wore thick glasses that helped her a little. In spite of her handicap, she adored going to the movies. It was a true passion with her; she could have spent her life at the cinema. I loved the Montez children;

the girl was thirteen, her name was Candelaria (we called her Candelita). Tall and thin, she was one of the most beautiful girls I had ever seen. She had a perfectly oval face, classic features, olive complexion, and skin as smooth as satin. But it was her eyes that were striking: they were of a rarely seen green, perhaps the color of light falling on a lily pond. People turned around to catch a better look at her when she walked, but she ignored their attention. She was extremely proud and acted like a queen. Only one time did I hear her return the catcalls of young men on the street.

"*Guapa!*" ("Beautiful!") they said.

"*Feo!*" ("Ugly!") she answered.

Her little brother, Jesús, was a curly-haired little devil, always in trouble. He and Candelita, who was his appointed babysitter, argued constantly.

It turned out that I stayed more than a month, thanks to a prolonged train strike that began just as I was ready to leave. I didn't mind at all. I loved Barcelona and the Montez family. Sometimes I went out with the children, but most often I set out by myself to visit everything I could: *la Sagrada Familia, el Pueblo Español* (the reconstitution of a Spanish village where artisans practiced their crafts), the Gothic District, the *Plaza Real,* the tall ship moored in the old port, Gaudi's *La Casa Milá,* or a wonderful museum of Romanesque frescoes lifted from old Pyrenean churches, a museum to which I returned several times to sketch details of the frescoes. I loved to walk past outdoor markets, which, to this day, are imprinted on my memory with their pyramidal displays of melons and watermelons of all kinds and colors. Sometimes I took a bus, any bus, and rode to the terminal to explore different districts. But some of my most memorable outings were the ones I went on with la Señora Montez.

"You come with me today, you and the children," Maria said.

She picked up a large double-handled bag, the kind she took to go shopping for food, and dropped cabbage leaves at the bottom. We followed her through cobbled streets that became narrower and narrower. We were in *"el Barrio Chino,"* the poor district of Barcelona, where, I was told, many Gypsies lived. Apartment buildings were in disrepair; beggars—some of them missing limbs—were sitting in doorways or lying on the ground; a few men worked at crafts, hammering metal trays. Straw was strewn all over the streets. It looked like a scene from *The Lower Depths*. Maria turned abruptly into a doorway, the children and I following behind. We climbed a dirty staircase, noise coming from behind the walls. She knocked on a door in a special way. A woman furtively let us in, making sure we were not followed. I sat in the kitchen with the children while Maria went to another room with the woman. When they returned, Maria's bag was completely full; the cabbage leaves were at the top, covering the contents. She quickly lifted the leaves to show me what was underneath. American cigarettes!

"You mustn't tell anyone or I would go to jail," she said.

Then we returned home, walking calmly, as if we had just been to the market.

Another time, I went to the movies with Maria and the children. Maria had been talking about it all week. We were going to see a movie in which the *Moros* (the Moors) were fighting the Spaniards. She couldn't wait; she had been saving her money. The movie house was crowded and extremely hot. The program consisted of three full-length feature films shown one after the other without interruption, except for a half-hour of live entertainment. We entered at about 3 pm and left around 9 pm. The movies were not very good. The crowd was extremely noisy, whistling, shouting and cheering for the Spaniards. During the entertainment, I believe I was the only one to be embarrassed when male comedians chased and groped women on stage while dancing couples pretended to copulate; everyone else laughed and clapped, even the children!

Sometime later, I wrote a story based on the Montez household. Since it shows Pablo on a day he was irritated, I want to point out that it was just a temporary state of affairs; Pablo was really a kind and patient man.

THE ENEMIES

Jesús was constantly harassed by his enemies, especially the Moors and the Indians of America. They never gave him any peace; they arrived in great numbers, on foot or on horseback. He always had to be ready for the attack. Generally in one day he killed a good hundred Moors and the same number of Indians. He knew how to fight and he had a good sword. His sword, he had made himself from a thin piece of wood painted pink that he had found in a street of Barcelona; while his mother and sister were sitting on the balcony fanning themselves he had taken a knife from the kitchen and split the pink wood into two pieces, one for the blade, and one for the handle; he had crossed the pieces and joined them with a couple of nails. The result looked somewhat like a dagger, but to Jesús, it was a sword.

It was hard for him to battle his enemies, with his mother, his father, and Candelita always in his way. One must admit that the Indians and their horses were especially attracted by Candelita. Impossible to kill them without turning around her, pushing her, blocking her passage! Sometimes the Indians were so close that he actually had to touch his sister with the sword. The more she screamed, the more furious the Indians got. Jesús loved it.

One day after lunch, several Moors suddenly appeared in the kitchen. Their skin was dark and they wore turbans. They looked exactly the way they did in the movies. For this important combat, Jesús had to climb on a chair. He was taking his enemies one by one. He had to be careful because each one of them was holding a sword in one hand and a knife in the other. He was attacking them bravely from the right, from the left, from above, from below. His sword sliced the air with frenzy. The kitchen was full of Moors killed or wounded. Now, only one was resisting; it was a long duel but finally, Jesús was going to deliver the fatal blow . . .

As he leaned to do so, Jesús bumped into his father's shoulder.

Pablo put down his newspaper and said, "If you don't put away this piece of wood right now, I will break it," and he seized the sword.

Delighted, Candelita chimed in, "Break it, Papa, break it!"

Jesús got down from his chair. He looked at his father straight in the eyes. He was absolutely motionless.

Pablo closed his hands tightly, one hand on each extremity of the sword.

"It would be easy, very easy; I would just have to press a little harder."

The wood bent and resisted more than expected. Now that he had delivered the threat, Pablo couldn't put down the toy, for, between him and the wood, a challenge had risen. One had to find the exact amount of pressure under which the plank would bend without yielding. It was a game. Pablo felt he had found the point where the wood was at its maximum resistance. It was tempting to go beyond the limit, almost irresistible. Crack! The sword broke in two.

Pablo threw the pieces on the table. Jesús remained silent. His mouth twisted, he left the kitchen and went to lean on the balcony. The street was blurry through his tears.

Candelita picked up an old magazine. Pablo said that it was time for him to go back to work and left.

3
A Party at Bernard's

In mid-December Bernard invited me to a party at his house. His parents were not going to be there, only his friends. He asked me to bring a few girls along. Françoise, a friend from Sophie Germain, was the only one who could come.

When I arrived Tante Yvonne and Oncle Marcel had not yet left. Tante Yvonne was still busy with the finishing touches. The carpet had been rolled up and the dining room furniture pushed in a corner to make room for dancing. On the table was an array of open-faced sandwiches, square or triangular, topped with ham, paté, or caviar and decorated with olives, sprinkles of eggs mimosa, or, for the caviar, dollops of crème fraîche. There were plenty of beverages (including champagne) to accommodate the guests. Soon Tante Yvonne and Oncle Marcel left and Bernard's friends began to arrive. One of these was Jean Joly, the son of my father's friend, Maurice (it had been both Papa and Maurice's dream that Jean and I would fall in love and marry—something not likely to happen as we were far from being compatible).

In one of my *petits papiers* I described the scene (again, a ridiculously vain piece of writing, but quite descriptive).

> Yesterday there was a party at Bernard's. I thought it was going to be full of little snobs but that wasn't exactly right. There were some of course, but to those, I paid no attention. I arrived early, a little before Jean Joly. Right after us came two boys and two girls, one of he boys looking like the perfect gigolo, and one of the girls like the perfect doll. Let's pass. We'll leave them in each other's arms. Others arrived. In all we were twenty six.
>
> I danced a lot, especially with Jean, who is a very good dancer. The light was turned off as soon as a dance began. I closed my eyes. With each step I took I felt as if I were opening the triangle of a star (that was probably due to the champagne). Jean was not tender yet. I danced with almost

all the boys, slow dances and boogies. A boy named Gérard told me I was gifted. He said that if I went two or three times to the *caves de Saint-Germain-des-Prés*, I would be *formidable*. When it got late, most of the boys left, as well as all the girls, except for two. The girls who remained were an ugly blonde who was taken over by a bearded guy (no less ugly) and my friend Françoise, whom Bernard claimed as his own. That left five boys and me.

It was then that Jean Joly became tender. He held me very tight and started kissing my neck. I had the feeling of being with a professional escort. The boy I liked best was Gérard, an immense guy with a mustache and a funny-looking red vest. He didn't try to kiss me and I am grateful to him for that. There was also a boy named Jacques. I asked him to dance because he was too shy to ask me. After that, he took his turn like the others. When we danced, he held me tight and kissed my hair. I don't know what he found in the taste of Bio-Dop!

Let's not forget Jean-Pierre, a friend of Bernard's, a handsome boy whom I had known for a long time. Whether I want to admit it or not, it was in his arms that I felt most comfortable. But Jean-Pierre, naughty one, also wanted to kiss

me! He had blue eyes, just like a celluloid boy-doll. He was very tall, as tall as Jean and Gérard; that is to say that he went from the floor almost to Tante Yvonne's dining room's light fixture. I let him kiss me on the lips without returning his kiss, then I kissed him on the cheek, and he said, "Well, you really are a funny one!" When the dances were over, it was a great fight; all the boys pulled me in every direction. It was fantastic! I danced with my arms around the neck of each one. What a job! At least, I can say that, all in all, I had fun, but I was tired, tired! Jean accompanied me to the métro and rode with me up to the Nation station. He was becoming more and more languorous, but he got on my nerves with his bland beauty and his long eyelashes. He told me I was made of ice!

This had been my first "real" party. Something had been revealed to me, which I was eager to duplicate. I decided to give my own party.

I didn't know how Bernard had convinced Tante Yvonne and Oncle Marcel to stay away for one evening, but I would have to ask the same thing of Papa and Fréda. It wouldn't be easy. Leaving their home? They had never heard of anything like that! They found my request very bizarre. I don't know how they finally accepted, perhaps because Papa talked to Tante Yvonne and she told him it was the modern thing to do.

Now, there was the question of the food. It hadn't been a problem for Bernard, as Tante Yvonne had been delighted to prepare open-faced sandwiches. I was getting ready to do something like that, but first, I had to consult my guests. At that point, besides Colette, I still had my friends of the villa de l'Ouest, as well as my new friends from Sophie Germain.

The party was set for New Year's Eve. As my parents were invited somewhere, it was the only night when they were willing to leave home for the evening. None of my friends of the villa (except Patrick perhaps) had attended a party such as the one I had been to. As soon as I discussed the food with Pierrette, Lili, Patrick, Jacqui, and Colette, I could see I had to forget about open-faced sandwiches. It had to be real food. I think we decided on hors-d'oeuvres, roast chicken, vegetables, salad, cheese and dessert. Everyone was assigned dishes to prepare, dishes that could be warmed up in my kitchen if necessary. Of course, we couldn't push off the dining room table in a corner to create a dance floor since we needed a table to eat on. Besides, it was too big and the room was too small. So, the table stayed where it was and we even had to use the extensions. This didn't leave very much room to walk around, especially since there was now a daybed on the right side of the dining room. But I still hoped that we would dance after eating. I owned *12th Street Rag*, the same Sidney Bechet record as the one that had played almost non-stop at Bernard's party. I also owned *Les Oignons*, by Claude Luter and Sidney Bechet, a Jazz tune I liked very much. Anyway, Patrick would bring his own records; he always had the best music.

I invited several friends from Sophie Germain, but only Jacqueline Heurtault came. I probably invited Jean Joly, but he didn't come. Of course, I invited Bernard, who brought a friend from his Lycée.

The atmosphere was not at all what I had expected. My party was nothing like Bernard's. As we were all sitting around the dining room table, eating out of my parents' pink porcelain set with the fancy silverware just taken out of its box, it looked very much like a traditional family dinner. We joked a little about our cooking—which was not bad, but not as good as our parents'. We drank wine during the meal, and champagne with the dessert. Drinking wasn't a big thing to us; we were all used to drinking in moderation.

I am sure that Bernard and his friend were disappointed. They didn't try to socialize with my friends of the villa de l'Ouest, probably thinking they were "too proletarian," since none of them attended a lycée. They spent the whole evening on the side of the room, talking and flirting with Jacqueline who was lying on the daybed

I don't remember that we danced. I think someone tried to turn off the lights once or twice, but it was just too dark and the lights were soon turned back on.

All my villa friends, as well as Colette and Jacqueline, had a good time. I had fun too, but I also learned two things. One: that I shouldn't have expected to generate a "cool" party out of a family-type dinner, and two: that I should be careful in how I "mixed" people. I did hope that my friends hadn't noticed that Bernard had snubbed them, but I wasn't going to bring up the subject. As for Bernard, had he known my friends better, he would have discovered, not only that they knew how to have fun, but also that some of them were children of the old bourgeoisie. Patrick, for one, not only had educated relatives, but he and his siblings had been brought up with all the proper values of the French middle class. The same was true of Colette. Her father, who came from the provincial bourgeoisie, could claim as a proof of the authenticity of his class the fact that his relatives had disowned him when he married Colette's mother, a woman of humble origins. But all that wasn't visible. Bernard and his friend, in their quick judgment, had probably felt that my friends were not of their milieu, and so, they had had nothing to do with them. (Here I want to add a note. When Bernard read this text, he objected to it, assuring me that he had not "snubbed" my friends. In fact I was perhaps being too sensitive. It is entirely possible that the reason he stayed close to his school friend was that they knew each other.)

At any rate, the question of social classes would become important later, especially in my future choice of a husband. I already vaguely realized that I wouldn't be able to pick a middle-class boyfriend, as he and his family wouldn't truly embrace Papa and Fréda's lifestyle (especially now that the plebeian "brothers-in-law" hovered in the background). On the other hand, the likelihood that I would be able to find a working-class boyfriend whose education corresponded to mine was rather remote due to the elitism of the educational system. For Bernard the transition would be smoother, as his parents already acted as if they were from the bourgeoisie, but for me, marriage into a more sophisticated class would unavoidably lead to conflict. Already, I instinctively knew that to solve this problem without hurting anyone (most of all, my father), my choice would be limited. Perhaps I would have to pick an artist, for whom class distinction would be irrelevant, or, better, a foreigner who wouldn't fit into the scheme of things.

At the moment, however, these social issues didn't preoccupy me greatly. I was ready to fall in love with whatever *galant* came my way. Pauper or prince, I didn't care.

4
Inside the Schuschmanns' Household

Talking about boys . . . My friend Colette and I still shared my cousin Miquette's confidences, avidly following the stories of her crushes and kisses. What we did not know was that these confidences were a small part of a larger picture.

There had been great changes for the Schuschmanns when their Sainte-Aubierge dream of living in the country had evaporated. Returning to Paris, they had moved into a cramped apartment of the 11th arrondissement, rue des Gravilliers, close to Place de la République. This apartment had belonged to Uncle Albert's father who had moved to Troyes (and, sadly, had died soon afterward). The Schuschmanns had gone back to their sweatshop-type sewing business. In the one-bedroom apartment, the workshop occupied the main room. Miquette hated this apartment where she had to sleep on a folding bed in a corner of the workshop.

"There were exposed pipes everywhere, some of them gas pipes. I was so unhappy in that place that many times I thought of opening one of the pipes and committing suicide," she confided in me a few years ago.

I had no idea she had such thoughts.

After a time, the family was able to move to a more spacious apartment in the 20th arrondissement, rue Courat, close to Place de la Nation. I would visit there, always enjoying spending time with Miquette. Her brothers Jacques and Claude I saw less often, as they still lived with their father, the ex-prisoner of war, and only came to see their mother every other weekend. Oncle Albert was as witty as ever. Tante Marthe was still made-up and perfumed, still jig-

Oncle Albert wowing Tante Marthe with a bunch of parsley. (1953)

gling her bracelets. But there was a change: the Schuschmanns now had television (they were the first in the family). Visiting them was not as fun as it used to be. We could no longer talk and joke as we did before. When they watched TV, Tante Marthe and Oncle Albert dimmed the lights and insisted on absolute silence.

It was years later that Miquette told me what had been going on inside the Schuschmann household. In my innocence, I had believed that their lives revolved around the movies (and now TV), science fiction novels, Gershwin concerts, and financial survival. Seeing them as a close-knit family, I never questioned anything about their life. My aunt was always pleasant, my uncle always ready to make a joke. I didn't, for instance, ask myself why my cousins were never given a voice as to their choice of career. Miquette's appointed role was to work at the power sewing machines and help with selling the merchandise. As for Claude and Jacques, both of them were placed in apprenticeship: Claude, as a tile-setter, and Jacques (whose dream was to be an engineer) as a mechanic for the bus company.

Besides my cousins' resentment about the way their future was carved for them, something else weighed on the family. I wouldn't learn of it until much later, a few years before Miquette's death in 2008.

"I adored Albert," Miquette told me, "I loved him as my own father. Actually he was the only father I had ever known knew since my biological father died at the same time I was born. When my mother married Yves, she sent me to live at Tante Valentine's. By the time I moved back with her, Yves had been taken prisoner by the Germans. It was during the five years he was held in Germany that Albert moved in with my mother; I was nine years old then. I always called him Papa. I found him *merveilleux*, and, to tell you the truth, I loved him more

My cousins Jacques, Claude and Miquette in Uncle Albert's car in front of my house. (1953)

than my mother. Little by little, I came to think of her as empty-headed, spineless, and a doormat to her husband. But one day, when we lived in Sainte-Aubierge, Albert came to me. 'I love you,' he said. 'It's only because of you that I stay with your mother.' He also admitted that it was out of jealousy that he slapped me one night when I came home late from dancing at the Sainte-Aubierge's fair. I was about seventeen then. From that day on, it was finished. Everything had changed for me. I couldn't be the same around him. Always on my guard, I could no longer talk to him as I had before (I suffered from that, and I know he did too). Now I was alone. I had nobody. When I told my mother about what Papa had said to me, Maman said, 'My little girl, I'm afraid you will have to leave. You must understand that I have to preserve my marriage!' And so, I was sent again to Tante Valentine's and stayed there for a couple of weeks, but of course that didn't help. I realized that my mother's only preoccupation was to keep her husband. She was incapable of living alone. This whole situation reminded me of the times when Albert got angry at her. Then, I would tell her, 'Why don't you go? You can leave him!' But she could never have left him; she was too wishy-washy. I hate women like that!"

Miquette and her brothers. (c. 1953)

I asked Miquette if Albert had behaved inappropriately toward her, if he had tried to make physical contact. She told me he had not. He had simply ruined their father-daughter relationship and shattered her world. It was something she would never forgive.

Reflecting on this later, I think that what Albert told Miquette (that he loved her and that she was the reason he stayed with her mother) was not true. He had a rocky but deep relationship with my aunt with whom he shared a kind of sinful complicity. Miquette was just a girl, more preoccupied with her beauty, her admirers, and her illustrated romantic magazines than with the various intellectual, artistic, and other cultural pursuits that my uncle relished—and that my aunt shared with him. It was obvious that the temptation was too strong and that he had been unable to resist Miquette's beauty and adolescent sensuality, but I don't think that, like Woody Allen, he would have left his wife to marry his step-daughter (who was almost of age). I am sure that all his life, he regretted his gesture. At least, I am glad that he showed some restraint. Of course, in Miquette's case, Albert, a father figure, would have done well to show total restraint.

Nonetheless, it seems that Miquette retained some daughterly feelings toward her step-father. On the rare occasions when Lydie, Albert's natural daughter, visited, Miquette told me she was a little jealous of the attention Lydie received from Albert. Poor Lydie! I will always remember her lovely face and striking green eyes. In the early sixties, not long after she got married, Lydie and her husband tragically died in a car accident. I was in America by then, more or less out of touch with the Schuschmanns. I did not learn of the accident until years later. Even then, Miquette was rather vague on the aftermath of these deaths. But knowing my uncle and the way he had of hiding his feelings to everyone but a few, I could well imagine his pain.

But let's go back to 1953. I am eighteen, Miquette is twenty-one. Claude and Jacques regularly visit their mother; Tante Marthe is very sweet to her teenage sons who have taken to calling her *Bichette*. There is much cuddling and kissing.

At that point the Schuschmanns were becoming restless again. Why stay in Paris? After having tasted country living in Sainte-Aubierge, they found out that they really didn't like the noise and pollution of the big city. They decided to move to Provence. There, they planned to lease a little store, live in a village, make friends with the local people, and, of course, be happy. While Miquette stayed in Paris, working as a salesgirl in a fashionable shop, Aunt Marthe and Uncle Albert set off for a small town north of Cannes that they had discovered during a vacation. Soon they were running a small toy and candy store. Tante Marthe attracted customers by giving candies to children. At first, everything seemed perfect.

But the local population turned out to be quite unfriendly toward these Parisian newcomers. The men of the village never once asked Oncle Albert to join them for a game of pétanque in the shady town square. Besides, it soon became obvious to the Schuschmanns that their finances were going from bad to worse. They decided to move to Cannes where Albert found a management position in a small firm. Now, he even had a secretary (Tante Marthe wasn't too happy about that!). Tante Marthe herself went back to work on her power sewing machine, now assembling, not work caps, but bikini bathing suits. It was around that time that Miquette, who had come to visit her parents, met her future husband, Gilbert. They soon would marry and settle in Nice.

Also living on the French Riviera, Miquette's younger brother, Claude, who had left Paris and his job as a tile-setter, was now working as a beach boy, parading his muscles and serving drinks to rich ladies. And like his brother, Jacques would soon leave his biological father's home and settle in Cannes near Tante Marthe and Oncle Albert.

Because of the physical removal of the Schuschman family to the south of France and my eventual departure for America, I stopped having contact with them except through New Year's cards or letters. Later on, when Miquette (whom, by then, we called Michèle), Claude, Jacques and I were in our forties, we re-connected and became close again.

5
Papa and Fréda

Fifty-three years old, in good health and forever youthful, my father seemed happy. He was still working at the printing shop with his old friends, and Fréda, a good wife, had pretty much become used to his ways. He couldn't complain about me: I was doing well—except for being in constant danger of falling prey to young men. Papa now socialized mostly with Fréda's family, going fishing or playing cards or pétanque with the jolly brothers-in-law. There was always plenty of laughter and kidding around, but also a lot of drinking: Pernods at aperitif time, wine at lunch and dinner, and many good excuses for a *p'tit verre* in between. Fréda and I knew my father was drinking too much, but there was nothing we could say to him.

My father's drinking was often an embarrassment to me. During the week, mornings and afternoons were fine. It was mostly in the evenings and on weekends that the situation was uncertain. When Kenneth Farrington's parents came to visit Tante Yvonne and Oncle Marcel, they were looking forward to meeting my parents. Had I been sure my father would remain sober, I would have loved for Ken's parents to come to our house—but it wasn't likely.

After visiting them in Paris, the Farringtons invited the Labbés to spend Christmas in London. Ken, Tante Yvonne, Ken's father and mother, Uncle Marcel. Trafalgar Square. (c. 1953)

And since it was not possible to invite the Farringtons without inviting the Labbés, I could clearly predict that Tante Yvonne's remarks and her tendency to "subtly" snub Fréda would not fail to irritate my father. With drinks flowing easily, I feared that some kind of scene would follow, with the poor Farringtons not knowing what to do. The sad part was that I was aware that the Farringtons were more akin to my parents than to the Labbés, and, if everything had gone well, they would have had a wonderful time. But the risk was too great. Proud as I was of my father sober, I couldn't bear for the Farringtons to see him "like that." And so, reluctantly, I managed to make an excuse so they wouldn't meet.

I had the same problem about bringing a boyfriend home. It might work, but it might not. Luckily, things hadn't reached that point: I had just met a boy I liked, but since he had not yet introduced me to his parents, there was no need to introduce him to mine.

I got along well enough with Fréda, but still addressed her with the formal "vous" as a way of making it clear to the world that she was not my mother. My father remained the center of the household. He decided on all important matters (although Fréda wasn't afraid to express her opinion), kept his budget books, recorded family events, planned trips and invita-

My father's crooked smile.
Later photo (c. 1965)

tions, talked trade-union and politics with me, and never failed to entertain Fréda and me with his many anecdotes, jokes, and songs (still his old pre-war favorites). I can still picture him when he was getting ready to go to work. Looking at his image in the mirror, he would carefully comb his sparse hair, splash eau de cologne on his neck, and, with his inimitable little smile, declare: *"C'est un péché d'être si beau!"* (It's a sin to be so handsome!)

Well-loved as I was, I had no reason to be unhappy at home. Yet, there was something I could barely stand: it was the fact that my father constantly repeated that he was "sacrificing" himself to send me to school. And what with my plan of going to the university? Wouldn't that require a still greater sacrifice? Since French university studies are practically free (there is no tuition; students only pay for their books, plus small fees for various services), what my father really meant was that, by going to school, I wasn't going to contribute to the family finances. I don't know why he was so concerned. After all, he earned a good salary; he had some savings even. We had a car, took nice vacations, our house was paid for; we had everything we needed. And it wasn't as if I didn't keep my spending to a minimum. I hardly ever bought new clothes since I was still getting hand-me-downs from Tante Yvonne. As for the books I read, they were either borrowed or given to me. His hammering about his "sacrifice" made me want to leave home as soon as possible. I didn't think that anyone noticed, but Tante Yvonne (who, in spite of what I believed at the time, always watched over me) told me later that she felt sorry for me whenever she heard my father carry on about his "sacrifice."

All this grumbling, I guess, was tied to the question of what I was going to do in life. Fréda, especially, tried to force me into deciding upon a career. I was only interested in literature, poetry, the theater, and the cinema. I suppose I could have told my parents (as I had at thirteen when I convinced my father to let me go to a lycée), that I planned to be a teacher—which, in the back of my mind, I still considered—but I came up with a much better idea: I decided to become an actress! The hard part was to announce it.

Why did I want to be an actress? Was it perhaps because I sang for the family as a child, got good grades in poetry recitation, and acted in plays in the villa de l'Ouest? Did I envy *"la Danseuse,"* a professional performer? Did I think of myself as irresistible? Or was it because I had the example of Ken Farrington, already a promising actor? I don't know. But I could see no other "solution" to the enigma of my future. What I wanted in life, according to a note I wrote to myself at the time, was "read, learn poems, listen to music, love, travel, be admired, have children." Only the theater, I concluded, could provide me with all of this (including children, I guess). I must add that I did have my doubts. "But, Colette," I asked myself, "do you believe the theater can give you the ideal life you dream of?" "No!" I answered. "The theater can mean unrewarded efforts, beaten-down pride, failures, stage fright; besides (I wisely added), one must have a calling." But did I really have a calling?

I decided to inform my parents of my career decision. Contrary to what I had feared, my father did not object. I think he could already see his glory in my glory. As for Fréda, she just smirked. Nothing more was said on the subject for several weeks. One day Fréda found me in a *Le Penseur's* attitude.

Ken in the Greek play *Trachinae*. (c. 1953)

"What are you thinking about?" she asked.

"My future," I said.

"Why think about your future? Live your life!"

"I can't! My future depends on the choices I make."

"Don't worry about it. You'll get married and have children."

"For what I want to do, I cannot think about that now."

"Because you know what you want to do? Your father and I would be glad to know too! Put yourself in our place. Do we have any idea why we should let you continue your studies? Maybe you want to be a doctor, a pharmacist! Now you are telling me that you know what you want to do, but every time we ask you, you answer that you don't know!"

"But I told you already!"

"Oh! Yes! I forgot! You want to be an actress!"

It was apparent she didn't take me seriously.

On one of the rare occasions when I complained about Fréda to Tante Yvonne, she gave me her own interpretation of the situation.

"Fréda would like to see you married as soon as possible," she said, "because she is anxious to enjoy her condition of wife. As it is now, all the available money is shared between you and her. And besides, she has to be at your beck and call. When you are gone, it will be her turn to reign. It's normal. At least, that's what I think."

After that, I stopped complaining. Tante Yvonne was probably right, but I didn't believe she had the complete picture: Fréda was a little rough, I didn't deny it, but, basically she liked me. In fact, there never were major problems between us, except for the cutting remarks she occasionally threw my way. But that's how she was. She couldn't help herself, I suppose.

I must admit that I kept score of Fréda's biting remarks. For instance, when my new boyfriend came to my house to pick up some of his records, Fréda met him briefly. After he left, she commented: "His hands are so white, one can see he doesn't do anything!" And I still couldn't forget what she had said about my friendship with Colette: that she feared the neighbors might interpret it as being of "the special kind."

6
Colette in Ireland

Actually, my friendship with Colette was as special as ever, albeit not in that sense. It was now two years since we had left the Cours Complémentaire de Vincennes. When I transferred to Sophie Germain, Colette didn't know exactly what to do. She ended up applying for an au-pair position in England for a year upon the recommendation of Mademoiselle Renard, our English teacher. It turned out that it was not in England, but in Ireland, that a position opened, and with a Dublin family that wasn't Irish: the wife was Canadian, the husband German. Colette was to help take care of the couple's six children. The mother was soon due to give birth to her seventh child.

During the time of Colette's stay in Ireland, she and I kept in close touch. I was worried and sometimes frightened by some of the letters she sent me. She often felt lonely, worthless, and terribly sad. At the time, I didn't recognize the signs which forebode the clinical depression that was to haunt her throughout her life. Then, one day, I could hardly believe my eyes when I read a long letter I had just received. It was written in the present tense:

> "Yesterday evening, at about eight-thirty, the children's father takes his wife to the clinic where she is to have her baby. At around eleven-thirty, the father's cousin calls me, asking me to tell him to give him a call as soon as he returns. At twelve-thirty the father arrives. I give him the message and he goes to another room to make his phone call. I wait until he is finished, as I want to ask him about his wife and the new baby.
>
> He comes back with a bottle of cognac and two glasses. He says he bought the cognac for me. I feel very uncomfortable. Then he says, 'I like you very much, Colette. I love you!' I am very surprised. I look at him and have the impression that he has been drinking. It's only an impression. I will never know for sure if had been drinking or was sober. He goes on, 'I like my wife and my children, but I love you.' He sits next to me and puts his arm

around my shoulders. I am a statue. I cannot take his arm away. I cannot move. From the moment he started talking to me, I have not stopped smoking. I cannot let my spirit fall asleep. I have drunk two glasses of Cognac. I tremble. He is next to me (I spare you no detail. It's repulsive). I feel his thigh against mine. He pants like an animal. He kneads my shoulder. My mind is fixed on a single thought: you are with a man who might be drunk and who is very strong. Don't lose your head, don't fall asleep. This is what I tell myself, and I keep on smoking. He takes my left hand and kisses it, then, he licks it. I am disgusted. His hand goes down against my right side; he takes my waist, leans toward me, and kisses my neck. I told you, I cannot react. I let him. He kisses my hair. I am very tired. It's about one thirty in the morning. I am frightened. I feel myself go. I cannot hold on. My head falls on his shoulder. What is he going to believe? I do not know. From the beginning I haven't said a word. He keeps on kissing me then, suddenly, he searches my lips. I start fighting; he holds me tight; I react, and he tumbles to the floor. It is not funny, it is not sad, it is disgusting. Then he picks himself up, goes away. I come back to myself and continue to smoke. He returns and turns off the light. I ask him to turn the light back on. He does, sits by my side and says, 'I love you, but do not be angry with me if I have been incorrect. I am a man. I am just a man. You are young, beautiful, you are nice to all of us, and I love you. Forget what I have done. I want to be your friend.' A moment like this is very nice after what went on. I accept his friendship."

Colette's letter threw me in turmoil. We had never faced anything like that! I thought it was repulsive, this man licking her hand! I wrote passionately supportive letters to her. Not long after these events, she left that family and moved in with another Dublin couple, a couple who had befriended her some time before. These people were wonderful; the husband was an actor, his wife a harpist. They were part of the movement to promote the Irish language and spoke Gaelic to their children. Colette was very happy with them and fell (innocently) in love with a poet, Niall, a friend of the family. But soon it was time to go home.

Back in Fontenay-sous-Bois, Colette, who seemed to have forgotten that she once was on the verge of turning communist, returned from Ireland a devout Catholic. She had become again the Catholic girl she had been in her youth, but now much more passionate. She often started her day by praying in a small chapel close to her house. I was very touched by that. I felt that devotion was an important part of my friend's personality. Although times would change and Colette would eventually devote herself to communism (something that caused a long interruption in our friendship), I have to say that, for the moment, our main interest was *les garçons*, and our main preoccupation *l'amour*. If we had not been so serious and modern, we would have been able to appreciate one of Papa's old sentimental songs, and, with a smile, we could have sung to our boyfriends:

> *Chéri, les jardins nous attendent*
> *Car ils ont besoin d'amoureux.*
> *Que feraient les pauvres rosiers*
> *S'ils n'entendaient pas nos baisers.*
>
> Darling, the gardens are waiting for us
> For they are in need of lovers.
> What would the poor rose bushes do
> If they didn't hear our kisses?

7
Bound for Other Things

I was now eighteen. While I was aware that my relatives did their best to surround me with love and care, I also felt that I longed for something else. Already I was taking some distance. I knew that my father felt that I didn't participate enough in family life (by that he meant Fréda's family life). I do admit that it was only once in a while that I made the effort to spend out-of-town weekends with him, Fréda and her clan. In contrast, it was with dutiful regularity that I visited Grand-mère Cessot, Tante Yvonne and Tante Valentine. But these family obligations began to seriously weigh on me. It was hard to find time to study, share my thoughts with Colette, or go out with my friends, both from the villa de l'Ouest and from Sophie Germain. And soon everything would become worse when every minute I had to spare was to be devoted to the one I loved. The one I loved? (A genius? A tyrant? A James Dean look-alike?)

Colette Gauthier Myles has a Bachelor's degree from the Sorbonne and a Master's from the University of California, Berkeley. After a career as a librarian in academic settings, she retired in Sonoma, California, where she writes, teaches French, and occasionally does portrait photography. She loves to collect old family photographs and spend time with her children and grandchildren.

www.ingramcontent.com/pod-product-compliance
Lightning Source LLC
Chambersburg PA
CBHW021958160426
43197CB00007B/169